GLOBAL LATIN/O AMERICAS

Frederick Luis Aldama and Lourdes Torres, Series Editors

Spanish Perspectives on Chicano Literature

Literary and Cultural Essays

EDITED BY
Jesús Rosales and Vanessa Fonseca

WITH A FOREWORD BY
Francisco A. Lomelí

THE OHIO STATE UNIVERSITY PRESS | COLUMBUS

Copyright © 2017 by The Ohio State University.
All rights reserved.

Library of Congress Cataloging-in-Publication Data

Names: Rosales, Jesús, 1955– editor. | Fonseca, Vanessa (Assistant professor of English), editor. | Lomelí, Francisco A., writer of foreword.
Title: Spanish perspectives on Chicano literature : literary and cultural essays / edited by Jesús Rosales and Vanessa Fonseca ; with a foreword by Francisco A. Lomelí.
Other titles: Global Latin/o Americas.
Description: Columbus : The Ohio State University Press, [2017] | Series: Global Latin/o Americas | Includes bibliographical references.
Identifiers: LCCN 2017011629 | ISBN 9780814213421 (cloth ; alk. paper) | ISBN 0814213421 (cloth ; alk. paper)
Subjects: LCSH: American literature—Mexican American authors—History and criticism. | Mexican American literature (Spanish)—History and criticism.
Classification: LCC PS153.M4 S68 2017 | DDC 810.9/86872073—dc23
LC record available at https://lccn.loc.gov/2017011629

Cover design by Larry Nozik
Text design by Juliet Williams
Type set in Myriad Pro

∞ The paper used in this publication meets the minimum requirements of the American National Standard for Information Sciences—Permanence of Paper for Printed Library Materials. ANSI Z39.48–1992.

9 8 7 6 5 4 3 2 1

CONTENTS

ACKNOWLEDGMENTS   vii

FOREWORD   From La Mancha to Aztlán: Spanish Approaches in Chicano Literature
    FRANCISCO A. LOMELÍ   ix

INTRODUCTION
    JESÚS ROSALES AND VANESSA FONSECA   1

PART I • SPANISH PERSPECTIVES *DE ACÁ*

CHAPTER 1   Reading, from *Don Quijote de La Mancha* to *The House on Mango Street*: Chicano/a Literature, Mimesis, and the Reader
    MANUEL M. MARTÍN-RODRÍGUEZ   19

CHAPTER 2   *Mestizaje* in Afro-Iberian Writers Najat El Hachmi and Saïd El Kadaoui Moussaoui through the Borderland Theories of U.S. Third World Feminisms
    CARMEN SANJUÁN-PASTOR   35

CHAPTER 3   Toward a Transnational *Nos/otr@s* Scholarship in Chican@ and Latin@ Studies
    RICARDO F. VIVANCOS-PÉREZ   58

CHAPTER 4   Tempted by the Words of Another: Linguistic Choices of Chicanas/os and Other Latinas/os in Los Angeles
    ANA SÁNCHEZ-MUÑOZ   71

CHAPTER 5	The Cultural Border, Magic, and Oblivion in *Bless Me, Ultima* (2013), *Obaba* (2005), and *Un embrujo* (1998)	
	JUAN PABLO GIL-OSLE	82
CHAPTER 6	*El Malcriado* (1964–1975): La voz impresa del campesino y su impronta	
	VÍCTOR FUENTES	90

PART II • SPANISH PERSPECTIVES *DE ALLÁ*

CHAPTER 7	Tendiendo puentes, compartiendo conocimientos: The International Conference on Chicano Literature in Spain (1998–2016)	
	JULIO CAÑERO	109
CHAPTER 8	Women's Literary Gardens as Eco-Spaces: Word Gathering with Anzaldúa and Hurston	
	CAROLINA NÚÑEZ-PUENTE	126
CHAPTER 9	*La Tierra*: Sense of Place in Contemporary Chicano Literature	
	CARMEN LYDIA FLYS JUNQUERA	139
CHAPTER 10	La narración de los linchamientos de los méxicoamericanos en el suroeste de los EEUU en el siglo XIX y principios del XX	
	ARMANDO MIGUÉLEZ	155

LIST OF CONTRIBUTORS	175
INDEX	181

ACKNOWLEDGMENTS

I WANT to thank my mentors, Francisco A. Lomelí, María Herrera-Sobek, and, especially, the late Don Luis Leal, all of whom served as an inspiration for this project. I also want to thank my colleague Vanessa Fonseca for coediting the book and Frederick L. Aldama for believing in its potential. More importantly, I thank my wife, María, and *nuestros hijos,* Angélica, Daniel, and Francisco, for all their love and support.

Jesús Rosales

I want to thank Dr. Jesús Rosales for extending the opportunity to collaborate on this project and for his unconditional guidance and friendship. I also want to thank Frederick L. Aldama for his excitement about the project and his encouragement throughout the submission process. Most importantly, I'd like to thank my family, my husband Raúl, and my son Kendyl for keeping me grounded and always supporting me.

Vanessa Fonseca

FOREWORD

From La Mancha to Aztlán
Spanish Approaches in Chicano Literature

CHICANO LITERATURE has overcome many obstacles in its development and evolution due to a series of complex circumstances and long-standing dilemmas: it didn't begin to become known as a body of literature until the late 1960s (and even then mainstream critics hesitated/resisted it until the 1970s); its definition took some time to gain acceptance because some feared the term Chicano was a recent social phenomenon; its premodern literary origins were not identified until 1973, when Luis Leal penned the foundation of its literary history in "Mexican American Literature: A Historical Approach";[1] a general notion persisted that peoples of Mexican descent up to the early 1970s were either invisible, insignificant, or both; and some Chicanos claimed that the literature's thematics had to be tied directly to the Chicano Movement agenda of social justice, civil rights, and race relations. As one can appreciate, pressures existed from within and from the outside. As a literature of endurance, it had to metamorphose more than once to gain a widespread acceptance.

Then there is the iceberg effect in which we realized we were only witnessing the tip of a larger literary legacy that had deep roots in the early written documents by Spanish subjects—who often referred to themselves as "españoles mexicanos" (Spanish Mexicans)—during the colonial era gener-

---

1. It appears in the first volume of *Revista Chicano-Riqueña* (1.1:6–13), founded by Nicolás Kanellos and David Dávalos.

ally known as the Hispanic Period, 1519–1821. Chicanos in the 1970s had to reconcile the fact that we are descendants of those early Spanish explorers and conquerors who eventually extended into northern Mexico, or what after 1848 became the American Southwest. The ideology of cultural nationalism in the 1960s and 1970s propelled an anti-Spanish rhetoric against the effects of the conquest, indigenous subjugation, cultural hegemony, the imposition of European values and aesthetics, land appropriation, and the creation of a social caste system that disadvantaged the conquered people—that is, *mestizos, mulatos,* and *criollos*.[2] A neo-indigenist philosophy emerged within the context of a revolutionary zeal, consequently romanticizing our indigenous cultural past while vilifying the Hispanic side. But in 1967 Rodolfo "Corky" Gonzales, in his epic poem *I am Joaquín,* made it clear that our identity is driven by the fusion of symbolic, paradoxical elements that are inextricably tied. In other words, we are both Indian and Spanish. Alurista, in his *Floricanto en Aztlán,*[3] was instrumental in promoting an Aztec aesthetics as a renewed connection with our ancestors while situating this new form of expression within the barrio.

Chicanos in 1970 clearly were divided. In California, for example, most assumed we were a product of recent waves of immigration, plus the chain of missions from the eighteenth century seemed far removed and exclusively part of Spanish colonization. Any connections we might have with the landholding Californios also seemed to be part of a fuzzy past. We sometimes uttered in silence: Are we the same people? Chicanos in California appeared to be uprooted, to have a shaky historical past, and as struggling to fit into American society via acculturation and assimilation. Other Chicanos, such as New Mexicans and Texans, shared another sense of history and belonging: they recognized a background that could be traced back for generations to the sixteenth century in New Mexico and the seventeenth century in Texas. Nonetheless, they too had to prove worthy of becoming part of the American Union.[4] Whereas most Californio descendants were either displaced, integrated (especially via intermarriage with elite Anglo Americans or representatives of the military), or co-opted by the late nineteenth century, their sense of community dwindled down to small pockets of inhabitants who were relegated to contribute in terms of services and physical labor. Albert

---

2. Although a complex system of caste classifications was used, in general these categories allude to racial mixtures between Europeans and Indians, Europeans and Africans, and finally Europeans born in the Americas, respectively.

3. Published by the Chicano Studies Center at UCLA, 1971.

4. It is no coincidence that New Mexico struggled to obtain statehood by 1912. Texas, on the other hand, was welcomed into the Union as a protest against Mexico, but Texans' Mexicanness continued to be a racially contentious issue for decades.

Camarillo describes this process as barrioization in his book *Chicanos in a Changing Society: From Mexican Pueblos to American Barrios in Santa Barbara and Southern California, 1848–1930*.[5]

While the Chicano Movement from the 1960s and 1970s temporarily distanced us from our Hispanic background in order to partly recover our indigenous past, we soon realized we could ill afford to dichotomize such a cultural legacy. Some militants believed Chicanos emerged in the 1960s, but others questioned that myopic historical notion as suggesting we had sprung up like mushrooms. Of course there had been figures such as Aurelio M. Espinosa in the first half of the twentieth century who espoused a strong connection with Spain, even claiming that much of the Chicano folklore, that is, *corridos* (ballads), *décimas* (poems of ten verses), *alabados* (religious hymns proper to Penitente brotherhoods), *pastorelas* (Christmas plays), and others were fundamentally derivations of Spain.[6] By the 1970s we began to come across early works that clearly attested to a long-standing literary tradition that contained both Hispanic and native Mexican elements. So, while the 1980s came to be known as the "Decade of the Hispanic," again, privileging our Iberian roots, some Chicanos resisted that characterization as neocolonialist. While the uplifting label of the 1980s turned out to be a mirage, the 1990s opened new possibilities of systematically exploring our literary past, thanks in great part to the Recovering U.S. Hispanic Literary Heritage Project based at the University of Houston. From this vantage point, we came to more fully appreciate and comprehend our mestizaje and how our Hispanic background fused and was enriched by our indigenous background, and vice versa. Spain once more came into view in 1992 when the Spanish government, in its efforts to celebrate or at least acknowledge the 500th anniversary of the Conquest of the Americas, sponsored a massive four-volume collection titled *Handbook of Hispanic Cultures in the United States* under the general directorship of Nicolás Kanellos and Claudio Esteva-Fabregat. The collection formed part of an Arte Público effort to gather foundational articles within anthropology, sociology, history, and literature and art. Such endeavors contributed to the "rediscovery" of a number of significant works that unveiled a whole new area of scholarship in which they exhibited a mestizo aesthetics: the early epic poem *Historia de la Nueva México*, by Gaspar Pérez de Villagrá (1610); poetry by Miguel de Quintana (1730s); the novel *Jicoténcal*, by Félix Varela (1826); the

---

5. Published in Dallas, Texas, by Southern Methodist University Press, 2005.

6. Other key Chicano folklorists, such as Américo Paredes, Luis Leal, María Herrera-Sobek, and José Limón, disagreed with this blanket assessment, offering a more balanced mixed-culture framework for the origins of much of Chicano folklore, which gave credence to a more localized or regional production of popular tradition.

novels *Who Would Have Thought?* (1872) and *The Squatter and the Don* (1885), by María Amparo Ruiz de Burton; the short novels *El hijo de la tempestad* and *Tras la tormenta la calma* (1892), by Eusebio Chacón; and later *Las aventuras de don Chipote o cuando los pericos mamen* (1928), by Daniel Venegas; *We Fed Them Cactus* (1954), by Fabiola Cabeza de Baca; *Pocho* (1959), by José Antonio Villarreal; and others.

The point is that as we expanded our critical lens beyond the cultural nationalist phase and the intense technical experimentations of the Quinto Sol Generation (1967–74) and the Postmodern Chicana Generation (1985–95), subsequently casting a wide net to encompass early works before 1965, researchers from other countries began to take notice. Among some of the earliest foreign scholars were a cohort of Spanish academics. Germans and French initiated the trend abroad, thanks in great part to the first international conference on Chicano literature and culture in Germersheim, Germany, in 1984 and then Paris, France, in 1986. However, by then Justo S. Alarcón and Armando Miguélez[7] in Arizona in the 1970s had already pre-empted their European colleagues within the United States. Spaniards in Spain, such as Manuel M. Martín-Rodríguez, Manuel Villar Raso, Federico Eguíluz, María Jesú Buxó Rey, Amaia Ibarrarán Vigalondo, Julio Cañero, María Antònia Oliver, Tomás Calvo Buezas, and others, later led a sizeable vanguard of critical studies in their country—often conflating their work into critical production within the United States. But it must be stated that José Antonio Gurpegui became the lightning rod and undisputed leader of this new field in Spain after he had traveled to New Mexico to study the short stories by Sabine R. Ulibarrí in 1986. His direct contact with Chicano/a critics in the first major conference on Chicano culture and literature in Torredembarra in 1988 near Barcelona cemented his keen interest in the field, and he quickly became instrumental in organizing and promoting conferences in Spain in 1990 and 1992, including those spanning from 1998 to the most recent in 2016. The Franklin Institute at the Universidad de Alcalá de Henares, which Gurpegui directed for a number of years, has become the principal center of Chicano literary and cultural studies outside the United States. It has replaced some of the attempts in Germersheim (Germany), Bordeaux (France), and even Universidad Nacional Autónoma de México in Mexico City, clearly exceeding and superseding what these other centers had accomplished through a consistent programmatic plan to institute Hispanic studies in Alcalá de Henares, which now includes a master's program. The result is a proliferation of Spanish critics among various

---

7. Professor Carlos Blanco Aguinaga at the University of California at San Diego in the 1970s also spearheaded efforts to deal with Chicano literature within traditional Spanish departments, although his role was viewed more as mentoring of upcoming Chicano/a critics.

generations who now dedicate a significant amount of critical scholarship on Chicanos/as, as this collection by Jesús Rosales and Vanessa Fonseca demonstrates. Although the United States possesses the largest grouping of critics conducting a steady stream of scholarly articles, journal issues, and books, Spain is undoubtedly in second place.

One logically might ask: Why such interest in Spain and among Spaniards? First, this is a result of the development of internationalization[8] in Chicano/a studies in general and in the study of Chicano literature specifically. Second, there is a growing relevance factor in which Spanish critics relate well to Chicanos, who often bridge the gaps between American and Latin America literatures. Third, Spanish critics, much like other international scholars, view Chicano literature as a viable vehicle to better understand the United States culturally. Fourth, many Spanish critics have studied and/or spent considerable time conducting research in the United States while pairing up with Chicano/a critics in the process. The result has produced a series of important partnerships and cross-fertilization of ideas and intellectual exchanges, sometimes leading to grants and seed money among the researchers. Spanish critics, then, have been invaluable in terms of putting certain theories to work on a larger stage by challenging Chicano/a premises and contributing to the overall enrichment of the ideas espoused. Chicano/a literature consequently benefits herein from the new vistas and approaches collected by the editors Jesús Rosales and Vanessa Fonseca in this excellent collection to document once and for all the range and depth of both the literature and its criticism in an international context, thanks in great part to Spanish scholars.

Francisco A. Lomelí

---

8. To further support this point, it is worth noting that Chicano literature has spread across the globe, as noted by Professor Tatiana Voronchenko's conference "Transborderland in the Changing World," situated in Chita, Siberia, in Russia in 2006, where we discovered that there were six doctoral students studying Chicano literature.

INTRODUCTION

JESÚS ROSALES and VANESSA FONSECA

ONE CAN argue that Chicano literary criticism evolved as a result of the Chicano social and political movement of the 1960s and early 1970s. Seminal Chicano literary journals, in particular *De Colores* (Albuquerque, New Mexico, 1973) and *Caracol* (San Antonio, Texas, 1974), were some of the first to publish literary criticism that analyzed and promoted Chicano texts of that significant period. With Gloria Anzaldúa's *Borderlands/La Frontera: The New Mestiza* (1987) and Ramón Saldívar's *Chicano Narrative: The Dialectics of Difference* (1990), Chicano literary criticism reached a sense of maturity and national and international exposure and acceptance. Today Chicano literature is a consequential subject of study at a number of academic centers in the United States and abroad. Since the late 1960s literary conferences centered on Chicano literature have been held in Mexico, Germany, France, Ireland, Turkey, and Spain, among other countries. Of the ones mentioned, Mexico and Spain have expressed a profound interest in augmenting their cultural and academic relations with Chicanos. For example, the National Association for Chicana and Chicano Studies (NACCS) annual conference met three times in Mexico: Hermosillo, Sonora (1991), Mexico City (1998), and Guadalajara, Jalisco (2006); and conferences on Chicano literature and culture have been organized in other Mexican cities, including Tijuana and Mérida. Inspired by the urgency of the Chicano Movement, the Universidad Nacional Autónoma de México (UNAM) initiated programs of study and research on Chicano studies. Furthermore, in an effort to bridge the cultural relations between Mexicanos and Chicanos, the Mexican government, in conjunction with the Raza Unida Party, sponsored Becas para Aztlán, scholarships that encouraged Chicanos to complete graduate studies at the UNAM. To complement these efforts, anthologies on Chicano literature, including the landmark *Chicanos: Antología histórica y literaria* (1980), and other academic studies and works by Chicano authors were published in Mexico by major editorial houses, including Fondo de Cultura Económica and Joaquín Mortiz.[1]

As far as Spain is concerned, Spanish scholars and the Instituto Franklin de Investigación en Estudios Norteamericanos of the Universidad de Alcalá have hosted ten international conferences on Chicano literature and culture. All were organized at different Spanish cities, including Granada, where the first conference took place in 1998; and Madrid, where the most recent one was held in 2016. A book of essays from the Málaga conference, *Perspectivas transatlánticas en la Literatura Chicana: Ensayos y creatividad*, was published in 2002, and the Instituto Franklin's journal *Revista Camino Real* consistently has published literary essays and works by Chicano critics and authors since 2009, the year of its founding. In addition, the Instituto Franklin, under the Colección Camino Real, has translated and published several Chicano texts, including Alejandro Morales's *El olvidado pueblo de Simons* (*The Brick People*, 2009), and Tino Villanueva's *Así habló Penélope* (*So Spoke Penelope*, 2013).[2]

More recently the Center of Study and Investigation for Decolonial Dialogues has annually hosted the "Decolonizing Knowledge and Power: Postcolonial Studies, Decolonial Horizons" summer course in Barcelona. A common theme discussed at all of these international conferences is the subaltern commonalities that Chicano culture shares with several European countries, specifically Spain. For example, Spanish cultural issues related to bilingualism, immigration, cultural nationalism, postcolonialism, queer studies, to name a few, are themes indisputably connected to the Chicano. In Spain, these matters are personalized by the country's diverse and unique multicultural landscapes (Galicia, País Vasco, Cataluña, Andalusia) and the voice of a flowing number of immigrants (from Africa, Central and South America) who reach its borders in desperate need of finding the fabled economic Promised Land.

---

1. The Fondo de Cultura Económica also has published *Mi lucha por la tierra* (Reies López Tijerina). The Universidad Autónoma de México's publications include *Antología de la literatura chicana* (Ed. María Eugenia Gaona, 1986) and *El bandolero, el pocho y la raza: imágenes cinematográficas del chicano* (David Maciel, 1994). Joaquín Mortiz published Alejandro Morales's first two novels, *Caras viejas y vino nuevo* (1975) and *La verdad sin voz* (1979).

2. Other titles include *George Washington Gómez* (Américo Paredes, 2012), *Loa a un ángel de piel morena* (Lucha Corpi, 2011), and *Los recuerdos de Ana Calderón* (Graciela Limón, 2010).

This book is part of a larger literary and cultural project that deals with the present and future of Chicano letters within a national and transnational context. The objective is not for Chicanos to present an inward personal reflection of their literature and culture (a book of essays written by Chicanos), but to present a collection written by non-Chicanos who present external perspectives that enhance the understanding and the appreciation of Chicano letters within the parameters of American mainstream literature and that of other dominant world literatures and cultures. It is imperative that Chicano ethnic issues are identified with global issues. This provides an opportunity to understand the social and political differences and similarities that both unite and divide nations. Engagement in social and political consciousness, for example, allows the Chicano to comprehend people's migrations through physical spaces around the world in search of economic opportunities and, in many cases, personal safety. With this in mind, it is fitting that Spain—the European country that conquered México and instilled in its people indelible cultural traits, fundamental to Mexican identity and, in turn, to Chicano identity—be an indispensable point of departure.

SPANISH LITERARY CRITICS' PRESENCE IN CHICANO LITERATURE AND CULTURE

As a result of the proclamation of the Plan de Santa Barbara, articulated in 1969 at the University of California, Santa Barbara, demanding, among other exigencies, the establishment of Chicano studies at colleges and universities in the United States, Chicano literature developed into an important academic field of study, primarily in the Southwest region of the country. Literary anthologies, journals, critical works, and PhD dissertations soon unearthed Chicano literary history and introduced major Chicano works at national and international forums. Literary scholars and institutions soon delved into Chicano literature, generating an enthusiastic interest in its authors and their literary production. The celebrated German scholar Wolfgang Iser, for example, published a book of interviews on Chicano authors, and in 1976 Rolando Hinojosa-Smith was awarded the prestigious Premio Casa de las Américas in Cuba.

With the growth and increasing presence of Chicano studies worldwide, Chicano literature, as a field of study, has captured the imagination of international scholars and general readers. More than any other country—outside of the United States—Spain has manifested a profound interest in Chicano literature since the mid-1960s; a sincere engagement that continues to this day. Many Spanish scholars left their country of origin specifically to study Chicano literature at national universities in the United States, many of them permanently making this country their home and devoting their academic career to Chicano literature and culture. Several of them were individually responsible for the field's growth and development at numerous academic institutions. For example, Justo S. Alarcón, who left his home country in the 1950s, helped develop Chicano studies at Arizona State University (ASU) and made it possible for Chicano literature to be a viable field of study in the school's Department of Spanish and Portuguese. Alarcón taught for more than forty years at ASU, founding *La Palabra: Revista Chicana*, a journal that contributed significantly to the growth of Chicano literature written in Spanish. In addition, he also wrote several books on Chicano literary criticism, as well as fictional works in the *literatura chicanesca* tradition.

One also must accentuate the significant work of Manuel M. Martín-Rodríguez, arguably the most influential Spanish literary critic of Chicano literature to date. Martín-Rodríguez, a native of Seville, not only has dedicated most of his academic life to the study of Chicano letters but also was instrumental in establishing and directing Latino/Hispanic studies centers at several institutions. At Texas A&M University, College Station, he helped create and directed Hispanic Studies; and at the University of Wisconsin, Milwaukee, he served as Director of the Roberto Hernández Center. In addition, Martín-Rodríguez is one of the founding faculty members of the University of California, Merced, self-proclaimed as "The first new American research university in the twenty-first century."[3]

Spanish Perspectives is divided into two parts. Part I, "Spanish Perspectives *de acá*" (Spanish critics from the U.S.), includes six essays from Spanish literary critics who received their graduate degrees from U.S. universities and live and work in this country, Chicano literature being, for some of them, an essential part of their research agenda; and Part II, "Spanish Perspectives *de allá*" (Spanish critics from Spain), includes four essays from Spanish literary critics who graduated from Spanish or American universities but live and work in their home country, studying Chicano literature within an overall North American literary context that is mostly comparative.[4] Both groups share similarities and differences, but unquestionably those from *acá* hold a

---

3. Martín-Rodríguez also has served on the National Committee of the Tomás Rivera Mexican American Children's Book Award and the Advisory Board of the University of New Mexico's "Pasó por aquí" Series; he is also co-editor of the University of California Latino Cultures Network.

4. A selected number of Spanish literary critics were invited to participate but due to circumstances beyond their control were not able to contribute to this volume. Justo S. Alarcón is one who needs to be mentioned and recognized, for he devoted most of his academic career

deep connection to Chicano culture, for they share the Chicano's day-to-day cultural life experience, even if they might feel at times, as Ricardo Vivancos-Pérez has suggested so vividly, painfully *enajenados* in the process.

THE ESSAYS

In the opening essay of Part I, "Reading, from *Don Quijote de La Mancha* to *The House on Mango Street*: Chicano/a Literature, Mimesis, and the Reader," respected critic Manuel M. Martín-Rodríguez examines the theoretical approaches of several scholars to discuss how reception and reading play a key role in the discourse of mimesis, a term that explores the relationship that exists between text and reality. This essay presents an initial analysis of the use of mimesis in early Chicano literature—late nineteenth century and early twentieth—including María Amparo Ruiz de Burton's novel *The Squatter and the Don* (1885), Eusebio Chacón's *Tras la tormenta, la calma* (1892), and Daniel Venegas's *Las aventuras de don Chipote o cuando los pericos mamen* (1928), but it focuses primarily on discussing Chicano Movement literature of the 1960s and early 1970s.

For Martín-Rodríguez, Chicano Movement literature is essentially mimetic in the sense that "it reveals strong and recognizable ties/references to reality." For him, the greatest originality lies in the way in which "it transforms the reader into the central element in the literary process." In other words, a group consciousness is formed, for the reader sees himself in the text. This, in turn, helps to contest stereotypes or distorted images of the Chicano so prevalent in the eyes of mainstream society. Martín-Rodríguez uses Tomás Rivera's, . . . *y no se lo tragó la tierra* (1971) as a good example to present his argument, for Rivera has the ability not only to "imitate" a Chicano reality that is familiar to the readers but also to narrate that specific reality in a way that is meaningful and respectful to the portrayal of his characters, an "Ethical obligation" that must be practiced and sustained.

These intimate connections between writer and audience will be challenged temporarily with the violent representation of the barrio in Alejandro Morales's *Caras viejas y vino nuevo* (1975) and in Ron Arias's surreal realities in his postmodern novel, *The Road to Tamazunchale* (1975). The connection, however, will re-emerge in full force by Chicana writers in the 1980s. Women writers, primarily Ana Castillo and Sandra Cisneros, offer a comforting communal Chicana experience in their narrative and poetry, highlighting

---

(more than forty years) to the study and promotion of Chicano literature at Arizona State University as a teacher, literary critic, and creative writer.

the beginning of a cycle in which mimesis contributes significantly to the formation of Chicana group consciousness. Martín-Rodríguez uses Cisneros's "The House of My Own" (from *The House on Mango Street*) to emphasize this possibility, for this selection explores the representational mimesis (one that intends to be faithful to the reality of the characters and readers) and its utopian possibility (one that represents what could or should be), all for the sake of "imagining better worlds."

Martín-Rodríguez, in his discussion of mimesis, uses examples of Don Quijote at the beginning of his essay before examining the Chicano literary works that he aptly analyzes. He is extremely conscious of linking both cultures, for it represents a symbolic gesture that sets in motion a Spanish and Chicano communal literary consciousness that hopefully will result in a cultural reconciliation of a difficult colonial past that historically has existed between Spain and Mexico.

Carmen Sanjuán-Pastor's "*Mestizaje* in Afro-Iberian Writers Najat El Hachmi and Saïd El Kadaoui Moussaoui through the Borderland Theories of U.S. Third World Feminisms" uses feminist *mestizaje* theories from the U.S.–Mexico borderland, specifically those voiced by Gloria Anzaldúa, Cherríe Moraga, Sonia Saldívar-Hull, and Chela Sandoval, to examine two texts produced from a *border* position by Catalan-Amazigh writers Najat El Hachmi and Saïd El Kadaoui Moussaoui: *L'últim patriarca* and *Límites y fronteras*, respectively.

Sanjuán-Pastor examines how these two novels confront feelings of "material and psychological" insecurities by Moroccan immigrants in Spain. Both writers use writing as a function to reconstruct the protagonist's mestizo identities. In *L'últim patriarca*, Sanjuán-Pastor argues that El Hachmi explores the formation of the self and collective consciousness of the narrator, emphasizing dual identities within the Moroccan-Amazigh social and cultural system, highlighting the immigrant community of Catalonia. In *Límites y fronteras*, the concept of the "eternal foreigner" (a notion intimately connected to the immigrant) is presented to discuss the author's explanation of the hardships and pains experienced by those who occupy borderlands. This experience is associated with "prison identities," for the borderland subject struggles to dismantle conflicting and harmful binaries ("foreigner/autochthonous, Moroccan/sick, European/normal") that exist in society.

Sanjuán-Pastor's essay provides an excellent example of the impact that Chicana literary critics and authors have established outside of the United States. Her use of Anzaldúa's concept of a "mestiza consciousness," of Moraga's "theory in the flesh," and of Cisneros's concept of writing as a form of liberation resonates among other nations that share common human conditions with Chicanos and Chicanas.

Ricardo F. Vivancos-Pérez's contribution to the collection, "Toward a Transnational *Nos/otro@s* Scholarship in Chican@ and Latin@ Studies," uses a highly personal narrative voice to present the trials and tribulations ("barbed wire of fear") that non-Chicano scholars of Chicano, feminist, and queer studies experience in this country.

To argue for the acceptance of the non-Chicano as a legitimate voice of Chicano studies criticism, Vivancos-Pérez discusses how Gloria Anzaldúa uses the concept of "nos/otras" and "nos/otros" ("us" and "others")—emphasizing "nos/otros"—to explain the contradictions that her readers encounter in her groundbreaking text, *Borderlands/La Frontera: The New Mestiza* (1987). For Anzaldúa, Vivancos-Pérez explains, "Nos/otros" implies inclusion. He feels that Anzaldúa's concept demonstrates that the two principles of Chicana feminism—tolerance and contradictions—need to operate on two levels: "both among Chicanas, and among Chicanas and outsiders—both within the group and outside the group." By doing so, the Chicano/a incorporates the voice of others. This implies, as Vivancos-Pérez suggests, the "democratization of Chican@ scholarship."

Using his personal life as an example of sharing and understanding Chicano social issues (Vivancos-Pérez was born in a border community—Málaga—in southern Spain, close to Morocco; he derives from a working-class background and experienced immigrant life and discrimination in the United States), Vivancos-Pérez understood Anzaldúa's writing as a call to action, a motivating force identified as "arrebatos" that led to stages of knowledge and transformations in the fight for social justice. This revealing process lead Vivancos-Pérez to accept his position as a non-Chicano studies scholar fully engaged in the construction of a radical feminist voice rooted in Latinidades and Hispanidades. The minute one speaks for others, Vivancos-Pérez argues, the non-Chicano scholar becomes a "proxy" that occupies and "outside-insider position" (as opposed to an "inside-outsider" or "participant-observer" position) within Chicana scholarship. The acceptance of the *nos/otros* scholarship in Chican@ studies, Vivancos-Pérez concludes, undoubtedly will enrich the dialogues about transdisciplinary methodological issues. He feels that for these debates to be fruitful, more outside-insider critically informed voices need to be legitimately accepted in Chicano discourse.

In "Tempted by the Words of Another: Linguistic Choices of Chicanas/os and Other Latinas/os in Los Angeles," Ana Sánchez-Muñoz explores Chicano Spanish and the Spanish spoken by other Latino communities that reside in Los Angeles, California, specifically, those from El Salvador and Guatemala.

Sánchez-Muñoz examines the various ways in which Chicano identity develops through language formation and the role it plays in other Latino groups. Sánchez-Muñoz highlights two important factors that are involved in Chicano Spanish formation that makes it unique. One, its connection to rural varieties of Mexican Spanish; the other, its intimate contact with English that results in the constant borrowing and convergences of both languages, culminating in a mixture known as "Spanglish."

Sánchez-Muñoz argues that despite the fact that Chicano Spanish is by far the most dominant Spanish spoken in Los Angeles (75 percent of the Latino/Hispanic population in Los Angeles is of Mexican origin), the Spanish that is spoken by other Latinos also has left its indelible mark in the city. For Sánchez-Muñoz, Central American Spanish differs from Chicano Spanish phonologically, syntactically, and lexically. She explores different theoretical frameworks to discuss these differences. These include an accommodation theory (where convergence or divergence play a major role), dialect leveling (strategies through which interlocutors adapt to each other's communicative behavior in order to reduce difference), koinéization (the mixing of features of different dialects, which leads to a new dialect), and diglossia (the specialization of use of two languages in contact within the same geographical area). Sánchez-Muñoz concludes that her research in Central American Spanish indicates that even though there is an adaptation or negotiation to Chicano Spanish, there exists a tendency toward bidialectalism rather than an adoption of a koiné; in other words, "Speakers are not merely *tempted by the words of another*, but through code-switching between languages and dialects, they make those words and codes their own." Sánchez-Muñoz argues that the forming of Spanglish (identified as a "linguistic third space") offers the freedom to borrow or reject words and linguistic codes. For her, bilingualism and bidialectalism are linguistic resources that best express the complex commonalities of the multifaceted immigrant experience.

In "The Cultural Border, Magic, and Oblivion in *Bless Me, Ultima* (2013), *Obaba* (2005), and *Un embrujo* (1998)," Juan Pablo Gil-Osle explores how three diverse Hispanic spaces located in the United States, Mexico, and Spain—all distinguished by their unique history of linguistic politics and rich culture—serve as the extraordinary background to three movies: *Bless Me, Ultima*; *Obaba*; and *Un embrujo*. All three share the common notion or feeling that its folk traditions are rapidly dissipating, being forgotten or, in the best of cases, undergoing drastic transformations. For example, *curanderos* (healers) are rapidly disappearing in New Mexico and Yucatán, and with them their Spanish and Mayan languages and cultural traditions. The same can be said of the narrator of *Obabakoak* (the novel *Obaba* is based on), who is beginning to lose his language—Basque—at the end of the story. Gil-Osle argues that all three narrations, in the novels and the films, experience a social violence, one that annihilates culture: a nonhealing magic. On the other hand, a wisp of hope does emerge for all three cultures to express their cultural magic in the form of border language identity as represented in the Spanish, Mayan, and Basque languages that are used by the protagonists.

Throughout the essay, Gil-Osle shares different characteristics that all three movies share. Some include the use of *la magia* and *lo maravilloso* (a type of magic realism) that is presented in a cathartic ritual; they are plurilingual; they have the potential to be asocial and ahistorical, in other words, an open-ended interpretation that transcends particular cultural borders and historical spaces. Gil-Osle, similar to Sanjuán, opens up Spain's cultural boundaries that question the need and/or the disappearances of cultural nationalisms across all borders: Chicano/U.S.; Cataluña/Basque/Spain. Language is key to identity, concludes Gil-Osle, as a means to warn us against the threats of the imperious forces of globalization that have jeopardized the integrity of the human condition.

The last essay of Part I is Víctor Fuentes's "*El Malcriado* (1964–1975): La voz impresa del campesino y su impronta." In this selection, Fuentes summarizes the most significant periods of *El Malcriado*, the official newspaper of the United Farm Worker (UFW), published from 1964 to 1989. The major themes of the newspaper deal with social-political, cultural, and artistic issues that concerned or identified the Union's goals. The essay explores the various general stages of the newspaper's publication development, but emphasizes two of the most important and significant ones: those published between 1964 and 1967, and those from 1972 to 1974.

Fuentes argues that in the 1964–1967 period, *El Malcriado*—published under the subtitle "Voz del campesino" (the farmworker's voice)—set the groundwork of the social and political goals of the UFW. Between 1967 and 1972, the newspaper passed through a stretch of inconsistent publications. The period 1972–1974 represented optimum years for *El Malcriado*. It improved its format, it was published bilingually, and it increased its national significance. In this period the newspapers published at least 30,000 weekly issues. Periods of more inconsistent publications followed until its demise in 1989. The essay focuses on the Spanish-language editions, highlights its history, and analyzes its most important characteristics at its various stages of development. Fuentes concludes that *El Malcriado* provided the reader with a mirror image of the history of the UFW union and of its iconic leader, César Chávez.

In sum, the essays collected in Part I address rich cultural themes that enhance the Chicano experience through the unique perspective of Spanish critics from both sides of the Atlantic. Their vision of Chicano culture transcends time and space. In these essays one catches a glimpse of the gallant knight *de la triste figura*—Don Quijote—who is personified in Esperanza, the young girl from a Chicago barrio living on Mango Street who yearns to find utopia in a world smothered with jarring realities as shown in Martín-Rodríguez's essay. Also examined are Spain's multicultural realities, as expressed in Spanish, Catalan, and Amazigh identities in Sanjuán-Pastor's contribution, as well as linguistic differences, Spanish and Basque, in Gil-Osle's. These parallel with the Chicano's Indigenous, Mestizo, and Anglo cultural makeup, and with the comparative linguistic manifestations of European and Central American immigrants in the vastly populated Mexican communities of the United States that are analyzed closely by Sánchez-Muñoz.

The *arrebato* or transgression of Chicano cultural nationalism has presented an array of possibilities for the study of Chicano literature and culture, resulting in the legitimization of a "transnational 'nos/otr@s' scholarship" proposed by Vivancos-Pérez. Last, a Spanish critic that takes on the task of chronicling a Chicano campesino newspaper from its battlegrounds, as Fuentes does, might seem a malign affront to close-minded Chicano cultural nationalists who dread a Spanish reconquest of their culture. This fear, however, is a travesty, for this phobia translates into a reckless effort to truncate the imminent growth of Chicano letters destined to catapult itself onto the world's center stage.

Part II begins with Julio Cañero's "Tendiendo puentes, compartiendo conocimientos: The International Conference on Chicano Literature in Spain (1998–2016)." In his essay, Cañero gives a brief overview of the International Conference on Chicano Literature (and Latino Studies), celebrating its tenth biennial gathering in May 2016. Crediting Dr. José Antonio Gurpegui as a key player in the formation of a Chicano critical consciousness in Spain, Cañero pays homage to the many Spanish scholars *de allá* who have contributed to an internationalized perspective of Chicano literature since the inception of the International Conference on Chicano Literature in 1998. Perhaps one of the most intriguing arguments Cañero makes is the necessity for Spanish scholars to better understand one of the largest Spanish-speaking populations in the United States and to strengthen relationships with Chicano scholars based on a shared history between Spain and the United States. As a result, the conference has grown in both attendance and critical readership of Chicano literature during the last twenty years.

The first international conference, at the Universidad de Granada, brought together first- and second-generation Spanish scholars interested in Chicano literature alongside reputed Chicano writers and critics. Second-generation

Spanish scholars tested the waters by presenting papers on canonical Chicano writers and internal colonization, while affirming the necessity to organize another conference in the future. The second international conference, held in 2000 at the Universidad del País Vasco, was not without political contention, as many individuals in the Basque Country held protests following the assassination of a local professor. The conference organizers used this opportunity to draw similarities between Chicano and Basque Country education efforts and the need for the conference to take place amidst political strife.

It was clear by the third conference, at the Universidad de Málaga, that the academic exchange between Spain and the United States was sustainable. Having witnessed the first PhD dissertation from Spain to focus on Chicano literature, the conference organizers and attendees continued to dissect topics such as Chicana feminisms and rap music in Chicano communities using interdisciplinary perspectives. The fifth conference, held at the University of Alcalá, was the first time the Instituto Franklin de Investigación en Estudios Norteamericanos worked together with Spanish scholars to organize a conference. Regarded as an important research center for Chicano and Latino studies, the Instituto Franklin has grown to be one of the major contributors to the International Conference on Chicano Literature.

Two major themes permeated the seventh international conference, at the Universidad de León: landscapes and language. Organized by Imelda Martín-Junquera, a well-known Spanish scholar focusing on ecofeminism and ecocriticism, the conference shifted nicely from environmental landscapes to linguistic landscapes. The ninth international conference, at the Universidad de Oviedo, saw a continued interest in conference participation by Chicano and Spanish scholars alike. Additionally, the conference now has an organizing hub—HispaUSA, whose focus is to increase scholarly dialogues and output from Spanish and American researchers in the area of Chicano and Latino studies.

The conference, over the past twenty years, has proved to be successful for Spanish and Chicano scholars alike, solidifying an important relationship in a common research area grounded on cultural background and mutual respect.

In "Women's Literary Gardens as Eco-Spaces: Word Gathering with Anzaldúa and Hurston," Carolina Núñez-Puente creates a cross-cultural and cross-genre dialogue between Chicano poetry and African American short story. Utilizing an ecofeminst perspective, she draws upon the many instances in which both authors evoke water as a way to demonstrate social injustices within garden spaces. Ecofeminism provides a lens with which we can understand the ways environmental literature written by women reflects the many historical, political, and social imbalances that are likely results of patriarchal and colonial practices in both communities. Núñez-Puente begins with a historical overview of the importance of gardening as woman's space in both Mexican/Chicana and African American traditions, despite the historical negation of environmental spaces and inclusion in the pastoral canon for African Americans who were viewed as possessions within the pastoral landscape under the slavery system. Núñez-Puente frames both Chicana and African American writing within environmental writing and notes that gardens have always been an important aspect of community building in both rural and urban spaces. Thus, ecofeminism, ecocriticism, and environmentalism are perfect points of departure for analyzing the literary works of Anzaldúa and Hurston.

In both works, Núñez-Puente draws upon the multiple references to water as a way to understand methods of oppression. In Hurston's short story "Sweat," the imagery of water is, at first, condemning to Delia, the main character. However, she finds the power within her to speak back to oppressions and, ultimately, to develop a sense of authority and security through her garden space, often invoking the help of her African ancestors through nature and rewriting traditional narratives, such as the Garden of Eden, to further her sense of empowerment. In Anzaldúa's poem "*sus plumas el viento*," social hardships are evidenced through farm labor and exploitation of Chicanos in the borderlands. Núñez-Puente demonstrates that themes of water, including sweat, blood, and tears, have always been a constant theme in Chicano/a literature, as Chicano ancestors have traveled across waters to endure backbreaking labor as "wetbacks." Núñez-Puente continues to demonstrate the cyclical lifestyle of Chicanos in positions of manual labor and the devaluation of this lifestyle by those who do not respect it, perhaps, as much as intellectual labor. In addition, nature is framed here not as pleasant, but as a site of violence for women. In the poem, Amalia is plagued by both past and present modes of oppression—as a member of the Chicano community and as a woman. As Núñez-Puente argues, Chicano/a literature seeks to denounce the very systematic violence that Amalia faces in "*sus plumas el viento*," utilizing ecofeminism as a theoretical tool.

The two readings by Hurston and Anzaldúa intersect at many moments, despite the more than fifty years that separate their publication dates. This is interesting when one considers the length of time women of color have endured environmental cruelties as evidenced through literary production. Núñez-Puente contends that eco-spaces are important centers of dialogue where scholars can use a comparative literature approach to demonstrate points of intersection among communities of color, promoting dialogue with "outer (green) and inner (hopeful) nature."

In "*La Tierra*: Sense of Place in Contemporary Chicano Literature," Carmen Lydia Flys Junquera analyzes a placed-based sense of identity in the works of three New Mexican / Chicano authors. Flys Junquera contends that despite any ongoing debate about what a sense of place entails, Chicano literature maintains a connection to the land as a marker of self and community. While Flys Junquera finds the closest translation to sense of place as *sentido de arraigo*, it is Rudolfo Anaya who equates the notion with *la tierra* (the earth) and the larger Chicano community that embraces both the physical *tierra* and the mythical Aztlán as homeland. In Jimmy Santiago Baca's story "The Importance of a Piece of Paper," siblings rival over traditional and contemporary feelings about the land. The struggle between tradition and modernity is evident here as Western and non-Western cultural beliefs collide over land-grant issues, ultimately demonstrating the subjective nature of attachment to the land. In a state that borders and conflicts with modernity, it becomes more evident that the entire community suffers when their sense of place is lost. Modernity often signals illness or death for the characters as a metaphor for the loss of tradition. In Ana Castillo's *So Far from God*, the characters advocate for a return to the land as a way to revitalize their communities, attempting to reclaim rural inheritance and relevance through land-based practices. However, as Flys Junquera shows, this is not an easy task, as local industries, such as factories, provide more consistent and immediate economic opportunities, although this also brings the risk of contaminants and subsequent illnesses for those that seek employment there.

Land loss sometimes is inevitable for Chicano communities and, with it, a sense of detachment and loss of heritage, as is evident in both Ana Castillo and Rudolfo Anaya's works. In "Matilda's Garden," by Jimmy Santiago Baca, Flys Junquera reflects on the central theme of gardening and the ways that threats to nature result in a subsequent threat to identity and self-worth for Chicano communities. This is demonstrated through many of Baca's stories.

Flys Junquera's essay finishes with renewed hope for the restoration of a sense of place in Chicano literature through the Sonny Baca detective series by Rudolfo Anaya. The protagonists are situated in a more urban/contemporary society and must learn to appreciate land and nature as necessary components of identity formation. This happens on a global and local level as Chicano communities learn to navigate a modern world through the eyes of ecocritical thought. Flys Junquera demonstrates that while older generations worked the land, contemporary Chicanos must find new ways to connect to concepts of nature and land and, ultimately, to the heritage of their ancestors.

In his essay "La narración de los linchamientos de los méxicoamericanos en el suroeste de los EEUU en el siglo XIX y principios del XX," Armando

Miguélez considers three types of lynchings most common in the United States during the nineteenth century: (1) spontaneous or repentant, (2) perpetuated by vigilant masses, and (3) crimes of the state. Miguélez documents the history and politics surrounding lynchings following the Mexican–American War (1846–48), noting around 700 lynchings of Mexican Americans in the United States between 1848 and 2000, though this number does not include undocumented lynchings.

Miguélez takes advantage of the historical information provided by the following publications: *El eco del Pacífico* and *El Nuevo Mundo* (San Francisco, CA), *El Clamor Público* and *Regeneración* (Los Angeles), and *El Ranchero* and *El Bejareño* (San Antonio, Texas). Miguélez demonstrates that the many atrocities committed against Mexican Americans living in the Southwest, particularly in California and Texas, were part of a larger colonial project to eradicate this population from newly acquired U.S. territories at the end of the Mexican–American War. In addition, as the periodicals show, the many editorials written by Mexicans argue for a more favorable system of justice from the new colonial powers that have continued to place the "población española" (mainly Mexican and Chilean) in a subaltern position. While Miguélez categorizes the lynchings in different ways, the end result is the same.

What is at stake in Miguélez's essay is a larger conversation about what civil participation entails in the nineteenth century and a discussion about what it meant to be of Mexican or Spanish origin in the United States during that period. Miguélez equates the victimization of the Mexican American population to perpetuation of genocide by the state, as stated. The Spanish-speaking periodicals during this time, as Miguélez argues, narrate the extent of these atrocities and provide a historical documentation for a period in which Mexicans were persecuted, tortured, and lynched in a system that often encouraged these actions as a strategy of eradication.

To review, the four essays from Part II enhance our understanding of the ways in which Spanish critics *de allá* engage with Chicano literature. The International Conference on Chicano Literature (and Latino Studies) has provided a space over the last twenty years for emerging Spanish scholars to grapple with themes and issues within Chicano literature, as Cañero demonstrates. An increased interest in Chicano literature and culture has resulted in a space where Spanish and non-Spanish scholars alike can engage in academic exchanges about two seemingly similar cultural models and histories.

There is a pronounced interest in female identity and eco-spaces as presented by critics *de allá*, recognizing parallels between Spanish, Chicano, and African American literary traditions. Ecocriticism, feminism, and a concern for nature abound the perspectives offered by Flys Junquera and Núñez-

Puente. Considering Miguélez's academic formation in the United States, it is not surprising to see his approach lean toward a historical and political analysis of Chicano print culture in the period following the Mexican–American War. While focusing solely on newspapers in the United States, his comparative approach echoes that of the other critics in Part II. Chicano literary scholars *de allá* speak to the nos/otros scholarship that Vivancos-Pérez describes in Part I, all while finding new and interesting ways to approach Chicano criticism in relation to other national and international minority literatures and cultures. The International Conference on Chicano Literature (and Latino Studies) likely will be a central place for the dissemination of this scholarship for years to come.

PART I

SPANISH PERSPECTIVES *DE ACÁ*

CHAPTER 1

Reading, from *Don Quijote de La Mancha* to *The House on Mango Street*

Chicano/a Literature, Mimesis, and the Reader

MANUEL M. MARTÍN-RODRÍGUEZ

IN GENERAL, studies on mimesis tend to concentrate on exploring the relationship between text and reality, paying less attention to other elements of the literary experience, such as the reader and the context of publication, to name just two. Most studies support themselves on Platonic or Aristotelian theory, which explains the focus of their analyses. Plato understood the mimetic as a means of (imperfectly) copying a reality that, in turn, is nothing but an imperfect copy of the ideal world. Aristotle modified Plato's theory by proposing that mimesis was in fact an imitation of a prior action or *praxis*.

It was only in the past few decades that scholarship on mimesis started to shift its focus from the reality/text relationship to other elements of the literary experience.[1] Such a move can be exemplified by the work of Varsava on mimesis and postmodern fiction (1990), as well as by Schad's study of mimesis, Dickens, and his readers (1992). For both Varsava and Schad, reception and reading play an important role in the discourse on mimesis, and they do so in ways that transcend Aristotelian catharsis and Platonic warnings against poets and their influence on readers, the two elements that dominated for centuries whatever consideration was given to reading and readers in this context.

---

1. The classic study on mimesis remains that of Auerbach, whose relativist historicism and implicit warning on the historicity of "reality" itself need to be taken into account by any succeeding study, this one included.

Indeed, after Plato's much heeded warning against poets, virtually all the bibliography related to mimesis and the reader focused on what different groups of people could or should read. In that sense, discussions of mimesis and reading were almost always tied to issues of legal, religious, or moral censorship. Although the history of censorship is well beyond the limits of this essay, some of its manifestations are of special relevance for my topic (mimesis, reading, and Chicano/a literature), and thus I will begin with two pertinent examples. First, it is worth remembering the prohibition against the exportation of novels and other secular books from Europe to the New World during much of the colonial period. As Leonard explored in detail, this interdiction did not stop the arrival of such books, but it succeeded in slowing down their entrance and dissemination. Later on, the initial ban was substituted by stringent normatives against particular groups of potential readers, women and the indigenous peoples in particular, who were not allowed to read certain books even after the legal restrictions against the importation of such books were lifted.[2] Illustrative in that regard are the troubles experienced in seventeenth-century New Mexico by Teresa de Aguilera y Roche, wife of Governor Bernardo López de Mendizábal. Inquisition records first brought to light by Eleanor B. Adams and France V. Scholes revealed that (among many other books) Aguilera owned a copy of Ariosto's *Orlando furioso* in Italian, a gift from her father so she could practice a language that she learned in her childhood. In her defense during the inquisitorial procedure, Aguilera stated:

> If the book had been evil, [my father] *would not have permitted me to read it*, nor would he have done so, for he was a very good Christian. And this book, according to what I heard from him and other persons, has been translated into our Castilian language, like the Petrarch, of which it is a companion volume although the style is different.
> (Adams and Scholes 220, emphasis added)

She also pointed out

> that [*Orlando furioso*] is current and widely read in both Italy and Spain by persons who understand it, for at the beginning of each chapter there is a statement called the allegory which says that only the good is to be taken from it and not the bad; and it inculcates great morality and good doctrine; and God help the witness who had such suspicions.
> (Adams and Scholes 220–21)

---

2. On restrictive policies and their effect, see Leonard, chapter 7.

The crucial element for our purposes is the sentence "by persons who understand it," which brings to the fore not only the issue of language fluency (Italian vs. the Spanish spoken by most New Mexican colonists) but, more importantly, that of the reader's competence, on which all ecclesiastical and lay restrictions rested. The fact that it was a woman who owned and enjoyed reading a book of poetry in 1660s New Mexico made the circumstances much more suspicious in the eyes of her accusers, and even Aguilera is forced to cite in her defense the fact that her father would not have *permitted* her to read the book if he had considered the book evil, thus properly illustrating the multiple levels of direct or indirect censorship affecting female readers at the time.

The second example I would like to discuss is a metaliterary episode in Miguel de Cervantes's *Don Quijote*. In it, the reader learns of the selective burning of Don Alonso Quijano's library by the religious authority in Don Quijote's hamlet.[3] The narration of that incident is marked by a certain irony, as Cervantes seems to play with Plato's warnings against the effects of poets and their works on the body politic. Don Quijote is said to have lost his mind because of his constant reading of chivalric novels, and his particular form of madness consists in the imitation of that earlier praxis which such novels narrate. Don Quijote, perhaps the most famous reader in literary history, confuses reality and its (extravagant) mimesis in the *novelas de caballerías* (chivalric novels) to such an extent that he transforms La Mancha and other surrounding regions in textual rather than geographical areas, seeing castles and giants where *ventas* and windmills stand. As the novel progresses, the limits between the physical world and its literary counterpart become less clearly defined, not just for Don Quijote but for the rest of the characters as well. Though some of the characters pretend to believe in the chivalric novel world only to amuse themselves at Don Quijote's expense, others—like Sancho—inhabit a greyer area between skepticism and the willful suspension of disbelief. Paradoxically, however, as the "madness" extends, Cervantes's readers soon realize that if Don Quijote had not read so extensively, and if he had not decided to imitate the heroes of his readings, he would have never been the splendid idealist character he becomes in the first part of Cervantes's novel, nor the magnificent moralist he is in the second part (a trait that is further accentuated by the way in which Cervantes surrounds him with corrupt and decadent noblemen and other questionable characters). The dangerous influence of chivalric novels in Don Quijote, therefore, ends up being beneficial to the republic as a vehicle of moral criticism and reformation.

---

3. Melberg suggests that in the episode of the library, Aristotelian poetics (as defended by the churchman) clashes with the also Aristotelian principle of mimesis as a reference to an earlier praxis (55).

Though clearly different, my two examples are intimately connected, because *Don Quijote* was one of the first books to circumvent importation restrictions in colonial Latin America, and one of the most widely read novels then and now.[4] But the main reason I wanted to stress these two moments in the history of mimesis and censorship is that I find echoes of both episodes in early Mexican American literature (i.e., that literature written in the United States by authors of Mexican descent that predates the Chicano Movement of the 1960s), and I would like to use them as a prologue to my analysis of mimesis and readers after the Movement.

One of the most well-known Mexican American writers from the nineteenth century is María Amparo Ruiz de Burton. Interestingly, Burton was the author of a five-act comedy adaptation of *Don Quixote*, published in 1876 and never reprinted since then.[5] She published two novels as well: *Who Would Have Thought It* (1872) and *The Squatter and the Don* (1885), both of which were recovered and edited in the 1990s by Rosaura Sánchez and Beatrice Pita, soon becoming central to the turn-of-the-century Chicano/a literary curriculum. These two works are, among other things, a keen protest against the disenfranchisement of the Californios and against discrimination for reasons of ethnicity, nationality, and gender. They represent one of the earliest defenses of the rights of women penned by a Mexican American. However, despite Ruiz de Burton's progressive stance on women's rights, and in spite of the fact that she was a well-read woman, her female characters are portrayed in ways that still reflect the traditional gender expectations on reading at the time. Keeping in mind the extraordinary significance of the fact that they *are* presented as readers, in the first place, I would like to interrogate nonetheless the class and gender aspects of this portrayal. As I have suggested elsewhere, Ruiz de Burton's *The Squatter and the Don* is marked by an elitist class bias that works to present the Alamar family as an example of Californio refined society ("Textual and Land Reclamations" 47). Young Mercedes Alamar, the heroine of *The Squatter and the Don*, reveals such an elite upbringing when we learn that she prefers reading to *siesta*, but the only book we "see" her read is a history of France: no novels or even poetry for her, as if the Spanish colonial ban on *libros de divertimento* (amusement books) were still operative in nineteenth-century U.S. California. The scene, involving Mercedes's French governess Madam Halier, is worth quoting:

---

4. See Leonard, esp. chapter 18. For its relevance in a New Mexican context, see Fray Angélico Chávez, *passim*, or, in more recent times, Thomas E. Chávez's adoption of *Don Quijote*'s literary model to structure his *Chasing History*.

5. In his "Early California Literature," Bancroft acknowledges her comedy as follows: "Mrs Burton reveals her innate Spanish taste in the five-act comedy of *Don Quixote*" (638).

"Mercedes's French novel must be very interesting," Carlota said.
"It is not a novel—it is French History," said Madam Halier. (120)

The ban against novels had long been lifted, as Carlota's comment makes clear, but the social value associated with each of the genres involved in her exchange with Madam Halier suggests that one (history) was more appropriate for upper-class female readers than the other. "A good girl must only read good books" seems to be the implied message in that scene, an idea that we see confirmed in an almost contemporary novel with another upper-class, female California protagonist: Gertrude Atherton's *Rezánov* (1906). In Atherton's novel, the female central character is a historical figure, Conchita Argüello (who later inspired Aurelio M. Espinosa's novella of that title). Ms. Argüello's education is praised as follows in *Rezánov*: "Concha had a larger vocabulary than other Californians of her sex, for she had read many books, and if never a novel, she knew something of poetry" (100). Californians, as these examples indicate, had succeeded in prolonging (under a class and gender basis) colonial censorship up to the late nineteenth century, at least as far as the upper-class, female readership was concerned.

In consequence, as an instructive and formative book, whatever history of France Mercedes read in *The Squatter and the Don* must be considered an "appropriate" choice for her within the parameters of her patriarchal society, one that would keep her mind focused on reality, preventing flights of fancy like those of Don Quijote, whose own fantasies about France—incidentally—had been recreated by Ruiz de Burton in her play *Don Quixote*, where she has the *hidalgo* say:

> I am he for whom dangers and great exploits are reserved. I am he who is destined to revive the order of the Round Table, that of twelve peers of France, and the worthies, and to obliterate the memory of the Platins, the Tablantes, the Olibantes, and Tirantes, "Knight of the Sun," and the Belianises, with the whole tribe of knights-errant of old. (19–20)

Ruiz de Burton's readers, especially those familiar with both of her works quoted here, cannot help but wonder about Mercedes's own destiny and how it might be related to reading and genre. If Don Quijote's incessant consumption of chivalric novels produced in him a desire to imitate that earlier praxis (to phrase it in Aristotelian terms), could we not argue that Mercedes's reading of history is behind her quick maturation process and her progressive acceptance of the historical forces that transform her (family) life? In that sense, Ruiz de Burton's own mixture of genres (romance for the story of Mercedes and Clarence, and political history for the critique of contemporary abuses against the Californios[6]) is not unlike Cervantes's strategy to ridicule the *novelas de caballerías* by weaving a parody of them into his masterpiece. Like Cervantes, Ruiz de Burton exposes the limitations of the romance for narrating the experiences of the Californios (thus rejecting the incipient co-optation of the Californio experience in sentimental and picturesque literature),[7] while embracing the committed discourse of denunciation and self-affirmation as a more suitable option.

In New Mexico, the Platonic warning against the dangerous effects of poetic mimesis finds a perfect example in Luciano, a character in Eusebio Chacón's *Tras la tormenta, la calma* (1892). Luciano represents Quixotic mimetism adapted to his own times and environment. Like Don Quijote, Luciano is unable to distinguish between reality and its discursive representation: "Todas aquellas cosas que leía le parecían á él haber pasado tal cual se pintaban, y nada creía más propio de la vida Estudiantil que todas aquellas blasfemias, indecoros, inmoralidades y faltas de honor" (38) ("He believed that all the things he read had actually happened as they were described and came to believe that the life of the student was just about blasphemy, shamefulness, inmortality, and breeches of honor" [87]).[8] As a consequence, the young Luciano adopts literary characters as veritable models of conduct:

> Era el tiempo de recordación para los exámenes finales, y él en lugar de atender á sus deberes gastaba su tiempo en leer El *Don Juan* de Byron, *El Estudiante de Salamanca* y otras composiciones por el estilo, de cuyas páginas iba cobrando una muy fuerte afición á las deshonestidades que en ellas se esparcen. De tal manera se despertó su fantasía que solo anhelaba la ocasión para probarse un temerario Don Juan, ó un Felix de Montemar. (38)

> It was closed week before final examinations, and instead of tending to his studies, Luciano spent his time reading [Lord] Byron's *Don Juan, The Student of Salamanca,* and other such works, becoming obsessed with the dishonest behavior that runs throughout them. In this way a fantasy was born in him that caused him to dream of the occasion he might prove himself a don Juan of a Felix of Montemar. (87)[9]

More a fool than a madman, Luciano lives his life as if he were a literary character (which ironically he is, of course, like Don Quijote), and that pro-

---

6. Cf. the subtitle: "A Novel Descriptive of Contemporary Occurrences in California."
7. See Padilla (*My History*), and Gutiérrez.
8. *Writings of Eusebio Chacón,* ed. A. Gabriel Meléndez and Francisco Lomelí 87.
9. See footnote 8.

duces the humor in this novella, when his aspirations and actions clash with those of the other characters, for whom books play virtually no role. Even though Luciano succeeds in marrying his love interest, Lola, Chacón uses this character to stress the superiority of "reality" over its literary mimesis: toward the end of the story, Luciano is publicly ridiculed and, like a second-part Don Quijote, he is brought back to the sanity of societal mores. In doing so, Chacón seems to warn against the dangers of recreational, unsupervised reading, thus raising the specter of censorship or, at least, of stricter controls for younger readers.

These and other examples of nineteenth-century Mexican American literature that we could explore reveal a large dose of traditionalism in their understanding of the relationship between reality, literature, writing, and reading. Even during the first half of the twentieth century, we find numerous examples of didactic writing in which moral lessons are foregrounded at the expense of the aesthetic pleasure of reading. This is the case of *Las aventuras de Don Chipote o cuando los pericos mamen*, published by Daniel Venegas in 1928, in Los Angeles, and in whose title and structure it is easy to perceive an allusion to Miguel de Cervantes's *Don Quijote*.

Like Cervantes's hero, Don Chipote leaves his village in search of "adventures" in Mexico's northern neighbor. An illiterate peasant, Don Chipote is moved not by the reading of novels or poetry, but by the stories he hears from his neighbor Pitacio: tall tales of a country in which money can be swept off the streets. Venegas, not unlike Ruiz de Burton a few decades earlier, combines a realistic (naturalistic at times) description of the experiences of Mexicans in California with moralizing digressions that help prepare the reader for the conclusion of the novel, that asserts that "los mexicanos se harán ricos en Estados Unidos: CUANDO LOS PERICOS MAMEN" (155) ("Mexicans will make it big in the United States . . . WHEN PARROTS BREAST-FEED" [160]).[10] In this warning against the danger of believing stories that say otherwise, Venegas continues exploring the tension between representation and reality that Ruiz de Burton and Chacón had examined as well. The radical difference in his case resides in the way in which he displaces the poetic referent from the world of high culture (to which both Ruiz de Burton and Chacón subscribed) to the (predominantly oral) popular culture of the Mexican masses. In other words, even if Venegas's title contains an allusion to a literary work, that reference belongs to the world of the author and the implied reader, but would be mostly incomprehensible for his characters, for whom cultural life centers on folkloric compositions and in the popular theatre scene that flourished at the

---

10. Venegas, *The Adventures of Don Chipote, or, When Parrots Breast-Feed* 160.

time in Los Angeles.[11] Don Chipote's only books are a *cancionero* and a book of poetry that he purchases with the intention of impressing a potential lover. As an illiterate man, he needs someone to read the books for him, and his own interaction with their contents seems to be restricted to memorizing, rather than understanding them: "No faltó quien, mediante una propina, le estuviera repasando las poesías hasta que se le metieron en el casco. Las canciones fueron cosa más difícil, pues el libro no traía las tonadas, por lo que de nada le sirvió el libro" (149) ("there was no lack of people willing to go over the lines of poetry with him, for a small fee, until he got them into his skull. The songs were more difficulty, because the book didn't include the notes, making the book not worth a darn." [150]).

The change of referent from the literary to the popular tradition that we see at work in Venegas's novel is of major significance, because it foreshadows much of what will later be the correlation between reality, mimesis, and readership in the literature of the Chicano Movement, including an emphasis on the working-class experience, a preference for popular language, a preeminence of the oral tradition, and an attempt to connect with working-class audiences. In fact, Mexican and Chicano/a workers became the inspiration for most literary characters during and (to a large extent) after the Chicano Movement, and they were seen as the ideal readership for many of those works as well.[12] As for mimesis, Chicano Movement literature is essentially mimetic in the sense that it reveals strong and recognizable ties/references to reality; but I would like to claim that its greatest originality resides in the way in which it transforms the reader into the central element in the literary process (including the very notion of mimesis).

In Chicano Movement literature, we perceive an undeniable effort to make the reader see him/herself in the text. Many of the works produced during the decades of the 1960s and the 1970s would have the reader feel that the main aspects of the plot are relevant not only to the characters' lives but also to those of the reader and his/her family. To a certain extent, this is also true of other ethnic literatures, in particular during their phase of affirmation. In them, as in Chicano/a letters, the literary recreation of clearly recognizable experiences serves as a catalyst for the formation of group consciousness, while simultaneously working to correct stereotypical and distorted images of the group in mainstream literature and the media. In the process, book sales and the dissemination of the new ethnic literature usually contribute to consolidating the emergent tradition by generating a continuous demand for that

---

11. For an assessment of the theatrical scene in Los Angeles at the time, see Kanellos 17–70.

12. I have explored this and many of the issues below in my book *Life in Search of Readers, passim*. This essay expands on my original research in those areas.

newer kind of literary representation. In the case of Chicano/a literature, as I explored elsewhere,[13] this resulted in the creation of Chicano/a presses, at first, and then in the increasing access by Chicano/a authors to mainstream publishing outlets, although at that point (or for those texts at least) the mimetic impulse had evolved into an entirely different kind of effort, often driven by a transcultural need to make the Chicano/a experience understandable to distant readers.

A good example of the Chicano Movement understanding of mimesis is found in the works of Tomás Rivera. In addition to illustrating it superbly in his novel . . . *y no se lo tragó la tierra*, Rivera wrote several essays on mimesis that are relevant for this discussion. In "Remembering, Discovery and Volition in the Literary Imaginative Process," for example, Rivera stresses the need to recreate a reality that is well known to the readers but also (and more importantly) to do so in terms that are familiar to the readers:

> I will discuss remembering first; I refer to the method of narrating which people used. That is to say, I recall what they remembered and the manner in which they told it. There was always a way of compressing and exciting the sensibilities with a minimum of words. New events were also being constantly added. Needless to say, this is what the oral tradition is all about. (*Tomás Rivera* 366)

Rivera's endeavor to "imitate" popular narrative forms should not be interpreted as just a stylistic resource. Rather, as I suggested above, it needs to be seen as a communicative strategy that seeks to engage the reader in an active process of literary (re)creation. Per his own implicit admission in "Remembering," Rivera's opting for a narrative mode that was familiar to his intended readers was of the utmost importance. While earlier novels such as José Antonio Villarreal's *Pocho* or John Rechy's *City of Night* initially failed to connect with a Chicano/a audience,[14] Rivera's success (aided, no doubt, by the efficient marketing strategies of the Grupo Editorial Quinto Sol) was based upon "imitating" not only a Chicano/a reality but his readers' storytelling practices and preferences as well.

Rivera's essays also emphasize the pleasure of reading as a ceremony of rejoicing in a shared experience. Even within . . . *y no se lo tragó la tierra*, the idea of a literary communion of sorts is explored through the figure of Bartolo, the itinerant bard:

---

13. *Life in Search of Readers*, chapter 1.
14. For Villarreal, see Bruce-Novoa; for Rechy, see Bruce-Novoa, and also Martín-Rodríguez, "Between Milton and Proust."

Bartolo pasaba por el pueblo por aquello de diciembre cuando tanteaba que la mayor parte de la gente había regresado de los trabajos. Siempre venía vendiendo sus poemas. Se le acababan casi el primer día porque en los poemas se encontraban los nombres de la gente del pueblo. Y cuando los leía en voz alta era algo emocionante y serio. Recuerdo que una vez le dijo a la raza que leyeran los poemas en voz alta porque la voz era la semilla del amor en la oscuridad. (113)

Bartolo passed through town every December when he knew that most of the people had returned from work up north. He always came by selling his poems. By the end of the first day, they were almost sold out because the names of the people of the town appeared in the poems. And when he read them aloud it was something emotional and serious. I recall that one time he told the people to read the poems out loud because the spoken word was the seed of love in the darkness. (215)[15]

This episode works in a specular manner for Rivera's own activity as a writer because, even if Rivera does not use the proper names of his own townsfolk, as Bartolo did, his novel can be said to reflect their lives through those of his characters.[16] As Julián Olivares rightly suggested, mimetic writing becomes for Rivera a kind of moral obligation:

We can perceive . . . [in Rivera's statements about his works] that Rivera had an ethical obligation to write of his people, to record their collective experience, to document the existence of a people. In this regard, he chose to write of the people with whom he was most ideologically and socially tied: the migrant workers. As a result, his people can read of themselves, and those who are aware of this type of existence can say: "sí, así era."
(in Rivera's *Tomás Rivera* 45–46)

In thus establishing a bond between author and reader, Rivera turns around Plato's admonition against poets and the moral effects of their works. In Rivera's mind, the poet's task is justified precisely as an ethical obligation: that of telling those stories that the official discourse had silenced, and telling them in a manner that is both meaningful to his audience and respectful of his audience's ways.

---

15. For more on Bartolo's poetry, see Martín-Rodríguez, "Paper Trails" 152–59.
16. The figure of Bartolo has generated considerable interest among critics. Morales, for instance, considers him a representative of community and of the oral tradition. As such, he emblematizes Rivera's desire to recreate reality as the oral tradition does.

Like Rivera, most Chicano/a writers in the 1970s attempted to document the experiences of their communities in a more or less mimetic way. Rolando Hinojosa's early works were perceived at the time as *costumbrista* (centered on the depiction of customs and manners) precisely because of their mimetic quality, although Hinojosa's experimentation with multiple genres precludes such a reductionist interpretation of his writings.[17] Even Rudolfo A. Anaya, who referenced myths and supernatural events in his fiction much more frequently than the other writers already discussed, seems to have embraced the need to reflect in his stories an experience familiar to his first and most immediate audience. Along with the universalistic dimension that myth may bring to *Bless Me, Ultima,* for instance,[18] we also find in that novel a careful description of folkloric practices that reflect those characteristic of New Mexican rural communities at the time. In his case, it is not the kind of anthropological or picturesque description typical of the works of Anglo American writers who visited New Mexico;[19] rather, Anaya adopts an insider's perspective in order to minimize the distance between characters and readers: what happens to the characters is something that could have happened to the reader as well or that, at least, is part of the audience's collective memory. Paraphrasing Olivares, a reader of Anaya could very well say "Yes, my grandmother told those kinds of stories as well."

The predominant mimetic drive that I am positing as typical of Chicano/a 1970s narrative had its exceptions from early on. In 1975, two rather successful novels seriously challenged the tenets of predictable reader's response. Alejandro Morales's *Caras viejas y vino nuevo* combined experimental techniques associated with the French *nouveau roman* with Spanish expressionism and *tremendismo* to portray an urban reality in almost hallucinatory ways. Though easily recognizable, the experiences depicted in *Caras viejas* do not allow the reader the kind of positive identification that was possible with Rivera's *Tierra,* since the characters are mostly drug addicts, alcoholics, and violent youngsters. Moreover, the novel's presentation techniques are far from the folk practices of the oral tradition, which further complicates the reader's emotional involvement with the storyline.

Ron Arias's *The Road to Tamazunchale,* on the other hand, is as far from the populist mimetism of the books published by Quinto Sol as it is from Morales's expressionism. Perhaps the first postmodern Chicano writer, and

---

17. Martín-Rodríguez, *Rolando Hinojosa y su "cronicón" chicano,* chapter 2.
18. On the universalism of myth in Anaya, see Cazemajou 256.
19. Padilla ("Imprisoned Narrative?" 45) analyzes this Anglo American discourse on New Mexico.

one of the earliest postmodern authors in the United States,[20] Arias delights in playing with the ontological limits of reality in a way that disrupts mimesis in its most traditional sense. Still, *Tamazunchale* would fit well with the newer understanding of postmodern mimesis that Varsava explores:

> Postmodern fiction is a *representation* of [the] questioning of the values and preoccupations of our epoch; in this lies its mimesis, its mimetic function. The literary ramifications of this questioning include the thematization of uncertainty, ambiguity, undeterminacy and a consequent concern for *form* that emphasizes the latter as a potentially liberating phenomenon. (182, original emphasis)

Indeed, the boundaries between the real and the unreal are extremely fuzzy in *Tamazunchale*: characters seemingly die but they keep reappearing in subsequent chapters as if they were still alive; they transform themselves into books or flowers; some of them come not from "reality" but from previous books by other authors, as is the case of David, the drowned man found in a dry riverbed. In this sense, *Tamazunchale* represents a more radical challenge to traditional mimesis than *Caras viejas* does, since Morales's reader may still recognize a well-known reality beyond narrative distortions, while the reader of Arias is thrown into a much more literary world (or a *formalist* world, in Varsava's sense of the term) that is, by necessity, further removed from everyday experience, even if geographic and cultural elements are still recognizable.

From that moment on, the mimetic literature that was so successful in constructing an image of Chicanas/os as a group started diversifying to the point where no dominant style or trend could be identified.[21] At the same time, the increasing visibility of Chicana literature, first heralded by works by Estela Portillo-Trambley, Berta Ornelas, Isabella Ríos, and Bernice Zamora in the 1970s, is emblematic of a shift from the pursuit of commonalities and group identification to an interest in the exploration of internal differences. The ensuing boom of Chicana narrative in the 1980s and beyond produces an interesting phenomenon in which new mimetic works begin to appear. These works, in particular those produced during the 1980s, position themselves at a special juncture that allows them to be a commentary on both reality and literature. In the latter sense, novels like Sandra Cisneros's *The House on Mango Street* and Ana Castillo's *The Mixquiahuala Letters,* because of the multiple ways in which they respond to a largely patriarchal literary

---

20. See my "Border Crisscrossing" 198.
21. Tatum provides some useful categories and groupings in chapters 5–7.

tradition (which includes 1970s Chicano literature), can be said to "read" and comment on previous texts, to the extent that we can almost hear the implied authors say "no, así no era" when confronting previous male Chicano depictions of family and society, which they now problematize and rephrase. In the former sense, books by Chicana authors share with their female readers the kind of bond that Rivera and Anaya, among others, sought to create with a gender-undifferentiated Chicano/a audience. Thus, in most works by Chicanas, female readers find a recognizable feminine, Chicana experience that they may perceive as "real" and/or as part of their experience as well. This is what poet and essayist Pat Mora refers to as "elements of commonality" that Chicana authors share with their readers.[22] As a consequence, the 1980s signal the beginning of a new cycle in which mimesis contributes to the formation of a Chicana group awareness by bringing authors and readers together in the creation of a new literary reality. This is best exemplified by Sandra Cisneros's *The House on Mango Street*, in which the author explores the tension between representational mimesis (that is, one that attempts to be faithful to the reality that characters and/or readers inhabit) and its utopian counterpart, understood as a literary mode that attempts to represent not what the world is like but what it could or should be. Since I have explored the metaliterary aspects of *Mango Street* elsewhere,[23] there is no need to repeat my arguments here. I will only add that utopian mimesis, as defined above, is best described in the story "A House of My Own," especially in its oft-quoted final paragraph: "Only a house quiet as snow, a space for myself to go, clean as paper before the poem" (108). For the reader of *Mango Street*, the stories in the book are an artistic rephrasing of social realities well known to most Chicanas (and many other readers): marginality, substandard living conditions, domestic and gender violence, an education that teaches girls to "grow down,"[24] and poverty, among other salient aspects. But "A House of My Own" opens up (and never closes) the possibility of other texts and other realities. The blank page is not dependent on a prior reality or praxis; rather, it stands as a yet-to-be-fulfilled potentiality; it seems to suggest that literature has a role in portraying the world we inhabit, but also in imagining better worlds. Considered from a reader's perspective, the blank page also works metaphorically as the

---

22. Mora talks about poetry specifically: "A Chicana poet also uses elements of commonality with her listeners: the importance of family, the retelling of familiar tales" (127). I believe that the same can be said of all other genres, and that several other common elements could be added to the list.

23. *Life in Search of Readers* 76–81.

24. The idea is borrowed from Annis Pratt's work on the female bildungsroman (14).

ultimate statement against censorship and other forms of social control. The blank page astutely circumvents the issues confronted by Teresa de Aguilar y Roche centuries earlier: if the book has no content, no parent or authority figure can determine it unfit for the female reader. In a book where patriarchal authority is almost absolute (cf. the stories about Sally, Minerva, Marin, and most of the women in the neighborhood), the utopian emptiness of the blank page signals the possibility of alternative subject positionalities and of an alternative literary praxis. Paraphrasing Cisneros's text, we could define this new praxis as not that of a man's nor a daddy's, but one in which people like Teresa de Aguilar, Mercedes Alamar, Esperanza Cordero, and others, would encounter freedom and openness, rather than barriers and censorship; one in which literary discourse would not only reflect the world outside but create new worlds from scratch.

WORKS CITED

Adams, Eleanor B., and France V. Scholes. "Books in New Mexico, 1598–1680." 1942. *With a Book in Their Hands: Chicano/a Readers and Readerships Across the Centuries*. Ed. Manuel M. Martín-Rodríguez. Albuquerque: U of New Mexico P, 2014. 207–31. Print.

Anaya, Rudolfo A. *Bless Me, Ultima*. Berkeley, CA: Quinto Sol, 1972. Print.

Arias, Ron. *The Road to Tamazunchale*. Reno, NV: West Coast Poetry Review, 1975. Print.

Atherton, Gertrude. *Rezánov*. New York: The Authors and Newspapers Association, 1906. Print.

Auerbach, Erich. *Mimesis: The Representation of Reality in Western Literature*. 1946. Trans. Willard R. Trask. Princeton: Princeton UP, 1971. Print.

Bancroft, Hubert H. "Early California Literature." *The Works of Hubert Howe Bancroft: Vol. 29, Essays and Miscellany*. San Francisco: The History Company, 1890. 591–668. Print.

Bruce-Novoa, Juan. "Canonical and NonCanonical Texts." *The Americas Review* 14.3–4 (Fall–Winter 1986): 119–35. Print.

Castillo, Ana. *The Mixquiahuala Letters*. Binghamton, NY: Bilingual Press, 1986. Print.

Cazemajou, Jean. "The Search for a Center: The Shamanic Journey of Mediators in Anaya's Trilogy, *Bless Me, Ultima*, *Heart of Aztlán*, and *Tortuga*." *Rudolfo A. Anaya*. Ed. César A. González-T. La Jolla, CA: Lalo Press, 1990. 254–73. Print.

Cervantes, Miguel de. *Don Quijote de la Mancha*. 1605. Madrid: Alhambra, 1983. 2 vols. Print.

Chacón, Eusebio. *El hijo de la tempestad. Tras la tormenta, la calma*. Santa Fe: Tipografía del Boletín Popular, 1892. Print.

———. *The Writings of Eusebio Chacón*. Ed. A. Gabriel Meléndez and Francisco A. Lomelí. Albuquerque: U of New Mexico P, 2012. Print.

Chávez, Fray Angélico. *My Penitente Land: Reflections on Spanish New Mexico*. Albuquerque: U of New Mexico P, 1974. Print.

Chávez, Thomas E. *Chasing History: Quixotic Quests for Artifacts, Arts, and Heritage*. Santa Fe: Sunstone Press, 2013. Print.

Cisneros, Sandra. *The House on Mango Street*. Houston: Arte Público Press, 1984. Print.

Espinosa, Aurelio M. *Conchita Argüello: Historia y novela californiana*. New York: Macmillan, 1938. Print.

Gutiérrez, Ramón A. "Charles Fletcher Lummis and the Orientalization of New Mexico." *Nuevomexicano Cultural Legacy: Forms, Agencies, and Discourse*. Ed. Francisco A. Lomelí et al. Albuquerque: U of New Mexico P, 2002. 11–27. Print.

Hinojosa, Rolando. *Estampas del Valle y otras obras*. Berkeley, CA: Quinto Sol, 1973. Print.

Kanellos, Nicolás. *A History of Hispanic Theatre in the United States: Origins to 1940*. Austin: U of Texas P, 1990. Print.

Leonard, Irving A. *Books of the Brave: Being an Account of Books and of Men in the Spanish Conquest and Settlement of the Sixteenth-Century New World*. 1949. Berkeley: U of California P, 1992. Print.

Martín-Rodríguez, Manuel M. "Between Milton and Proust: John Rechy's World of Lost Angels and Time Remembered." *The Textual Outlaw: Reading John Rechy in the Twenty-First Century*. Ed. Manuel M. Martín-Rodríguez and B. Hernandez-Jason. Alcalá de Henares: Instituto Franklin-Universidad de Alcalá de Henares, 2015. 85–93. Print.

———. "Border Crisscrossing: *The* (Long and Winding) *Road to Tamazunchale*." *Cross-Addressing: Resistance Literature and Cultural Borderlands*. Ed. John C. Hawley. Buffalo: SUNY P, 1996. 181–206. Print.

———. *Life in Search of Readers: Reading (in) Chicano/a Literature*. Albuquerque: U of New Mexico P, 2003. Print.

———. "Paper Trails: Recovering Mexican American Popular Poetry from the Early Twentieth Century." *Aztlán* 42.1 (2017): 139–62. Print.

———. *Rolando Hinojosa y su "cronicón" chicano: Una novela del lector*. Sevilla: Universidad de Sevilla, 1993. Print.

———. "Textual and Land Reclamations: The Critical Reception of Early Chicano/a Literature." *Recovering the U.S. Hispanic Literary Heritage*. Vol. 2. Ed. Charles Tatum and Erlinda Gonzales-Berry. Houston: Arte Público Press, 1996. 40–58. Print.

Melberg, Arne. *Theories of Mimesis*. Cambridge: Cambridge UP, 1995. Print.

Mora, Pat. *Nepantla: Essays from the Land in the Middle*. Albuquerque: U of New Mexico P, 1993. Print.

Morales, Alejandro. *Caras viejas y vino nuevo*. México: Joaquín Mortiz, 1975. Print.

———. "'*Y no se lo tragó la tierra*': palabra y estructura en una cultura postmoderna." *Culturas hispanas de los Estados Unidos de América*. Ed. María J. Buxó Rey and Tomás Calvo Buezas. Madrid: Cultura Hispánica, 1990. 494–500. Print.

Olivares, Julián. *Tomás Rivera: The Complete Works*. Houston: Arte Público Press, 1991. Print.

Padilla, Genaro. "Imprisoned Narrative? Or Lies, Secrets, and Silence in New Mexico Women's Autobiography." *Criticism in the Borderlands: Studies in Chicano Literature, Culture, and Ideology*. Ed. Héctor Calderón and J. D. Saldívar. Durham: Duke UP, 1991. 43–60. Print.

———. *My History, Not Yours: The Formation of Mexican American Autobiography*. Madison: U of Wisconsin P, 1993. Print.

Pratt, Annis. *Archetypal Patterns in Women's Fiction*. Bloomington: Indiana UP, 1981. Print.

Rivera, Tomás. *Tomás Rivera: The Complete Works*. Houston: Arte Público Press, 1992. Print.

Ruiz de Burton, María Amparo. *Don Quixote de la Mancha: A Comedy in Five Acts, Taken from Cervantes' Novel of That Name.* N.p.: n. pag., 1876.

———. *The Squatter and the Don: A Novel Descriptive of Contemporary Occurrences in California.* 1885. Houston: Arte Público, 1993. Print.

———. *Who Would Have Thought It?.* 1872. Houston: Arte Público, 1995. Print.

Schad, John. *The Reader in the Dickensian Mirrors: Some New Language.* New York: St. Martin's Press, 1992. Print.

Tatum, Charles M. *Chicano and Chicana Literature: Otra voz del pueblo.* Tucson: U of Arizona P, 2006. Print.

Varsava, Jerry A. *Contingent Meanings: Postmodern Fiction, Mimesis, and the Reader.* Tallahassee: Florida State UP, 1990. Print.

Venegas, Daniel. *Las aventuras de Don Chipote o cuando los pericos mamen.* 1928. México: SEP, 1984. Print.

———. *The Adventures of Don Chipote, or, When Parrots Breast-Feed.* Houston: Arte Público Press, 2000. Print.

CHAPTER 2

Mestizaje in Afro-Iberian Writers Najat El Hachmi and Saïd El Kadaoui Moussaoui through the Borderland Theories of U.S. Third World Feminisms

CARMEN SANJUÁN-PASTOR

IN THIS ESSAY, I use feminist *mestizaje* theories from the borderland (Moraga and Anzaldúa; Anzaldúa; Saldívar-Hull; Sandoval)[1] as a lens through which to examine two texts produced from a border position by Catalan-Amazigh writers Najat El Hachmi and Saïd El Kadaoui Moussaoui: *L'últim patriarca* and *Límites y fronteras*.[2] These two novels address the feeling of material and psychological insecurity experienced by the daughters and sons of Moroccan immigrants in Spain who are confronted with contradictory sociocultural demands and belongings. Both authors fictionalize these anxieties in the form

---

1. My use of *mestizaje* as a lens in this essay follows two specific analytical perspectives found in Anzaldúa's own use of this term. First, Michael Hames-García has distinguished "the historical process of racial mixing (through sexual relations) in Latin America (*mestizaje*) from Anzaldúa's theoretical extrapolation from *mestizaje*: [. . .] understood as any mixing of cultures, languages, or philosophies" ("How to Tell" 109). Second, Yvonne Yarbro-Bejarano has proposed to study Anzaldúa's "*mestiza* consciousness" as "a constructionist project" "that gives voice and substance to subjects rendered mute and invisible by hegemonic practices and discourses, and is understood as the necessary prelude to political change" (Trinh T. Minh-ha, *Women, Native, Other,* 87) (Yarbro-Bejarano 13). Furthermore, Paula Moya has contextualized this analytical project as part of Anzaldúa's contribution to developing "a woman of color identity and politics" (*Learning* 65–66). In this essay, I link feminist *mestizaje* theories from the borderland to the practice and theories of third world feminisms (Chandra Talpade Mohanty, "Cartographies").

2. It is estimated that 80 percent of the Moroccans that live in Catalonia are of Amazigh origin ("Imazighen en la sociedad"). Akioud and Castellanos explain that the original inhabitants of the North of Africa are the Imaziguen (the plural form of Amazigh). Although they are also known as Berbers, this term has negative connotations (7). For more information, also see Holgado and Razgalla.

of a fractured subjectivity and point to writing as a way of reconstructing the multicultural self. Yet, even though both texts seem to address a similar form of pain associated with the complex lived realities of the border subject, the authors construct the confusion and isolation felt by their main characters in substantially different ways, both theoretically and creatively. I argue that in her investigation of "the gradual incarceration" (*The Last Patriarch* 245)[3] that looms over her central protagonist, El Hachmi sheds light on the silences and marginalizations felt by those individuals who fall through the cracks of normative identities—in this case, the daughters of Moroccan-Amazigh immigrants from The Rif. I read this exploration of living with multiple marginalities through the concept of *mestizo* or border thinking as articulated by women of color and Chicana feminist theory. The first-person voice in *L'últim patriarca* imagines writing as a way of recreating "one's own identity narrative" (*relato identitario*) (El Hachmi, "El inherente" 156–57).[4] I propose reading this "identity narrative" as the product of multiple negotiations and as a form of addressing various manifestations of personal and social violence. Similarly, Ismaïl, the main character of *Límites y fronteras,* writes a first-person account of his own process of reconstituting his subjectivity after suffering a psychotic break in hopes of understanding and healing the pain he feels. El Kadaoui Moussaoui nonetheless is less interested in exploring the multiple social realities that constitute the border self, and instead focuses on exploring the danger that essentialized identities or "prison identities"[5] pose to developing his own political thinking. I approach his creative elaboration of a borderland identity through the theories of two authors the writer himself has cited as his influences: Amin Maalouf's discussion of identities and individualism, and Kwame Anthony Appiah's views on cosmopolitanism and ethics. Moreover, I point to the limits of this apparatus to integrate true cultural diversity and a reflection on social justice.

L'ÚLTIM PATRIARCA

L'últim patriarca is conceived structurally in two parts comprising thirty-eight and thirty-nine vignettes or short chapters respectively and preceded by a

---

3. All quotes are from the English edition: *The Last Patriarch* (2010).

4. In "El inherente espacio de la creación literaria," El Hachmi has explained this state of "identitary schizophrenia," which daughters of immigrants often feel to an extent that impedes their ability to develop their own "identity narrative," "in order to not become either devoured by the paternal narrative or overly diluted by alternative discourses of the "host society."

5. El Kadaoui Moussaoui defines "prison identities" as "monolithic and rigid." "Identidad prisión," *El País,* 7 Oct. 2010. http://elpais.com/diario/2010/10/07/sociedad/1286402403_850215.html.

chapter zero, which functions as a prophecy of sorts, told in a narrative style imitating that of storytellers, that warns us: "This is the story of Mimoum, son of Allal, son of Mohammed. [. . .] It is his story and the story of the last of the great patriarchs who make up the long line of Driouch's forebears"(vii). This false prophecy, though, ultimately winds up straying toward another story: that of Mimoum's daughter (vii). In this prologue, El Hachmi already suggests a number of the themes that she revisits throughout the novel and that I seek to analyze: the essentialist gaze toward Arab-Islamic cultures, the role of "narratives"—"whether determinist or pseudo-magical in character" (vii)—in the creation of one's own identity, and the construction of gender identities within the specific Moroccan-Amazigh social and cultural system—located first in the rural zone of The Rif and later in the immigrant community of Catalonia. The two parts that form the body of the novel weave a singular reflection upon the origin and nature of Mimoum's power, which is presented from the point of view of his daughter. Both parts, however, respond to different creative criteria. The first section of the novel takes place in The Rif and describes events to which the narrator lacked direct access or was too young to remember. This part of the story is narrated in a distant tone by a narrative voice that seems aware of the motivations that drive the characters who inhabit the familial stories she chooses to share. Through an analysis of the various clues suggested by the narrator, the reader can reconstruct the moments in which she gained access to these familial stories, heard and repeated in different intimate family circles, along with traces of explanations offered by the protagonists and the language in which these explanations were codified ("I will get rid of all the djinns he's got inside him [16]," "whores who needed a male the way bitches or doe rabbits do [42]"). When viewed collectively, these narrative fragments reveal the ideologies upon which the characters operate and also must negotiate on a day-to-day basis. The second part of the novel, however, is narrated with a less-certain pulse. The first-person voice does not order the pieces of a puzzle from a distance but rather tackles her own partial comprehension of the material and discursive relations that regulate her social position as the daughter of Moroccan-Amazigh immigrants in Spain. El Hachmi represents, in a movement of great complexity, the narrator's process of reconciling differing aspects of her multicultural self, first through the perspective of a child and later of a young woman, while at the same time addressing various manifestations of personal and social violence that she experiences in her liminal position.

In my argument, in *L'últim patriarca* El Hachmi shows the process of forming the "self and collective consciousness" (Mohanty, "Cartographies" 33) of the first-person voice that ties together the narrative. I suggest that this process can be read alongside the theorization of a "multiplicitous subjectivity" (Ruiz-Aho 357) provided by "'U.S. Third World Feminists'(Moraga and Anzaldúa 1981; Sandoval 1991)" (351).[6] Theoretical constructs such as Gloria Anzaldúa's *"mestiza* or borderland consciousness" (*Borderlands/La Frontera*) or Cherríe Moraga's "theory in the flesh" (*This Bridge Called My Back: Writings by Radical Women of Color*) emphasize the notion of a subjectivity "structured by multiple determinants—gender, class, sexuality, and contradictory membership in competing cultures and racial identities" (Yarbro-Bejarano 11). Moraga explains how this critical approach not only signals the *physical realities* (Moraga and Anzaldúa 23) experienced by the border subject as a source of knowledge about the oppressions she suffers, but also calls for an articulation of these relations of oppression: "Here, we attempt to bridge the contradictions in our experience. [. . .] We do this bridging by naming ourselves and by telling our stories in our own words" (23).

Two facets of this critical apparatus merit further commentary in order to develop my argument regarding the theory of *mestizo* or border thinking that I read in *L'últim patriarca*'s narrative composition. First is the need to situate this theorization of *mestizaje* in the realities that exist at the U.S. and Mexican border (Yarbro-Bejarano 8–9, J. D. Saldívar 152). Chicana feminism should not be understood as a reflection on "'signifying spaces,' but [rather on] material geopolitical issues that redirect feminist discourse" (Saldívar-Hull 208). A second area of interest is the way in which feminist thinking has been defined under this formulation. Chandra Talpade Mohanty has explained how third world women have delineated a feminist ideology and practice, independent of their rejection of this label in various instances due to its association with cultural imperialism or "shortsightedness in defining the meaning of gender in terms of middle-class, white experiences, and in terms of internal racism, classism, and homophobia" (7). Rediscovering the feminist interventions and practices of third world women in their daily experiences or in their histories requires, as Mohanty suggests, "reading against the grain of a number of intersecting progressive discourses (e.g., white feminism, third world nationalist,

---

6. Jessica Folkart already has indicated the plurality inherent in the border position from which the narrator in *L'últim patriarca* speaks, one she suggests reading through the lens of the border theories of Anzaldúa, Homi Bhabha, and Parvati Nair. Likewise, Cristián H. Ricci and Folkart, reading *L'últim patriarca* through the lens of Abdelkébir Khatibi's key concepts of "penseé-autre" and "double critique," have pointed out that El Hachmi's narrator questions "the logocentrism of the unitary Cartesian subject of the Occident as well as the metaphysical Islamic subject of the Orient" (Folkart 360). My reading complements their interpretation by pointing out U.S. third world feminism's emphasis on challenging the "individualist subject of much of liberal feminist theory" (Mohanty 36) or of ethnic nationalist movements (Moya, *Learning* 65–66) that are primarily focused on the analysis of gender relations or of racism, at the cost of rendering invisible the simultaneously occurring oppressions experienced by women of color.

and socialist), as well as the politically regressive racist, imperialist, sexist discourses of slavery, colonialism, and contemporary capitalism" (4). Positioned at the interstices of the different worlds in which they live, women of color do not feel safe "within the inner life of her Self" (Anzaldúa 42) and often must pause during the performance of their daily activities to evaluate the power relations that determine the options available to them.[7] In this process of comprehending the complex discursive framework that can obscure or invisibilize the hegemonic structures that regulate their lives, the role of memory and writing possesses a fundamental importance "as a space for struggle and contestation of reality itself" (Mohanty 35). The use of private memories and personal stories that imply a political act of consciousness-raising is one of the key processes that allow for the creation of "*mestiza* consciousness" in *Borderlands* (Yarbro-Bejarano 14).

Similar to the narratives written by women of color that I employ as critical reference, I suggest that *L'últim patriarca* can be studied as "a space of contestation about reality" (Mohanty 35). I argue that El Hachmi creatively tackles this analysis through a type of literary artifice that reflects the thoughts of the character telling the story. This artifice simulates oral expression and allows the writer to embed fragments of conversations and forms of speaking and explaining reality into the narrative, all of which are linked by an interpretive framework that reveals the work of a posteriori reconstruction by the narrative voice. In my reading, this artifice stems from three diegetic sources, all of which have a profound impact upon the subjective constitution of the protagonist. The formal composition, for example, recalls Mercé Rodoreda's writing style in *La plaça del diamant* (1962), which Carme Arnau has described as "a way of writing that reflects the voice of the character who is speaking, thus necessitating the use of a complicated literary artifice that evokes orality" (Rodoreda, *Obres completes* xxxii).[8] The apparent simplicity of this writing style allows El Hachmi to create an intimate dialogue with the reader. We can also see an example of a first-person meditation by a female character "about her own world" (Rodoreda, *Obres completes* xxxiii) in the second diegetic source: *The House on Mango Street* (1984) by Sandra Cisneros. In addition, critics have interpreted this novel as an example of "reading against the grain" (Mohanty 4) of the very discourses that attempt to invisibilize the pain that young Esperanza feels.[9] The references to Cisneros's novel

---

7. In this essay I follow Chandra Talpade Mohanty's views on "the inherently political definition of the term *women of color* (a term often used interchangeably with *third world women*)" (7).

8. All translations from sources originally written in Spanish into English are mine.

9. See Saldívar-Hull (1991), Haydee Rivera.

appear in the second part of *L'últim patriarca* in which, unlike the first part of the novel that focuses on the interpretive apparatus that the protagonist's family circle provides, the narrator begins to create her own interpretive paradigms based partially on a collection of texts written by women of color and by Catalan women writers who have reflected upon notions of belonging and representations of national and cultural identity in their works. Both novels also contain vignettes narrated from the perspective of an adolescent who must face the confusion that often results from growing up as a minority both racially and culturally. Ramón Saldívar highlights the rhetorical strategy that Cisneros employs in order to represent, "from the simplicity of the childhood vision, the enormously complex process of the construction of the gendered subject" (181). The richness of Cisneros's technique is pulled into focus as we explore the strategies that El Hachmi uses to expose the multiple layers of mediation that filter her subject's access to reality, such as when the young protagonist reflects aloud about her difficulty recognizing the origin of her own memories as a result of having heard them repeated countless times by her mother. This awareness, however, does not alter the narrator's belief that there are both better and worse "views that explain the world" (*The Last Patriarch* 223). Thus, the final source that influences the construction of the literary artifice that drives the narrative and captures the narrator's process of subjective constitution emerges: the strategies that the women belonging to the protagonist's family and cultural community in The Rif have developed in order to circulate information. In a context characterized by a separation of the sexes and the confinement of women to the private sphere, young girls learn the rules and language in these female spaces that allow them to share "pertinent" information in one space and undesired information in others.[10] In *L'últim patriarca,* El Hachmi recuperates this situated act of resistance by women as a strategy that requires a political reading of the social relations that constrict their spaces of agency and that can be read through the feminist definition of *epistemic privilege.*[11]

Just as the women in her family must decipher the mixture of ideas, personalities, and social realities that have an effect on their personal develop-

---

10. See Holgado Fernández and Razgalla, Aceval.

11. In my analysis, I reference the definition of *epistemic privilege* offered by postpositive realism (Mohanty, *Literary* 1999), one that is constructed on a cognitivist vision of experience and whose emphasis rests upon the subject's interpretation of her own experience. A cognitivist vision of experience, in the words of Satya P. Mohanty, assumes that experience can be both a source of knowledge about social hierarchies as well as error: "our social locations facilitate or inhibit knowledge by predisposing us to register and interpret information in certain ways. Our relation to social powers produces forms of *blindness* [my emphasis] just as it enables degrees of lucidity" (234).

ment, Mimoum's daughter understands that her survival depends upon her ability to interpret her own experience. In my analysis, I propose that the protagonist's *mestizo* thinking operates on a political rereading of versions of reality offered by different individuals within her intimate circle and an evaluation of their consequences. Facing the task of expressing this reconstruction in the creative realm, El Hachmi employs a range of strategies that supplement the artifice that drives the narrative. I pay special attention to three: (1) the emphasis on illuminating spaces of blindness or higher epistemic perception of the characters in accordance with "their relation to social power" (Mohanty, *Literary* 234);[12] (2) the interruption of misogynistic, racist, or classist ideologies that guide the behavior of certain characters by inserting their comments or reasoning within a framework that destabilizes them,[13] through either a facetious or ironic tone of the narrator or a distant tone that manifests her ulterior judgment (another dimension of this strategy also includes displaying the effect of these ideologies on the day-to-day lives of the same individuals who champion them);[14] and (3), the inclusion of relevant contextual information that frames the memories or descriptions of events that have been recuperated by the narrator.

---

12. See the definition of a cognitivist vision of experience in previous note.

13. Jessica Folkart already has proposed this reading of the use of "double voicing" in *L'últim patriarca*, which presents the violent acts or the language of authority of the patriarchs in the novel alongside "ironic" or "matter of fact" comments that have "the effect of uncovering the threads and gaps that undergird the surface design of the text(ile) of patriarchal authority" (364). Folkart theorizes El Hachmi's "cross-cultural" voice as an example of "bilingual writing" using Abdelkéebir Khatibi's formulation of "double critique" (360). In her reading, female oral storytelling, which she reclaims as a subversive narrative of written law following Fatima Mernissi's discussion in *Scheherezade Goes West* (2001), is that which filters the written Catalan language of the protagonist (360–64). In my reading of this "double voicing" strategy, however, the critical gaze does not derive from a subversive oral narrative that precedes or filters the subjectivity of the narrator, but rather from a political investigation developed by the mestizo subject who explores the best and worst explanations of her world. Yet, I agree with Folkart that the subversiveness of the oral narrative of the women from The Rif is one of the fundamental influences upon the protagonist's critical gaze.

14. My reading of this strategy parallels a comment by author Junot Díaz in an interview with Paula Moya ("The Search for Decolonial Love"), in which he discusses the influence of narratives by women of color on his prose and the compositional technique that he employs in his collection of short stories, *Drown*. In the collection of writings, Díaz strives to go beyond simply describing racist and sexist violence and instead creates a "hidden underlying countercurrent" in his texts that reveals how oppressive discourses shape his characters: "are Yunior's gender politics, his generalizations and misogyny, rewarded in the book's 'reality'? [. . .] it appears to me that Yunior's ideas about women, and the actions that arise out of these ideas, always leave him more alone, more thwarted, more disconnected from his community and from himself" (Moya, "The Search" 2012).

The protagonist returns to the past in search of "determinist or pseudo-magical explanations" (El Hachmi, *The Last Patriarch* vii) that consolidate the patriarch Mimoum's power and dictate the terms of the "prison" (245) in which he has enclosed her. Along the way, the protagonist reclaims experiences and knowledges that she has lost in Catalonia. *L'últim patriarca* explores the impact of a historically prevalent ideological interpretation of Islamic sexual morality on the construction of gender identities and the organization of domestic and social life within the Moroccan-Amazigh community in which Mimoum has been educated, as well as the way in which this interpretation reproduces itself within the narrator's familial circle in Catalonia.[15] As Fatima Mernissi explains, "Islamic sexual ideology is predicated on a belief that women's inherent sexual power, if left uncontrolled, would wreak havoc on the male-defined social order—hence the necessity to control women's sexuality and to safeguard Muslim society through veiling, segregation, and the legal subordination of women" (Rassam and Worthington). Note that this threat toward the Amazigh and Arab patriarchal system is perceived not only on the level of sexuality but also on that of thought. The Amazigh imaginary accords to "female nature, the power of *fitna*—an Arabic word that means 'the power of seduction [. . .] and anarchy—combined with *kayd*, a form of intelligence that is essentially feminine and is devoted to the calculated destruction of the system" (Holgado Fernández and Razgalla). Significantly, the novel constructs Mimoum's personality through a stylization of specific ideas belonging to this common imaginary. A reading of this ideological substratum in conversation with feminist critics of Islam permits not only to contextualize Mimoum's obsession with "domesticating" his wife: "The woman he'd choose [. . .] would be faithful to him even in her thoughts. And if she wasn't [. . .] he'd soon tame her" (*The Last Patriarch* 28) but also the subversive potential shown by the decisions made by various female characters regarding the control of their own body, sexuality, and imagination.

A crucial aspect of El Hachmi's creative approximation to her character's Riffian memories is that, while she roots the vignettes within a distinct cultural reality, she also highlights the habitual negotiations that take place in porous societal systems inhabited by individuals who possess differing values and interests. For example, after his first sexual experience with his adult cousin Fatma, twelve-year-old Mimoum decides to marry her and "make her respectable." Fatma, on the other hand, has several lovers and is in no hurry to marry. While for Mimoum, Fatma's unsatisfied desire confirms her

---

15. Read Fatima Mernissi's study of this ideology that spans "all the cultures of the Islamic tradition, even those whose language is not Arabic" (*Islam* 176).

inescapable betrayal, for Fatma, sex is about pleasure. Practicing anal or oral sex protects her virginity and creates a space of agency "within a culturally structured discourse that expresses personal conflicts in cultural terms and therefore terms that are intelligible and acceptable to the larger social group" (Plantade cited in Holgado Fernández and Razgalla).[16] In different interviews and talks, El Hachmi has linked her own imaginative process with the stories, or oral literature, that her mother used to tell her and has characterized the women in The Rif "as creators."[17] Specifically, in her prologue to the edition of *Cuentos libertinos del Magreb* (2011), by Nora Aceval, El Hachmi presents oral fables passed on through generations of women as part of their process of negotiating social conventions in the domestic sphere. As Aceval further explains: "In these fables, the obscenity that exists does not neglect a larger social critique, one that does not avoid the political nor religious order, such as the example of the goat who loses her virginity and searches for a husband. The irony is often cruel" (16). Another way in which El Hachmi incorporates forms of oppositional thinking in the text is by saturating it with different versions of the same facts that circulate in the various intimate circles of the Driouch family as a way to counteract the patriarch's control on the familial narrative.

From a critical point of view, it is important that Mimoum's daughter is the first woman who *openly* questions the patriarch in the private sphere at the end of the novel. The adult narrative voice understands the danger of "[yielding] to his [father's] blackmail" (*The Last Patriarch* 49) and confronts him about her mother's supposed betrayal. Yet, as relevant as resisting his father's vision of reality is as an expression of political feminist *mestizo* thinking, it is equally significant that Mimoum's daughter also challenges him to face his own contradictions. She realizes that she needs to look at the factors limiting her father's own personal and social development in order to expose both his own pain and the pain that he inflicts on others. In the process, her relational perspective also challenges the reader who seeks to confirm the discourse of cultural difference in the text (Sommer). We can observe the originality of the narrative's literary artifice through the novel's articulation of young Mimoum. An example of this relational perspective arises during the account of Mimoum's trips to Spain. While the sexual ideologies of the future patriarch do not change during his first experience abroad, the narrator's ironic discourse transforms

---

16. See Holgado Fernández and Razgalla for an analysis of the different symbolic languages used by women to "appropriate their own time and space within the public sphere," (Holgado Fernández and Razgalla).

17. El Hachmi, "Writing from the Borderland," 2010.

the landscape through which Mimoum moves while in Spain into contested terrain for the reader. The *mestizo* thinking of his daughter—who through anecdotes and memories alludes to the educational deficits, poverty, and rural isolation that shaped young Mimoum while living in the small village of The Rif—weaves a textual framework in which Mimoum's loneliness and ignorance are drawn against a background of racism, economic exploitation, and the fetishization of North African bodies in the industrial Catalan city.[18] The narrator's distant tone seamlessly bridges Mimoum's out of touch explanations of the strange behavior of Spaniards with the larger stereotypes that still pervade the Spanish imaginary about Moroccans (such as stories of Moroccan beheaders during the civil war), just as she makes sure to allude to the severity of the economic inequalities in European society that are silenced by the modern social veneer: "He [. . .] went to the bar in the square where he was fascinated by the music blaring from the fruit machines while the television, covered in olive oil stains, displayed images of the world where he supposed he must be living" (73). Mimoum's interpretive tools do not adequately prepare him to understand the complexity of the social framework in which he must exist. Yet, the narrator, who has grown up as a daughter of immigrants in Spain, knows it well.

The second part of the novel continues El Hachmi's exploration of sources of knowledge that may help the first-person narrator of *L'últim patriarca* build the interpretive tools she needs to understand her pain and sense of confusion and to address them. The inability of the protagonist's mother to guide her though life in Catalonia and the scarcity of her relationships with other young people leads her to search for interpretive perspectives in literature. Novels by Mercè Rodoreda and Víctor Català accompany Mimoum's daughter during her childhood and help her to understand the way in which her father's absolute power has destroyed both him and her mother.[19] The family's move to another town and the arrival of adolescence opens up a new realm of literary references. The themes that appear in this moment of the protagonist's social and psychological development depict a gendered experience:

---

18. For an analysis of *L'últim patriarca,* and specifically the character of Mimoum-Manel, in the context of a criticism of the discourse on European multiculturalism that fails to deal with the economic factors that feed it and the subsequent cultural instrumentalization and deispersonalization of immigrants, read Palmar Alvarez-Blanco.

19. An example is the way in which the young protagonist imagines her mother's transformation since her arrival in Catalonia vis-à-vis the experiences of Mila in *Solitud* (1905) and Natalia in *La plaça del diamant* (1962). For an analysis of the rich intertextual dialogue in *L'últim patriarca* with works by Víctor Català and Mercé Rodoreda, see Ricci, Everly, Campoy-Cubillo, and Folkart.

I talked to her about crises, crises I still couldn't recognize as being about *identity* [my emphasis], about breasts that grew too much, a mother who didn't want me to depilate and who'd thrown my tampons away, just like that, without telling me, for fear I might lose my virginity, [. . .] . I told her about father being obsessed with me not seeing boys outside of school. (247)

The decision to make the young female protagonist's discovery of the impact that her sexuality has on the way she is perceived as a woman both socially and within her own home coincide with her arrival at "our house on Mango Street" (210) illustrates the author's preoccupation with showing how women of color—in this case the protagonist of *L'últim patriarca*—should ultimately create their own "identity narrative *(relato identitario)*" ("El inherente" 156–57). Meaningfully, El Hachmi paints the narrator's "ruptured subjectivity" (Ruiz-Aho 354) through terms of "confusion:" "That was how everything was changed into transgression and tinged with fear. [. . .] I couldn't understand what was wrong with that" (248). As Ruiz-Aho has noted: "It is [the] constant clash of differently-positioned cultural norms that make lived-experience painful for postcolonial subjects" (354). The narrator's need to work through the consequences of occupying a gendered, racialized, and classed position in her Catalan neighborhood further accentuates the relevance of the diegetic links she creates between her experiences and those of the central characters in novels such as *The House on Mango Street* (1986) or—less emphatically—*The Color Purple* (1982) by Alice Walker.[20]

Just like Esperanza in her alley on *Mango Street,* it is within books that Mimoum's daughter finds a community of women whose experiences allow her to understand how sexual violence operates in conjunction with racial and economic ideologies (Saldívar, *Chicano* 186). The loneliness of this border subject, who warns us about her house in her new neighborhood, "but no Lucy and no *chicanos*" (210), pushes her to search for "theories" (Saldívar-Hull 206) that can help her create an alternative space in which to develop her own subjectivity (Saldívar, *Chicano* 186), first through reading (233–34) and later through writing as an act of political reflection. Writing is conceptualized in *L'últim Patriarca* as a space of resistance (Moraga and Anzaldúa 23), as well as a way of creating the very community that the protagonist lacks: "a space

---

20. *L'últim patriarca*'s first person voice also connects her experiences to characters from Zadie Smith's *White Teeth* (2000)—which explores postcolonial identities within Britain's multicultural society, and Leïla Houari's *Zeida de nulle part* (1990), which has been theorized as an example of Beur literature in France. See Josefina Bueno Alonso for an analysis of El Hachmi's work in dialogue with this literary corpus. *L'últim patriarca* only refers to the film version of this novel.

to share my own experiences with everyone else" (*The Last Patriarch* 248). As the second part of the novel progresses, El Hachmi focuses on the silences and deficits that are part of the daily lived reality of her main character and other young border women ("He intentado") like her, including, for example, the experiences that she cannot share with her supposed best friend because they seem "too serious" (*The Last Patriarch* 233), the reasons for her well-being that doctors do not understand (291), the low expectations of the Catalan educational system for the daughters of Muslim immigrants (252), or the failure of traditional Riffian cultural codes to help young women survive intergenerational changes that occur both in Morocco and in the immigrant community in Spain (El Hachmi, "El inherente" 156). This is, in fact, a story about their "loneliness" (El Hachmi, *Gent de paraula*).

El Hachmi configures the final part of the novel as a succession of ineffective "routes to liberation" for her protagonist (287). This creative solution offers the reader access to some of the narrator's "forms of epistemic blindness" (Mohanty, *Literary* 234) that result from her liminal position, as well as to the consequences of her difficulty to read "against the grain" (Mohanty, "Cartographies" 4) of the different ideologies that limit her personal development. At various times, El Hachmi has spoken of the burden that falls upon the daughters of immigrants due to "the loss of 'our' customs, which are identified with decency and religious compliance" (El Hachmi, "El inherente" 155).[21] The novel provides a space to reflect on how these two social and familial narratives (religious compliance and decency) may function in a context of immigration to help bridge the main character's border self. Nonetheless, *L'últim patriarca* barely touches upon the religious practices of Muslim Moroccan immigrants in Spain.[22] El Hachmi seems more interested in exploring how the process of migration has contributed to the creation of the narrator's dysfunctional family. One way in which she delves into this subject is by overemphasizing Mimoum's social hypocrisy "with regard to religion, that double life, that double moral" ("Mimoum").[23] Mimoum is a failed patriarch who "chooses" what interests him from "his culture of origin:" "Drinking doesn't have as much importance because after you drink, you can repent and transform yourself into a regular mosque-goer. Toying with the family's

---

21. See Hassan Aikioud and Eva Castellanos.

22. The author has reflected on her Muslim identity in the context of her Catalan-Amazigh identity in other texts, especially in *Jo també sóc catalana* (2004) and in "Navidades Musulmanas" (2011). In addition, her analysis in *Jo també sóc catalana* delves into some of the challenges encountered by Spain's Islamic communities.

23. El Hachmi explores the "social hypocrisy" of the patriarch in conversation with an earlier literary corpus: "The writer Naguib Mahfuz, in his 'Cairo Trilogy' very often deals with this type of character. The boss of Mahfuz's family is similar to Mimoum" ("Mimoum").

honor is a different story" ("De Nador al Liceu"). El Hachmi thematizes the incoherencies that exist in the Driouch household by exaggerating seemingly arbitrary facets of the patriarch's personality, such as his fondness for Bud Spencer and Terence Hills films. The author herself has pointed out that this strategy allows her to highlight the connection between processes of social disintegration and this type of "trivialized violence" ("De Nador al Liceu"). Within this context, Mimoum's daughter's futile attempt "to be a good Muslim, the best" (*The Last Patriarch* 206), as a way of finding order and peace at home, is constructed in the novel as out of step with the family's dynamics. The patriarch's "social hypocrisy" alongside his wife's remote popular religiosity bring to an end their daughter's hopes that religious compliance may help her break out of her "gradual incarceration" (*The Last Patriarch* 245). The other social and familial narrative, that of decency, emerges as an alternative "way out": "the only one I thought was left to me, the one that was to reconcile my worlds" (*The Last Patriarch* 287). Significantly, marriage with a Riffian man is linked in the text not only with traditional expectations but also with the latent, essentialist gaze in Catalan society toward Moroccan women: "I'd been told so many times about how in your culture women shift from being under their father's tutelage to being under their husband's, I'd come to believe it" (298). The *mestiza* or *fronteriza* narrative thus implicates various parties in the process of eroding the self-esteem of this young woman (268).

The accumulation of familial pressures and misguided decisions drives the main character to a state of extreme fatigue that ultimately triggers a rupture of subjectivity: "I only wanted to sleep, not have that perpetual queasiness in my guts, [...] not think I was the worst person in the world. I still had those pills you put under your tongue and I started to swallow them" (*The Last Patriarch* 293). This near-death experience is nevertheless transformed in the text into a moment of clarity. Through her writing and reflection, the narrator has achieved a fuller understanding of the social relations that oppress her and is able to discover a way out of her own "prison."[24] She first confronts her father about his lies and the pain he has caused her and her mother. Then, she enters into a marriage that allows her to "simply look ahead for the first time in my life" (297). Just to add, though: "it was Paroxetine, not optimism" (297). It does not come as a surprise that shortly thereafter, she ends up getting a divorce and clearly states: "It was then I began to think I had to make my own destiny" (303). The echoes

---

24. My reading of this process of consciousness-raising is in dialogue with Moya's postpositivist realist interpretation of Anzaldúa's "conception of *mestiza* consciousness": "Significantly [...] [it] provides her with a more accurate perspective on the world than she previously had, enabling her to see the 'Chicana anew in light of her history' and to see 'through the fictions of white supremacy' (87)" (*Learning* 78).

of *The House on Mango Street* return in *L'últim Patriarca* through the connection that Cisneros establishes between writing as a form of liberation for Esperanza: "You must keep writing. It will keep you free" (*Mango* 61), and the knowledge that even if she finally manages to leave her neighborhood, writing will be her "ineluctable tie to community" (Saldívar, *Chicano* 84). Cisneros's sense of a collective and precarious struggle resurfaces in *L'últim patriarca*, which ultimately draws attention to the difficult set of expectations and constraints this border woman must navigate. A case in point may be the fragility of the protagonist's final steps toward "emancipation" (El Hachmi, *Gent de paraula*) or even more so, the symbolic violence that the text reintroduces in the final vignette, "Revenge with a vengeance," in which the centrality of sex in El Hachmi's construction of the end of the patriarchy for her protagonist and its association with pain, pleasure, betrayal, and liberty leaves the ending open to numerous interpretations, as Folkart has discussed (370).

However, as I have argued already, the author seems equally invested in creating a narrative landscape that sheds light upon a complex array of social violences that are visible from this particular borderland location.[25] An illustrative example may be that while the protagonist's husband reproduces her father's patriarchal ideologies, it is not by mistake that the descriptions of their relationship are accompanied by the background noise of Spanish television programs about "stories of deceptions and abuse" (288). From her unique position, Mimoum's daughter can observe ideologies of inequality that operate in Spanish society and that tend to be rendered invisible by discourses of racial and cultural difference, especially when contrasting the experiences of working-class women with those of North African immigrant women. This is a form of political critique that El Hachmi already began to develop in her first book, *Jo també sóc catalana* (2004).

LÍMITES Y FRONTERAS

In *Límites y fronteras*, El Kadaoui Moussaoui fictionalizes the condition of the "eternal foreigner" (27) that characterizes the immigrant experience. The novel seeks to explore the effects of essentialized definitions of cultural identity on Ismaïl's inability to forge a subjectivity inclusive of multiple sociocultural belongings. The author textualizes this premise in the first pages of the book by situating Ismaïl as a patient in a psychiatric clinic in Barcelona, to which he is admitted after suffering a psychotic break. Right from the start, the reader

---

25. See Paula Moya's realist definition of epistemic privilege correlated to minority identities (*Learning* 60), as presented in footnote 10.

is exposed to a wealth of stereotypes about Arabs, Imaziguen, Spaniards, and Catalans, all of which are interiorized and shouted by the sick protagonist as he wanders through the streets. Upon arriving at the clinic, Ismaïl begins a process of "delving into the written word" (84) as a way of understanding his pain and ultimately healing it. *Límites y fronteras* is conceived as a first-person account of this healing process told retrospectively by Ismaïl from a present, when some truths have been uncovered, and he feels hopeful. The principal uniting thread of this narrative is Ismaïl's internal monologue, facilitated by conversations with his therapist, Doctor Jorge, which, on occasion, he literally transcribes, although they are always framed by Ismaïl's own comments. Additionally, the narrative is composed of pages from Ismaïl's diary, poems, fragments of articles, or stories written by himself, as well as fragments of other conversations that he remembers. The protagonist attempts to access "pieces of my life that not even I knew that I knew, that I remembered and that were so important to understanding something about who I was in those instants" (27). This dialogue, however, takes place in a closed space, not only in the hospital but also in the closed space of Ismaïl's mind. I argue that *Límites y fronteras* is a novel that presents various contradictions. On one hand, although this is a text written through the remembrance of the pain and trauma of the immigrant experience, it paradoxically moves almost immediately to a level of abstraction that makes it difficult to access the causes that have provoked this pain. On the other hand, the narrative seeks to dismantle a series of binaries that exist in society, not simply in the mind of the patient, that have contributed to the rupture of his subjectivity—foreign/autochthonous, Moroccan/sick, European/normal—but instead, the text activates other dualistic conceptions; for example, a vision of culture as high culture or literary culture versus cultural practices understood as "signs that identify you to the outside world" (*Cartes* 48) and that El Kadaoui Moussaoui associates with "prison identities."

The psychotic break that Ismaïl suffers leads him to experience "total disorientation" (15). In my study of *L'últim patriarca*, I discuss "the contradictions in our own experience" (Moraga and Anzaldúa 23) felt by postcolonial subjects or women of color. *Mestizo* thinking, theorized by third world feminism, "emerges from the material reality of multiple oppressions and in turn conceptualizes that materiality" (Yarbro-Bejarano 6). The confusion felt by Mimoum's daughter or Esperanza, the narrative voice in *The House on Mango Street*, requires that they "read" (Mohanty, "Cartographies" 4) and "write against the grain" (35) of the different discourses on race and gender that converge at their position on the interstices of various cultures and social realities in order to develop their own voices. In contrast, the vision of a borderland subject that El Kadaoui Moussaoui portrays in *Límites y fronteras* is associated with two concepts introduced at the beginning of the novel: that of country or homeland (30) and that of culture. The form in which El Kadaoui Moussaoui presents both concepts reintroduces in the text a tendency to search for an authoritative subject that coincides with "the dominant Western philosophic and humanist paradigm for understanding selfhood [. . .] whose inner workings as a rational mind can be made transparent through introspective reflexivity" (Ruiz-Aho 354). While the identification with this stable subject allows Ismaïl to articulate social and political demands, the ultimate effect is the silencing and marginalization of other experiences of oppression and resistance in the text.

The feeling of having a "double nationality" (*Límites y fronteras* 97) is explained, for example, as an inferiority complex that has accompanied Ismaïl since childhood and that leads him to become angry and defend "Morocco when he is in Spain and Spain when he is in Morocco" (29). As for Ismaïl's views on culture, there is no reflection in his narrative on day-to-day practices and struggles within communities that share cultural values as theorized by feminist *mestizaje* thinking from the borderland. A notion of culture that is relevant for Ismaïl corresponds with what Josefina Bueno Alonso has called a "pluricultural doxa" ("Hispanisme" 42), referring to a type of knowledge privileged by El Kadaoui Moussaoui in his second book, *Cartes al meu fill. Un català de soca-rel, gairebé* (2011).[26] Bueno Alonso has described *Cartes al meu fill* as "a polyphonic text from a cultural, intellectual, and existential point of view" (42). Ismaïl's thinking and narrative seem to already be incorporating elements of this "pluricultural doxa," even if it is clearly skewed toward authors of "universal literature" (Bueno Alonso 41) who write in the West: "I enjoyed reading Baudelaire, José Agustín Goytisolo, Hölderlin, Gioconda Belli, Pushkin, Chekov, Saint-Exupéry and his little prince, and many more" (*Límites y fronteras* 61). Other authors that populate Ismaïl's imagination and narrative are Fatima Mernissi and Mahoud Darwich alongside Leo Tolstoy, Gustave Flaubert, Fyodor Dostoyevsky, Jorge Luis Borges, or references to the sculptures of Michelangelo. Ismaïl's fascination with these works of art or authors seems to derive from their ability to capture some part of the common humanity of their subjects or characters, something that can be accessed from and by all cultures. It is therefore significant that the only mention of a literary work authored by a Moroccan writer, *Dreams of Trespass: Tales of a Harem*

---

26. Some of the authors that form this "doxa" in *Cartes al meu fill* are: Kwamey Anthony Appiah, Víctor Català, José Agustín Goytisolo, Abdallah Laroui, Claude Lévi-Strauss, Amin Maalouf, Joan Margarit, Miquel Martí i Pol, Malika Mokkedem, Edgar Morin, Hanif Kureishi, Edward Said, Wole Soyinka, George Steiner, Mohammed Talbi, Leo Tolstoy, Mario Vargas Llosa, and Virginia Woolf.

Girlhood (1995), by Mernissi, appears in order to speak about "fantastical stories" that "transported women far from the walls" of the harem. Furthermore, Ismaïl connects the brief mention of Mernissi's book with the nostalgia that he feels for the stories that the women in his family told in his presence when he was a child in which "they got revenge on men, converting them into punch lines for their jokes" (123–24). Ultimately, Mernissi's book comes to serve in *Límites y fronteras* the function of establishing or perhaps reaffirming for the reader "a cruel truth": "the lack of liberty and the submission of women" (124), a "truth" that serves as a prelude to an even larger one: "Sometimes all of Morocco comes to be that for me. A world of traditionalisms that stifle freedom" (124). The contextual emptiness and exotic framework in which the oral tradition of women in Maghreb is introduced reinforces, as noted before, the absence of a reflection on negotiations of power and agency developed by individuals within culturally structured discourses and practices (Mohanty, "Cartographies" 35; Plantade cited in Holgado Fernández and Razgalla).

This example reveals a pattern that repeats itself in the text. Morocco is constructed in Ismaïl's narrative as a series of dreams or memories told by a narrator who positions himself as a "documentalist" (125) of practices and traditions that take place in small towns of The Rif that lack "light or running water" (98) or in the city of Nador. Ismaïl becomes progressively aware that these images (97–99) respond to his own anxieties, which he seems to link to his ignorance about a "homeland" that he had to abandon as a child, or to the clichés about "Moroccan culture" that both Spaniards and Moroccans have internalized (191). Nevertheless, Ismaïl's identification with the liberal subject becomes clear when, after arriving at a number of conclusions on the lack of freedom of Moroccan women, illustrated in his mind by Mernissi's book, Ismaïl himself speaks up to denounce the use of the veil as an imposition of traditionalism in an article that he writes for the clinic's magazine (124). Through this article, Ismaïl posits an idea that El Kadaoui Moussaoui later explores at the end of the novel, as well as in *Cartes al meu fill*: "There are different cultures and there are different norms. Freedom will never be a cultural difference" (124). Ismaïl's narrative nonetheless fails to communicate other points of view—particularly those of women—regarding how the veil is used in a Moroccan or Spanish context.

Límites y fronteras offers an explanation of what causes the pain experienced by those occupying a borderland position. In one of Ismaïl's conversations with Don Jorge, Ismaïl declares that "my own demons are those that make me feel inferior" (30). The implication of this assertion is further clarified when El Kadaoui Moussaoui chooses a quote by Amin Maalouf for the epigraph of *Cartes al meu fill*, a book that is both autobiographical and theoretical, in which Maalouf states: "For it is often the way we look at other people that can imprison them within their own narrowest allegiances. And it is also the way we look at them that may set them free."[27] Ismaïl associates his experiences of rejection in Spain to the pervasiveness of "simplistic" identities in the public imaginary, understood as a response given by a population that feels threatened or humiliated (Maalouf 35). Just as his Moroccan family members are *imprisoned* by an impoverished vision of "culture," Ismaïl provides anecdotes about the perception of Moroccan culture or Islam as signs of "a backwards world" (166) in Spain.[28] Daniela Flesler has studied the effect of the arrival of immigrants from North Africa, and specifically from Morocco, to Spain in the last three decades, on the adoption of "European discourses of 'new racism'" (5),[29] as well as the reactivation of images belonging to the collective imaginary about the "Moor" as a threatening and radically different figure (4–5). Flesler explains that it is not the difference exactly but rather the proximity and similarity of the Muslim immigrant (8–9) that activates "the anxiety over symbolic and literal boundaries, which results in an attempt to establish Spanish identity as unequivocally 'European' and set up clear cut differences with those deemed as outsiders" (10).[30] One of El Kadaoui Moussaoui's central preoccupations, in both *Límites y fronteras* and *Cartes al meu fill*, is to denounce the artificiality of these "symbolic and literal" barriers that, in the Spanish context, are perpetuated by Spaniards, Catalans, and Moroccan immigrants alike.

The first of two ideas developed by El Kadaoui Moussaoui in *Límites y fronteras* and later in *Cartes al meu fill* as a theoretical response to the danger posed by essentialized or "prison" identities to the construction of a multicultural subjectivity is that of portraying identity as "a dress that you make for yourself as you go" (*Cartes* 61). In *Cartes al meu fill*, El Kadaoui Moussaoui enters into conversation with Maalouf in order to explain to his son that "each individual identity is unique, complex and irreplaceable" (Maalouf, qtd. in *Cartes* 11) and a compendium of "different mixtures and influences, some

---

27. Maalouf, *In the Name of Identity and the Need to Belong*, 25.
28. I use the concept of imprisonment in this context, following El Kadaoui Moussaoui's El Kadaoui's definition of "prison identities." See footnote 28.
29. Flesler uses Étienne Balibar's explanation of this phenomenon to describe how "this new or differentialist racism replaces the belief in biological inferiority with that of the presumed incompatibility of different cultures, lifestyles, and traditions" (*Return* 5). She further contextualizes this term in the analysis provided by Martin Baker, Étienne Balibar, Pierre-André Taguieff, Robert Miles, and Paul Gilroy (5).
30. Read Martin-Márquez for a study that delves into different representations of the Andalusian legacy, the Spanish colonial project, and their influence on the "performance" of Spanish national identity.

of them quite subtle or even incompatible with one another" (Maalouf, qtd. in *Cartes* 11).³¹ El Kadaoui Moussaoui seeks to structure his argument around his right as an individual to exercise a critical opinion without feeling that he is "betraying" his Moroccan or Imaziguen roots (*Límites* 185, *Cartes* 67). In his vision of border identity, the subject should be free to choose between "a diversity of ideas, of sounds, of music, of smells [. . .] of languages that others do not have" (*Cartes* 68). The second idea addresses the rejection of cultural relativism. In *Cartes al meu fill*, El Kadaoui Moussaoui suggests the concept of "cosmopolitanism," theorized by Kwame Anthony Appiah, as the best way to integrate cultural differences: "It deals with a cosmopolitanism that does not advocate for a dialogue between static and closed cultures but rather whose primary goal is respect for human dignity and personal autonomy" (66). Paul Jay explains that the vision of cosmopolitanism that Appiah suggests in the book that El Kadaoui Moussaoui references, *Cosmopolitanism: Ethics in a World of Strangers* (2006), "wants to look beyond cultural and 'identitarian' differences in the interests of fostering a view of identity organized around shared human traits, values, and rights" (*Global Matters* Kindle file).

Límites y fronteras and *Cartes al meu fill* are two texts full of profound tensions related to the notions of culture and identity that are activated. While, at certain points, El Kadaoui Moussaoui points to the possibility that democratic ideals may have originated within various cultures (*Cartes* 116), in general he tends to assimilate the democratic project with the liberal project (67, 151) and with an abstract perspective separated from local knowledge about the definition of violence, justice, and values. In addition, although he mentions the European "imperialist" (*Cartes* 67) past, he isolates democracy as "a bright idea" that Europe should "export" (151). El Kadaoui Moussaoui delineates a project, in this sense, similar to Appiah's, one that is susceptible to the reproduction of a Eurocentric conception of modernity.³² Moreover, El Kadaoui Moussaoui fails to illuminate acts of resistance in *Límites y fronteras*

---

31. Cristián H. Ricci has analyzed *Límites y fronteras* as an example of a text written from a "paradigm of the formation of cultural identities that are marked by immigration, hybridization, and *creolité*" (*Moros* 25). Ricci appreciates the ability of the text, in agreement with Maalouf's criticism on murderous identities, to "reach a universality of values and at the same time avoid the categorization of a single identity (101, 117)" (*Moros* 245).

32. See Paul Jay's reading of Appiah's concept of cosmopolitanism through the prism of Walter Mignolo's theory of critical cosmopolitanism. According to Jay: "Traditional European forms of cosmopolitanism dating from the Enlightenment, like the one invoked by Appiah, can only be 'thought out from one particular geopolitical location: that of the heart of Europe, of the most civilized nations' with their ideals of 'justice, equality, rights, and planetary peace' ([Mignolo] 735–36)." However, he insists, "it remains difficult to carry these ideas further without clearing up the Renaissance and Enlightenment prejudices that surrounded concepts of race and manhood (736)" (Jay, *Global Matters* Kindle file).

that exemplify his interest in showing cultures as porous entities that are continually evolving. Finally, his rejection of an essentialized definition of cultural identity that impedes the psychological survival of the borderland subject ultimately leads him (and Ismaïl) to a constructivist vision that does not allow him to theorize and make visible the contradictions this border subject confronts on a daily basis.

CONCLUSION

In "Another Way to Be: Women of Color, Literature, and Myth" (2010), Paula M. L. Moya proposes the study of literature written by "marginalized peoples" (483) as a way to conceptualize social justice projects. Moya explains: "Some works of literature can help readers understand [. . .] how the social processes of gender, race, and ethnicity become materialized in individual lives" (488). She has also posited that works of literature written from minority positions may give access to forms of knowledge rendered invisible by dominant discourses: "Examining minority identities is [. . .] central to the project of discovering new—or reviving old—forms of knowledge that might help chart a way out of an oppressive society or social formation. (Mignolo 2000; Moya 2002; C. Mohanty 2003; Hames-García 2004; Teuton 2008; Siebers 2008)" (Moya, "Another Way to Be" 485). In this essay, I suggest that *Límites y fronteras* successfully elaborates the dangers of being imprisoned by "dualistic thinking" (Anzaldúa 80) but fails to articulate the complex set of oppressions and silences that bring Ismaïl to suffer a psychotic breakdown. The novel also tends to overlook views of the self or of agency that have been developed by individuals through day-to-day practices within culturally structured discourses. *L'últim patriarca* (2008), meanwhile, creates a nuanced narrative of the ways in which the border subject may negotiate (though not always competently) her way through "the different worlds she inhabits" (Anzaldúa 20). Moreover, the text constructs representations of sexuality, storytelling, or writing as spaces of interpellation or negotiation of dominant relationships carved out by women on the margins of different hegemonic systems.

WORKS CITED

Aceval, Nora. *Cuentos libertinos del Magreb*. Madrid: Editorial Planeta, 2011. Print.

Akioud, Hassan, and Eva Castellanos. *Els amazics: una història silenciada, una llengua viva*. Valls: Cossetània, 2007. Print.

Alvarez-Blanco, Palmar. "De etnomanías y otros terrores: literatura e inmigración en la España del siglo XXI." *Contornos de la narrativa española actual (2000-2010). Un diálogo entre creadores y críticos*. Ed. Palmar Alvarez-Blanco y Toni Dorca. Madrid: La Casa de la Riqueza, 2011. 55–65. Print.

Anzaldúa, Gloria. *Borderlands/La Frontera: The New Mestiza*. 2nd ed. San Francisco: Aunt Lute Books, 1999. Print.

Bueno Alonso, Josefina. "Género, exilio y desterritorialidad en *L'últim patriarca* de Najat El Hachmi." *De Guinea Ecuatorial a las literaturas hispanoafricanas*. Ed. Landry-Wilfrid Miampika and Patricia Arroyo Calderón. Madrid: Verbum, 2010. 213–26. Print.

———. "Hispanisme et catalanité: enjeux méthodologiques et littéraires d'un transnationalisme maghrebin." *Expressions Maghrébines* 11.2 (2012): 27–43. Print.

Campoy-Cubillo, Adolfo. *Memories of the Maghreb: Transnational Identities in Spanish Cultural Production*. New York: Palgrave Macmillan, 2012. Print.

Català, Víctor. *Solitud*. 15th ed. Barcelona: Selecta, 1976. Print.

Cisneros, Sandra. *The House on Mango Street*. New York: Vintage Books, 1991. Print.

El Hachmi, Najat. "De Nador al Liceu." *El periódico*. 5 Mar. 2008. Web. http://medios.mugak.eu/noticias/noticia/136089.

———. *Gent de paraula*. RTVE.es. 7 Apr. 2011. Web. http://www.rtve.es/alacarta/videos/gent-de-paraula/gent-paraula-najat-hachmi/1068292/.

———. "El inherente espacio intercultural de la creación literaria." *Quaderns de la Mediterrània* 17 (2012): 155–58. Print.

———. *Jo també sóc catalana*. Barcelona: Columna, 2004. Print.

———. *The Last Patriarch*. London: Serpents Tail, 2010. Print.

———. "Mimoum." Diario Siglo XXI. 16 Feb. 2009. Web. http://www.diariosigloxxi.com/texto-diario/mostrar/37792#.VERZ-EuRB95

———. "Navidades Musulmanas." *Dossier Cuentos de Navidad. Letras Libres* (December 2011): 8–11. Print.

———. *L'últim patriarca*. Barcelona: Editorial Planeta S. A., 2008. Print.

———. "Writing from the Borderland." YouTube. 13 Oct. 2010. Web. https://www.youtube.com/watch?v=gPT_027R2sk.

———. "He intentado alejarme de unos orígenes que duelen." *El país*. 2 Feb. 2008. Web.

El Kadaoui Moussaoui, Saïd. *Cartes al meu fill. Un català de soca-rel, gairebé*. Badalona: Ara Llibres, 2011. Print.

———. *Límites y fronteras*. Lleida: Editoral Milenio. 2008. Print.

Everly, Kathryn. "Immigrant Identity and Intertextuality in *L'últim patriarca* by Najat el Hachmi." *Cuaderno Internacional de Estudios Humanísticos y Literatura (CIEHL)* 16 (2011): 142–50. Print.

Flesler, Daniela. *The Return of the Moor: Spanish Responses to Contemporary Moroccan Immigration*. West Lafayette: Purdue UP, 2008. Print.

Folkart, Jessica. "Scoring the National Hym(en): Sexuality, Immigration, and Identity in Najat El Hachmi's *L'últim patriarca*." *Hispanic Review* 81.3 (2013): 353–73. Print.

Hames-García, Michael. "How to Tell a Mestizo from an Enchirito: Colonialism and National Culture in the Borderlands." *Diacritics* 30.4 (2000): 102–22. Print.

Haydee Rivera, Carmen. "Breaking the Rules: Innovation and Narrative Strategies in Sandra Cisneros' *The House on Mango Street* and Ana Castillo's *The Mixquiahuala Letters*." *Ethnic Studies* 26.1 (2003): 108–20. Print.

Holgado Fernández, Isabel, and Hend Razgalla. "La mujer beréber o el vacío de la identidad femenina." *Africa Internacional* 19. Web. http://www.eurosur.org/ai/19/afr1916.htm. 10 Feb. 2014.

"Imazighen en la sociedad actual catalana." *Imazighen: un pueblo invisible*. Asociación Tamazgha-Catalunya. Web. 10 Feb. 2014.

Jay, Paul. *Global Matters: The Transnational Turn in Literary Studies*. Ithaca: Cornell UP, 2010. Print.

Kwame, Anthony Appiah. *Cosmopolitanism: Ethics in a World of Strangers*. New York: Norton, 2006. Print.

Maalouf, Amin. *Las Identidades Asesinas*. Madrid: Alianza editorial, 1999. Print.

Martin-Márquez, Susan. *Disorientations: Spanish Colonialism in Africa and the Performance of Identity*. New Haven: Yale UP, 2008. Print.

Mernissi, Fatima. *Islam and Democracy: Fear of the Modern World*. Boston: Addison-Wesley Publishing Company, 1992. Print.

———. *Scheherezade Goes West*. New York: Washington Square, 2001. Print.

Mignolo, Walter. *Local Histories/Global Designs. Coloniality, Subaltern Knowledges, and Border Thinking*. Princeton: Princeton UP, 2000. Print.

Mohanty, Chandra Talpade. "Cartographies of Struggle: Third World Women and the Politics of Feminism." *Third World Women and the Politics of Feminism*. Ed. Chandra Talpade Mohanty, Anne Russo, and Lourdes M. Torres. Bloomington: Indiana UP, 1991. 1–47. Print.

Mohanty, Satya P. *Literary Theory and the Claims of History: Postmodernism, Objectivity, Multicultural Politics*. Ithaca: Cornell UP, 1997. Print.

Moraga, Cherríe, and Gloria Anzaldúa. *This Bridge Called My Back: Writings by Radical Women of Color*. San Francisco: Aunt Lute Books, 1981. Print.

Moya, Paula. M. L. "The Search for Decolonial Love: An Interview with Junot Díaz." Boston Review. A Political and Literary Forum. 30 March 2014. Web. http://bostonreview.net/books-ideas/paula-ml-moya-decolonial-love-interview-junot-d%C3%ADaz.

———. "Another Way to Be: Women of Color, Literature, and Myth." *Doing Race: 21 Essays for the 21st Century*. Ed. Hazel Rose Markus and Paula M. L. Moya. New York: Norton, 2010. 483–508. Print.

———. *Learning from Experience: Minority Identities, Multicultural Struggles*. Berkeley: U of California P, 2002. Print.

Rassam, Amal, and Lisa Worthington. "Mernissi, Fatima." *The Oxford Encyclopedia of the Islamic World*. Oxford Islamic Studies Online. 19 Sep. 2014. Web. http://www.oxfordislamicstudies.com/article/opr/t236/e0527. 10 Feb. 2014.

Ricci, Cristián H. *¡Hay Moros en la costa! Literatura marroquí fronteriza en castellano y catalán*. Madrid: Iberoamericana, 2014.

———. "*L'ultim patriarca* de Najat El Hachmi y el forjamiento de la identidad amazigh catalana." *Journal of Spanish Cultural Studies* 11.1 (2010): 71–91. Print.

Rodoreda, Mercé. *Obres completes. 1967–1980*. Vol. 3. Barcelona: Edicions 62, 1984. Print.

———. *La plaça del diamant*. 1962. Barcelona: Club Editor, 1982. Print.

Ruiz-Aho, Elena. "Feminist Border Thought." *Routledge International Handbook of Contemporary Social and Political Theory*. Ed. Gerard Delanty and Stephen P. Turner. New York: Routledge, 2011. 350–60. Print.

Saldívar, José David. "Border Thinking, Minoritized Studies, and Realist Interpellations: The Coloniality of Power from Gloria Anzaldúa to Arundhati Roy." *Identity Politics Reconsidered*. Ed. Linda Martín Alcoff, Michael Hames-García, Satya Mohanty, and Paula M. L. Moya. New York: Palgrave, 2006. 152–70. Print.

Saldívar, Ramón. *Chicano Narrative: The Dialectics of Difference*. Madison: U of Wisconsin P, 1990. Print.

Saldívar-Hull, Sonia. "Feminism on the Border: From Gender Politics to Geopolitics." *Criticism in the Borderlands: Studies in Chicano Literature, Culture, and Ideology*. Ed. Hector Calderón and José Saldívar. Berkeley and Los Angeles: U of California P, 1991. 203–20. Print.

Sandoval, Chela. "U.S. Third World Feminism: The Theory of Oppositional Consciousness in the Postmodern World." *Genders* 10 (1991): 1–24. Print.

Sommer, Doris. *Proceed with Caution, When Engaged by Minority Writing in the Americas*. Cambridge: Harvard UP, 1999. Print.

Yarbro-Bejarano, Yvonne. "Gloria Anzaldúa's *Borderlands/La frontera*: Cultural Studies, 'Difference,' and the Non-Unitary Subject." *Cultural Critique* 28 (1994): 5–28. Print.

CHAPTER 3

Toward a Transnational *Nos/otr@s* Scholarship in Chican@ and Latin@ Studies

RICARDO F. VIVANCOS-PÉREZ

> El poeta no pide benevolencia, sino atención,
> una vez que ha saltado hace mucho tiempo
> la barra espinosa de miedo que los autores
> tienen a la sala
>
> The poet does not ask for benevolence, but for attention,
> once a long time has passed since he jumped
> over the barbed wire of fear that authors
> have of the audience.
>
> —FEDERICO GARCÍA LORCA, PROLOGUE TO *LA ZAPATERA PRODIGIOSA*

MY BOOK *Radical Chicana Poetics* (2013)[1] is about the emergence of new subject positions under the category Chicana since the late 1970s to the present. It is about how a group of Chicana feminists has been defining, both theoretically and artistically, their new subject positions by recognizing their being perceived as "dangerous beasts." In the process of doing this, these writers have expanded the scope of the story Chicana in multiple ways and with multiple approaches, but always highlighting creativity, aesthetics, and imagination. At the core of their thought, there is a metapoetic discourse about their own mission and methodology that includes theoretical reflections about their occupation as writers, activists, and scholars.

So one cannot write a book about Chicana feminisms without addressing one's own position since positionality is at the core of every discussion, every notion, every character, and every metaphor in Chicana cultural production. This has always been a serious concern during my career as a non-Chicano

---

1. This essay is a modified and expanded version of the "Disclaimer" and the "Epilogue" of my book.

Chican@ studies scholar. Should I position myself? Should I avoid it or just ignore it? How can I avoid reflecting upon my own positionality when positionality is an essential subject matter and shaping component of Chican@ and Latin@ scholarship?

I have been going back and forth mulling over these questions during my almost seventeen years of research, writing, and teaching in the fields of Chican@, Latin@, and Latin American studies. My senior male mentors, whom I admire and to whom I am respectful and grateful, have always advised me that I should not address my position in my scholarly writing; whereas my female mentors, and especially some of the authors whose work I study—Alicia Gaspar de Alba and Cherríe Moraga—have urged me to explain, from the beginning, what my position is in order to recognize my privileges and (dis)identifications. They have encouraged me to do so as an exercise of honesty and commitment that truly portrays my own process of transformation into an ally and a proxy. Only by doing that would I be able to engage the reader, and to argue my ideas in the most powerful way possible. Both subscribing to and separating from traditional scholarship beliefs and classical tropes, this is what I am doing in this *captatio malevolentiae*, asking for the reader's attention, and for both their benevolence and their malevolence, once I have gone over the "barbed wire of fear" that, according to Federico García Lorca, exists at the border between authors and audiences.

Self-reflection and self-critique, as well as a primary focus on articulating the specificity of one's oppression, are at the core of radical Chicana feminist thought, what I call "dangerous beasts poetics" following Gloria Anzaldúa's words in the groundbreaking anthology *This Bridge Called My Back: Writings by Radical Women of Color,* which she co-edited with Cherríe Moraga: "*A woman who writes has power. A woman who writes is feared.* In the eyes of the world this makes us dangerous beasts" (Moraga and Anzaldúa 182; emphasis in the original).

In addressing my positionality as a non-Chicano Chican@ studies scholar, I am not simply displaying an analogy between my approach and the methodologies offered by radical Chicana artists, but rather the processes of transformation that may habilitate my own as another voice that desires to engage in the construction of a radical feminist poetics rooted in Latinidades and Hispanidades. This is such a radical assertion coming from the subject position of a scholar who initially does not appear to belong to the social and cultural group or communities that he aspires to preserve, voice, and represent. But isn't dangerous beasts poetics essentially radical risk taking in constructing new subject positions that are initially preconceived as those of impossible monsters?

SO HERE I GO . . .

My book is about women of color's feminist thought written by a white man. It is a book about Chican@ culture written by a Spaniard. It is a book about queer, lesbian cultural production written by an ally, but nonetheless "straight" man, according to traditional "normalizing" categorizations. Did I have the right to write this book? Who can speak about something as culturally specific and politically charged as radical Chicana poetics? Only radical Chicanas? Only those feminist-oriented Chicanos who share their political aspirations? Only those progressive women who share some of their concerns and who participate in similar battles against oppression? These are questions I have been reflecting upon since I had the *arrebato* (rapture) to engage in the study of Chicana and Latina cultural production. The process of rumination starts over every time I read a new text, or experience new artistic expressions. More food for thought leads to more reformulation, and more accumulation to more inclusion and expansion.

The exploration and construction of dangerous beasts poetics involve a performative process of altering, discarding, adding, and reshuffling that has no end, and in which looking for ends, definite outcomes, or fixed truths should be a mistake. It goes through many tensions, struggles, and states of "psychic unrest" that constantly ameliorate what Gloria Anzaldúa calls the path of *conocimiento* (knowledge), but those are nonetheless necessary stages toward transformation in a holistic, organic sense—as activists, scholars, citizens, and persons. Dangerous beasts poetics is a methodology of creative emancipation rooted in the body—radical—and the imagination—a poetics. The writing process is one example or representation of the path of *conocimiento* in its broadest sense of spiritual, holistic transformation.[2]

Chicana feminist thought is, for the most part, about what Emma Pérez and others call writing Chicanas into history, and about historicizing their cultural practices and political interventions. But as Gloria Anzaldúa reminds us, a feminist philosophy that aims at empowering border women is also about empowering *atravesados* or border subjects in general, with borders being understood as the space occupied by the marginalized. Anzaldúa uses the term *nos/otras* or *nos/otros,* playing with the word "we" in Spanish and splitting it into "us" and "others" (*Borderlands*). For her, the word *nosotros* is a split signifier—*nos/otros*—whose parts are constantly looking for each other—"nos" searching for "otros," and "otros" searching for "nos." She even conceives the two as necessarily interchangeable.

---

2. For a detailed analysis of the six stages toward "conocimiento," based on Anzaldúa's theorizations in several of her essays after *Borderlands*, see Vivancos-Pérez 33–35.

Nos/otros, a notion that Anzaldúa was developing in her later works, serves to explain some of the apparent contradictions that some readers find in her seminal work *Borderlands/La Frontera.* Anzaldúa's aggressive rejection of racists, machistas, homophobes, and xenophobes does not mean excluding the possibilities for white Anglo Americans, men, and/or heterosexuals to become allies, or to enter the conversation about liberation and social justice. Furthermore, Anzaldúa's ideas about inclusion are controversial for some members of her own group, as shown for example by her disagreements with Cherríe Moraga, who refused to participate in the sequel—*This Bridge We Call Home* (2002)—to the anthology—*This Bridge Called My Back* (1981)—after knowing that it would include pieces by men and white women.³

In this regard, what Anzaldúa's concept of *nos/otros* shows us is that one of the tenets for Chicana feminists—tolerance for contradictions—has to operate on two main levels: both among Chicanas, and among Chicanas and outsiders—both within the group and outside the group. This is a fundamental challenge for scholars in ethnic, feminist, queer, and disability studies: overall, for those of us who are constantly scrutinized and sometimes stigmatized as "the school of resentment" by some reactionary scholarship. Anzaldúa reminds us to ask ourselves: Are we ready to face our own internalized "resentments?" Are we ready to include the voices of others in our discussions, or should we keep some venues, such as ethnic and/or feminist anthologies, as safe spaces just for women, lesbians, or ethnic groups? Are we ready to move on?

By asking us to change the "we" into *nos/otros,* Anzaldúa is inviting us—*nos/otros*—both to recognize our internal split and to include the voices of the others. In other words, by substituting the "we" for *nos/otros,* we can envision part of the answers to the questions above in the articulation of the questions themselves: Are *nos/otros* ready to address our own internalized "resentments?" Are *nos/otros* ready to include the voices of others in our discussions, or should *nos/otros* keep some venues, such as ethnic and/or feminist anthologies, as safe spaces just for women, lesbians, or ethnic groups? Are *nos/otros* ready to move on?

Nos/otros addresses, overall, the tensions involved in the processes of democratization of Chican@ scholarship, and their repercussions for Chicanas, border subjects, and their allies. Anzaldúa is both encouraging and questioning, first, the use of the "we" by most Chican@ scholars who strive to authenticate their voices as members of the group as well as to legitimize their approaches; and second, the right to speak about Chican@ culture by

---

3. For a reflection on how the turbulent personal relationship between Moraga and Anzaldúa is representative of their understanding—and of other Chicana feminists—of collective creativity, see Vivancos-Pérez 73–77.

those who do not belong, and who tend to obviate their own positionality in their writings.

Anzaldúa herself set up an example for border writers on how to position oneself in her preface to *Borderlands/La Frontera*. Her gesture—placing herself into the discourse by means of the "I"—is indicative of the consolidation of the story Chicana in writing and scholarship over the years:

> I am a border woman. I grew up between two cultures, the Mexican (with a heavy Indian influence) and the Anglo (as a member of a colonized people in our own territory). I have been straddling that *tejas*-Mexican border, and others, all my life. It's not a comfortable territory to live in, this place of contradictions. Hatred, anger and exploitation are prominent features of this landscape.
>
> [. . .]
>
> This book, then, speaks of my existence. My preoccupations with the inner life of the Self, and with the struggle of that Self amidst adversity and violation; with the confluence of primordial images; with the unique positionings consciousness takes at these confluent streams; and with my almost instinctive urge to communicate, to speak, to write about life on the borders, life in the shadows. (Anzaldúa *Borderlands* n.p.)

Many Chicanas/os and border writers have followed Anzaldúa's example as a valid vehicle for individual empowerment. However, Anzaldúa also is pointing at the split between the real "I" and the authorial "I"; that is, the presence of each individual voice within a collective entity represented by the "I's" in the text.

In *Radical Chicana Poetics*, I focus on the creation of this fictional and theoretical "I"—the "I" of the Chicana writer—as the dangerous beast; and on how radical Chicanas build their own poetics from this subject position. The "I" of the Chicana writer is in fact both an "I" and a "we." The body of one—the otherized, marginalized, ethnoracialized, and sexualized female body—is also the body of the collective. Anzaldúa and other Chicanas use the notion and the image of the Aztec goddess Coyolxauhqui to explain the dismembering and re-membering of the body as a constant reformulation of the abstract entity called "Chicana," accounting for both the individual and the collective reconstruction or what Norma Alarcón explains as "identity-in-difference."

These notions shed light on the first contradiction pointed out by the concept of *nos/otros*. But, then, we have its second level of operation, the one dealing with the voice of the other as part of the collective other. In this regard, what interests me is the intermediate position of the non-Chicano, male, and/or white scholar who decides to engage in the study of Chicana cultural production.

I agree with Gayatri Chakravorty Spivak when she says that the minute we speak for others, we are both becoming a proxy for and providing our own account of ourselves; that is, we manage to occupy an intermediate outside-insider position. Political representation has two sides that become inseparable at the discursive level: "*Representing*: proxy and portrait, as I said, there are two ways of representing. Now, the thing to remember is that in the act of representing politically, you actually represent yourself and your constituency in the portrait sense, as well" (Spivak, *Postcolonial* 108; emphasis in the original). Renato Rosaldo and Deena González have studied the position of the Chican@ scholar as a participant-observer, and an "inside-outsider," but there is a clear tendency to avoid and ignore talking about the non-Chicano Chican@ studies scholar, whom I prefer to call "outside-insider" (Vivancos-Pérez 14).

As a Chican@ and Latin@ studies scholar, I am occupying, theorizing, and advocating for my own position as an outside-insider. I reclaim mine as a much-needed perspective, but nonetheless just one more to complete a multidimensional, tensional approach. During my writing process, I have been tempted to use "we" to explain Chicana poetics many times. This, I believe, has to do with my desire to empathize with the communities that are the subject matter of my analyses, but it is also an effect of radical Chicanas' desire to consider my thoughts and my story seriously. The *nos* and the *otros* attract each other just as the dismembered body parts look for each other in the monstrous representation of Coyolxauhqui. Can you disregard, then, my voice as part of a feminist philosophy of *nos/otros*? Can you obviate desire and the *arrebatos* involved in and provoked by dangerous beasts poetics?

ARREBATOS

In her descriptions of the path of *conocimiento,* Anzaldúa includes a series of calls to action or *arrebatos*. Anzaldúa defines those experiences that ignite our desire for action instead of reaction. *Arrebatos* mark our early stages of *conocimiento* or transformation. They agitate us into action by compelling us to write our story anew.

I can remember many *arrebatos* that have called me to engage in reading and writing about Chicana poetics over the years. Personally, I have always felt like a kind of *atravesado*. I grew up at the border between Spain and Morocco, in a working-class neighborhood of Málaga, a provincial town where tourism and African immigration were considered—and still are by many—a threat to traditional conservative worldviews. I was born the year the dictator died, and have experienced the transition into democracy in different ways. As far as the educational system and educational views in Spain are concerned, I belong to a "guinea-pig" generation. They experimented with us at home, in school, and in college. Growing up as a child in the times of *la movida*—sex, drugs, and rock and roll—sexual liberation, and changing views on the family is something that I appreciate now as enriching, but that I remember as confusing for me as a kid. Additionally, having to deal with an abusive father, and being raised by my mother in a feminocentric environment, gave me a unique perspective into my multiple experiences of transition into democracy, into new conceptions of the family, gender, sexuality, multiculturalism, and so on. No wonder that when I first read Gloria Anzaldúa's *Borderlands* and Cherríe Moraga's plays, I had an *arrebato*!

Then I became an immigrant in the United States, where I have suffered language discrimination many times, and many times I have been treated as a pet, or *animal de compañía,* whenever I am around Anglo Americans. This new dimension of my position as *atravesado* got me even closer to dangerous beasts poetics. Being perceived as the "Spanish conquistador" by Latinos, and as a "Mexican with a thick accent" by Anglos, together with my background as a feminist-oriented border subject have led me to being politically and culturally engaged with Chicana feminist thought.

I especially remember those *arrebatos* that relate to my becoming an outside-insider in Chican@ studies. My first advisor gave me the first warning. He said something like: "Are you sure you want to write about Chicana feminists? Are you aware of your outsider position as a Spaniard, and everything it implies? You really need to decide now, before it is too late, whether you want to do this or something else." This was not new, since I had already been experiencing the abnormality of being a male researcher doing Feminist studies in Spain, where the strongly patriarchal and disciplinary views in academia were being contested by feminist scholars with separatist views that were equally excluding—men were not allowed in Women Studies organizations, men could not get grants to do feminist research, and so on. But now I was arriving into an almost unknown political arena for me—that of U.S. academia. There was anxiety and *la barra espinosa de miedo.*

A year later, when I was writing on Alicia Gaspar de Alba's works, a senior Chicano professor asked me: "How are you going to convince me that your work is worth reading?" He allegedly was addressing my writing style, but in fact he was referring to my right to speak for Chicana lesbians. "You are supposed to be the expert on Chicana lesbian writing. You need to convince us that you are a reliable expert, a real expert on this literature." But how could I claim to be an expert if I did not belong? Reading Sor Juana Inés de la Cruz's works gave me the clues. Her personal story allowed me to envision and articulate my position as an expert or a proxy.

SOR FILOTEO

I realized that what I was experiencing while writing about Chicana feminisms was a process of transformation that involved what one could call discursive transvestism. A crucial episode in Sor Juana's life helps to explain this discursive strategy.

In Sor Juana Inés de la Cruz's most controversial work, *Carta Atenagórica*, the Novohispana nun criticized a sermon about Jesus Christ's finezas, or acts of love, published by Antonio de Vieira, an influential Portuguese Jesuit of the times. Manuel Fernández de Santa Cruz, archbishop of Puebla, published Sor Juana's letter without her permission in 1690. The text was dedicated to Sor Filotea de la Cruz, and included a preface by Sor Filotea herself. In fact, Sor Filotea was Fernández de Santa Cruz's pseudonym. He used the letter as part of his rivalry with another archbishop, Aguiar y Seijas. By publishing Sor Juana's letter, Fernández de Santa Cruz placed the nun against Aguiar y Seijas, who was famous for his misogyny (Paz 511–33).

This important event in Sor Juana's life, which is recreated in detail by Gaspar de Alba in her novel *Sor Juana's Second Dream* (1999), shows how discursive transvestism—that is, adopting a gender identity that is not yours within discourse—may be used to perpetuate and reinforce traditional patriarchal values. The episode made me realize that I was practicing a discursive transvestism of a very different kind. I was questioning and defying traditional academic values that have seriously limited literary and cultural studies in many ways. Writing about Chicana lesbians and homoeroticism was, and is, still problematic or weird for many if you are not Chicano, a woman, or gay.

In my case, I became aware that I was taking on the position of the feminist scholar and the Chicano scholar without being a Chicano, a woman, or queer, but that I was not hiding my real identity. Rather, I was asserting my right to speak, and the validity of my perspective "from the outside." I was not Sor Filotea, but Sor Filoteo. I was empowered by my position in academia and by my identity to speak about and for others, but I wanted to recognize my position as an "outside-insider." But isn't Sor Filoteo an impossible, fictional character?

Pioneer U.S. Latinomericanist and Chican@ cultural critic Don Luis Leal helped me with this question. When I first met him and told him about my projects, he was very supportive and added a revelatory note of humor. With well-intended and optimistic honesty, he pointed out how I was becoming "¡un scholar lesbiano!" (a lesbian scholar). I realized that in my work, I am occupying the impossible position of "lesbiano" or Sor Filoteo. I am adopting feminist discourse to make it my own, but at the same time I am constantly revealing the illusory quality of my positionality. In this way, I am faithful to the perspective on sexual and cultural identity that is present in the cultural production of radical Chicana feminists. My research inevitably includes a kind of transvestism in a discursive and metaphorical sense.

Today, after ten years of expanding my research on Chicana poetics, I can recall so many additional *arrebatos* in my process of transformation into Sor Filoteo. The *arrebatos* were not only professional—as an outside-insider in U.S. academia—but also personal—as an immigrant-first-generation-college-student-Hispanic-feminist-oriented-male-writer. It is in this ongoing process of transformation that my theoretical "I" has emerged. I have overcome my initial fears, but I recognize that my position as non-Chicano Chicano scholar, displaced Spanish immigrant, and *lesbiano* in fact represents the convergence of the fictional and the real. In a way, and following the irresolvable discussions on the separation of fantasy and reality in literature, I am situated in the blurred boundaries from which the fantastic arises. My position as a scholar is an impossible one from a "normalizing" realistic point of view. It is perceived as dangerous, and it is in constant state of scrutiny. It is marked by anxiety. But when I recognize the fictional constructedness of my position, I can overcome some of the anxiety. In those moments of consciousness, I am able to appreciate the works of the imagination and the mutually enabling desire between *nos* and *otros*.

So, as a Chican@ and Latin@ studies scholar, I write from a position as a critic that may be perceived as a fictional construction, or as one of many possible figurations. By figurations I mean transgressive political fictions, following feminist cultural critic and philosopher Rosi Braidotti. Since her earlier works in the late 1980s and early 1990s, Braidotti has argued that feminist thinkers need to formulate figurations, "a style of thought that evokes or expresses ways out of the phallocentric vision of the subject. A figuration is a politically informed account of an alternative subjectivity" (*Nomadic Subjects* 1).

The process of explaining and analyzing dangerous beasts poetics has shaped a figuration of my own subject position as a dangerous beast. My *captatio benevolentiae* is also a *captatio malevolentiae*. By blurring the distinction between benevolence and malevolence, I am just asking for *nos/otros* to pay attention to imagination, and to the processes of narrativization and a metaphorization involved in what I call *nos/otros* scholarship.

A *NOS/OTROS* SCHOLARSHIP

Speaking for others is a common practice in academia that should not be addressed too much unless we want to single ourselves out, play with the double binds of political correctness, or defy traditional conventions about elitism and authority. However, in the many fields within ethnic and feminist studies, the practice of speaking for others has always been suspicious, or at least the object of severe scrutiny for obvious and many times justified reasons. In one of the essays included in *Who Can Speak?* (1995), Andrew Lakritz explores how authority functions when intellectuals speak for others. Analyzing the cases of Ralph Ellison and Hannah Arendt, who at some point spoke for Black women from their own positions as a Black man and as a Jewish woman, Lakritz explains how notions of authority in academia generally reflect two positions: (1) that scholars launch their critique from their own experience as authentic members of the group, claiming that outsiders have no access to the truths of their culture; and (2) that the critic "owns authority by their long and careful study of research" (25). As products of their time, Ellison and Arendt did not have to address their condition as outsiders because they enjoyed what Ellison called "Olympian authority." This is not exactly the case in ethnic and women's studies since their creation as academic disciplines in the late 1960s.

Today in Chican@ studies, in a stage that goes beyond ethnonationalism, non-Chicano Chican@ studies scholars are welcome to participate. Their names and their initiatives and collaborations are desirable as part of organizations and publications in order to establish global connections. Chican@/Latin@ scholars have consolidated permanent collaborative networks in Europe—mainly in Germany, France, Spain, and Russia—and even in the Arab world (Bost and Aparicio 107–30). However, the situation is slightly different with regard to non-Chicano scholars who do Chican@ studies in the United States.

As I mentioned earlier, my experience, as that of many others in my situation, has been contradictory and caught up in double binds. On one hand, I have been welcomed generously with *brazos abiertos* (open arms) by Chicana/o scholars as a researcher who writes about them, and who even admires them. On the other, I have been scrutinized and treated with disregard when, for example, I have sent my research for publication in their journals. Moreover, when important academic and even hiring decisions are to be made, my diasporicity does not help. When I applied for a Chicano studies position in a top southwestern university, one of the members of the search committee openly asked: "How can we hire a Spaniard to teach Chicano studies in an English Department?" As an outside-insider I have to constantly be aware of these double binds. My situation gets even more complicated, being a supposedly straight man specializing in radical feminist thought.

What happens in the context of postnationalistic ethnic and gender identities is complex. Gender and ethnic groups in academia replicate some of the domesticating strategies of dominant groups. They want to get credit for including your name as an outsider, collaborator, and admirer, but will not let you access their hard-won and exclusive circles of power. The phenomenon is similar to what happens with the idea of nation and nationalism. There is a desire to go beyond ethnonationalistic views, but certainly not to really be postnationalistic. It does not matter whether the term is understood as beyond nationalism or antinationalism. In the case of Chican@ studies, everyday language reflects a more or less unconscious nostalgia for the ethnonationalistic approaches of the early Chicano Movement. Researchers still have a strong tendency to generalize the use of Chicana/o scholar, instead of Chicana/o studies scholar, which would include both Chicanas/os and non-Chicanas/os.

Going back to Lakritz's discussion, questions of authority vary substantially depending on the rank, or the level of politicization, of the field you work in. Doing interdisciplinary or transdisciplinary work across highly politicized fields can be a source of tremendous anxiety. But what interests me about Lakritz's reflections is his conclusion. He argues that, in general, in the 1990s multiculturalist academic environment—what we may call today postnational or transnational or global—the crucial question for the outsider critic is "how to write about others" rather than "who can speak." His optimistic approach in the early 1990s is surprising. In her book *An Aesthetic Education in the Era of Globalization* (2012), Gayatri Chakravorty Spivak still feels compelled to address her positionality, even though she enjoys "Olympian authority" in postcolonial Feminist studies. And she does so because of still being continually interpellated to give an account of herself as a scholar speaking for others:

> I repeat that I find it tedious to go on endlessly about my particular diasporicity. Come what may, I cannot think of what used to be called "the brain drain" as either exile or diaspora. I feel that as a literary intellectual, I am here to use my imagination, not only to imagine the predicament of diaspora, exile, refuge, but also to deny resolutely that the manifest destiny of

the United States is (to appear) to give asylum to the world. As such, I often have to confront the question of "speaking for" groups that are not my own.

I have responded to this question so many times that a particular reference would be silly. Yet I seem never to be heard. Let me repeat then. Why has this Enlightenment model of parliamentary democracy (representing a constituency, "speaking for" them) become the master-model for rejection of diasporic academic work? Why has the imperative to imagine the other responsibly been lifted? (Spivak, *Aesthetic Education* xiv)

In this context, I believe it is time to move on toward debating the possibilities of *nos/otr@s* scholarship in Chican@ studies and in feminist and queer studies. This also would be a debate that would enrich dialogues about transdisciplinary methodological issues. For these debates, we need more figurations of the outside-insider critical subject; that is, more critically informed voices from different locations to be accepted and incorporated.

WORKS CITED

Alarcón, Norma. "Conjugating Subjects in the Age of Multiculturalism." *Mapping Multiculturalism*. Ed. Avery F. Gordon and Christopher Newfield. Minneapolis: U of Minnesota P, 1996. 127–48. Print.

Anzaldúa, Gloria. *Borderlands/La Frontera: The New Mestiza*. 3rd ed. San Francisco: Aunt Lute Books, 2007. Print.

———. "The New Mestiza Nation." *The Gloria Anzaldúa Reader*. Ed. AnaLouise Keating. Durham: Duke UP, 2009. 203–16. Print.

———. "now let us shift . . . the path of conocimiento . . . inner worlds, public acts." *This Bridge We Call Home: Radical Visions for Transformation*. Ed. Gloria Anzaldúa and AnaLouise Keating. New York: Routledge, 2002. 540–71. Print.

Bost, Suzanne, and Frances R. Aparicio, eds. *The Routledge Companion to Latino/a Literature*. New York: Routledge, 2013. Print.

Braidotti, Rosi. *Nomadic Subjects: Embodiment and Sexual Difference in Contemporary Feminist Theory*. New York: Columbia UP, 1994. Print.

Gaspar de Alba, Alicia. *Sor Juana's Second Dream*. Albuquerque: U of New Mexico P, 1999. Print.

González, Deena. "Speaking Secrets: Living Chicana Theory." *Living Chicana Theory*. Ed. Carla Trujillo. Berkeley: Third World P, 1998. 46–77. Print.

Lakritz, Andrew. "Identification and Difference: Structures of Privilege in Cultural Criticism." *Who Can Speak?: Authority and Critical Identity*. Ed. Judith Roof and Robin Wiegman. Urbana: U of Illinois P, 1995. 3–29. Print.

Moraga, Cherríe L. *A Xicana Codex of Changing Consciousness*. Durham: Duke UP, 2011. Print.

Moraga, Cherríe L., and Gloria E. Anzaldúa, eds. *This Bridge Called My Back: Writings by Radical Women of Color*. 1981. 3rd ed. Berkeley: Third Woman Press, 2002. Print.

Paz, Octavio. *Sor Juana o las trampas de la fe*. México: Fondo de Cultura Económica, 1982. Print.

Pérez, Emma. *The Decolonial Imaginary: Writing Chicanas into History*. Bloomington and Indianapolis: Indiana UP, 1999. Print.

Roof, Judith, and Robyn Wiegman, eds. *Who Can Speak? Authority and Critical Identity*. Urbana: U of Illinois P, 1995. Print.

Rosaldo, Renato. *Culture and Truth: The Remaking of Social Analysis*. Boston: Beacon P, 1989. Print.

Spivak, Gayatri Chakravorty. *An Aesthetic Education in the Era of Globalization*. Cambridge: Harvard UP, 2012. Print.

———. *The Postcolonial Critic: Interviews, Strategies, Dialogues*. Ed. Sarah Harasym. New York: Routledge, 1990. Print.

Vivancos-Pérez, Ricardo F. *Radical Chicana Poetics*. New York and London: Palgrave Macmillan, 2013. Print.

CHAPTER 4

Tempted by the Words of Another
Linguistic Choices of Chicanas/os and Other Latinas/os in Los Angeles

ANA SÁNCHEZ-MUÑOZ

THIS ESSAY EXPLORES Chicana/o (and other Latino/a) identity formation through the use of language. It examines the vocabulary choices and communicative exchanges in the vernacular varieties of Latino immigrant groups. The main goal is to investigate the negotiation of ethnic and linguistic identity as different languages and dialects come into contact sharing the same multicultural urban space.

Previous research has identified patterns of dialect change and formation in the Spanish used by different Latino groups in Los Angeles (Parodi "Contacto de Dialectos," "Normatividad y Diglosia," "El otro México"). This essay adds to the existing literature by exploring how language ideologies, attitudes, and accommodation (or lack of it) are intertwined, contributing to the complex linguistic fabric of the city, defying the idea that there is only one Latino speech community (Spanish-speaking). For example, Central Americans may resist more dominant varieties of Mexican Spanish in California. Each group's linguistic behavior has a different meaning in the construction and negotiation of a distinctive Latino identity.

In particular, this essay references the way in which Chicanas/os construct a unique identity through language as well as how their vernacular influences other Latino groups (mainly Central American). Language use plays a specific role in the negotiations, a symbol of identity to represent different social meanings within their own Latino community.

L.A.: THE CITY OF (SPANISH-SPEAKING) ANGELS

Los Angeles is a natural sociolinguistic lab: From Korea town to Little Armenia, from Chinatown to Little Ethiopia, L.A.'s many distinct neighborhoods evidence the huge ethnocultural and linguistic diversity of the city. But among the many sounds heard around town, two linguistic "giants" dominate the urban landscape: Spanish and English. These two colonial languages have been coexisting in California since the 1800s when English started moving west. Despite the fact that English gradually replaced Spanish as the language of economy and power, Spanish continued to be spoken and used by Californians, especially in the south of the state. To this day, Spanish is the most-spoken language in many areas of Los Angeles and San Diego Counties.

In addition to the long historical presence of Spanish in the area, immigration from Latin American countries, especially from Mexico and Central America, has kept on increasing. In the L.A. metro area, almost 50 percent of the population is classified as Hispanic/Latino (2010 U.S. Census). Spanish is the most frequently spoken language after English and the predominant language in many communities. Even though the majority of the Latino population is of Mexican descent or origin, the number of Central Americans has more than doubled since the 1980s. Table 1 offers a glimpse of the most recent Latino demographics for L.A. County.

TABLE 1
Latino/Hispanic origin in Los Angeles County U.S. Census, population estimates for 2015

ORIGIN	POPULATION	PERCENTAGE OF THE LATINO/HISPANIC POPULATION
Mexican origin	3,693,975	76.3%
Central American origin	795,799	16.5%
South American origin	131,802	2.7%
Caribbean origin (Spanish-speaking)	88,408	1.8%
Other (Latino/Hispanic)	126,435	2.7%

Because immigration brings high linguistic diversity, L.A. is an ideal place to examine the formation of new Latino speech communities, dialect contact areas, and dialect mergers. This essay examines Chicano Spanish and the contact between this and other varieties of Spanish that make L.A. their home. It also explores the ways in which ideologies and linguistic attitudes are revealed against the complexity of the urban linguistic landscape.

This essay begins with an overview of the most characteristic features of Chicano Spanish in Los Angeles. Next, it examines how contact between distinct Spanish dialects manifests in various L.A. communities, specifically between Mexican and Central American varieties spoken in the region (mainly by Salvadorians and Guatemalans). The essay concludes with a discussion on some of the ways in which speakers navigate their linguistic repertoire (different varieties of English and Spanish) to display their multifaceted *L.A.tina/o* identities.

THE SPANISH OF L.A. CHICANOS

The term Chicana/o was originally a derogatory term applied to the descendants of Mexican people in the United States. This term was later adopted as a term of ethnic pride and political consciousness during the civil rights movements of the 1960s. To identify oneself as Chicana/o as opposed to Mexican American or Latino or Hispanic means reasserting a unique ethnic and sociopolitical bond. It means claiming a distinctive culture, not just a mixture of two colonial pasts but rather a culture with its own history, aesthetics, music, and unique linguistic expression. The Chicana writer Gloria Anzaldúa writes about this in her *opus magnum Borderlands/La Frontera: The New Mestiza*: "We don't identify with the Anglo-American cultural values and we don't identify with the Mexican cultural values. We are a synergy of two cultures with various degrees of Mexicanness or Angloness" (85).

What are, then, the languages that Chicanos use to encode those various degrees of "Mexicanness" or "Angloness" that Anzaldúa wrote about? A distinct code, *Spanglish*, has been commonly associated with Chicanos and with Latinos in the United States in general. But even though the population at large uses the term *Spanglish* frequently and widely, there is no consensus in the literature as to what exactly this term refers to (see, in this regard, Dumitrescu 2010, which includes, among other things, a lengthy discussion about the perception of and the attitudes toward the term *Spanglish*). Some authors claim it to be a rather new American language, produced by the blending of two languages and two identities into a single one, usually referred to with the transparent acronym of *Spanglish* (Stavans). By contrast, many scholars (see for instance Otheguy and Stern or Lipski) believe that the term does not serve the Latino community well as it blurs many scientifically well-studied linguistic phenomena into a mesh of a half-baked language system. Regardless of whether we like the term or not, what is commonly referred to as *Spang-*

lish is namely code-switching, code-mixing, borrowings, and other language-contact phenomena, which I further explain below, commonly employed by bilinguals. Since Chicanos often inhabit bilingual and bicultural spaces, it is natural to expect that such features will characterize their linguistic expressions (Sánchez-Muñoz "Identidad").

Bilingual Spanish-English spaces are not so clearly defined either. The degree to which Spanish is spoken and maintained in the United States varies greatly from community to community and from family to family. Most Chicanos in the L.A. area are bilingual, although English is the dominant language. Speakers can function in Spanish, but theirs is a variety of Spanish characterized by those unique features that are not typical of monolingual varieties of the language.

So, what are some of the key ingredients that give Chicana/o Spanish its particular flavor? Parodi ("Contacto," "Normatividad," "El otro México") and her students at the CEEEUS research center at UCLA (Center for the Study of Spanish in the United States) have been tracking the formation and evolution of *Español Vernáculo de Los Angeles* (EVLA), a Spanish koiné in Los Angeles which has a distinct Mexican flavor spiced with those *Spanglish* features typical of the intimate contact with English: convergence, borrowings, calques, switches, and so forth. EVLA is the variety spoken by Chicanos in L.A., and, according to Parodi, it is also the one acquired by second-generation Latinos/Hispanics in the city regardless of their self-identification as Chicana/o or other.

There are two main factors that characterize EVLA as an urban ethnic dialect: its connection to rural varieties of Mexican Spanish and the aforementioned features of language contact. Regarding the first, its rural origins in Mexican ranchos of Querétaro, Guanajuato, Aguascalientes, and Jalisco (Parodi "Contacto"), we find syntactic features such as the generalization of the morpheme "-s" for the second person of the simple preterit (e.g., comiste<u>s</u> instead of the standard *comiste*) and archaisms such as *haiga* (instead of the canonical *haya*). Phonologically, processes typical of casual nonstandard production are normalized in Chicano Spanish, such as contractions of the definite article before a vocalic sound (e.g., *l'avena, l'alfalfa*); contractions or deletions of entire syllables in high-frequency connectors, prepositions, or verbs (e.g., *pa', pos, tá'* instead of *para, pues,* or *está*); or simplification of consonant clusters (e.g., *dotor* instead of *do<u>k</u>tor*). These features are traditionally stigmatized in monolingual varieties since they are typical of rural environments and associated with un- or undereducated speakers, and thus carry little or no linguistic prestige. However, in a situation of bilingualism where another language, English in this case, is the language of power, the variety of the most numerous minority (rural Mexican Spanish) becomes the one that carries more weight and enjoys covert prestige in the formation of a distinct immigrant dialect.

Regarding the linguistic phenomena that develop in language-contact situations, Chicano Spanish displays several well-known traits; among these, two are particularly salient: code-switching and lexical transfer. Code-switching is the moving back and forth between two languages in a single communicative exchange. It is the ubiquitous *entre idiomas* (between languages) that can be heard on the streets of L.A., in *mercados* (markets), buses, and several Latino TV and radio stations. Indeed, code-switching is a very common linguistic strategy present all over the world in bilingual and multilingual speech communities. The general category of "lexical transfer" can further be classified into single-word switches to English (items that preserve English phonology) and single-word borrowings (items adapted to Spanish phonology). In this latter group, we differentiate between loans (the transfer of forms with their meanings; for example *troca* 'truck'), and semantic extensions (the transfer of meanings only; for example *carpeta*, which in standard Spanish means "binder" or "file folder," used with the meaning from English "carpet"). Speakers of L.A. Spanish use these linguistic resources that set them apart from monolingual varieties of the language. Thus, Chicana/o speakers perform the various pieces of their cultural heritage in their language use, as a kind of linguistic *Nepantla* (Sánchez-Muñoz "Identidad").

Chicano Spanish can be heard in many L.A. barrios, sometimes together with Chicano English, another urban ethnic dialect of English, which is characterized by the contact with the Spanish of the region (for an in-depth analysis of Chicana/o English, please see Penfield and Ornstein-Galicia and Fought). But just as Chicano English is not the only variety of English heard on the streets of L.A., Chicano Spanish is not the only Spanish, either. A growing number of Central Americans have made their linguistic mark in the city, too. The following section discusses some of the consequences of dialect contact among speakers of Spanish from different regions of the Spanish-speaking world.

JUNTOS PERO NO REVUELTOS: DIALECT CONTACT, CONVERGENCE, AND DIVERGENCE

As mentioned earlier, according to the last U.S. census, half the population in Los Angeles is Latino or Hispanic (of course, if we took into consideration those not included in the official statistics, these numbers would be much higher).

Also, as indicated above, even though most Latino communities are bilingual, that does not necessarily imply that every member of the community speaks Spanish or English. There is indeed a continuum between recently arrived monolingual Spanish speakers and U.S.-born monolingual English speakers with various degrees of bilingualism between those poles. Additionally, there are many varieties of Spanish spoken in the city. Even though Chicano Spanish is the most widely spoken variety (Parodi "En torno"), Central American varieties are increasingly making their way in the linguistic landscape of Los Angeles. As shown in Table 1, the number of Central Americans in L.A. County, mainly Salvadorian and Guatemalans, is significant, at close to eight hundred thousand people (more than 16 percent of the Latino population).

Central American Spanish differs from Chicano Spanish phonologically, syntactically, and lexically. These differences correspond to dialectal variation between Spanish varieties of the highlands in Mexico, which is the base of Chicano Spanish, (Parodi "Contacto," "Normatividad," "El otro México") and the lowlands in Central America. Some of the main differences are summarized in Table 2.

TABLE 2
Differences between Central American and Mexican Chicano Spanish

	CENTRAL AMERICAN VARIETIES	**MEXICAN VARIETIES (N/BAJÍO)**
Phonological features	Aspiration s → h	No aspiration
	Velarization n → ŋ / p,b → k/___ ts	No velarization
	Epenthesis o → y	No epenthesis
Morphosyntactic features	Use of the second personal singular personal pronoun "**VOS**" and its verbal conjugation (*vos venís, vos comés*)	Use of the second personal singular personal pronoun "**TÚ**" and its verbal conjugation (*tú vienes, tú comes*)
Lexical features (great variation in vocabulary)	Examples: *Ayote* (pumpkin) *Chumpa* (jacket) *Chele* (light-skinned person) *Yinas* (sandals/flip-flops) *Pacha* (baby bottle) *Piscucha* (kite)	Examples: *Calabacita* (pumpkin) *Saco/Chamarra* (jacket) *Güero* (light-skinned person) *Chanclas* (sandals/flip-flops) *Mamila* (baby bottle) *Papalote* (kite)

Just as language contact results in a number of unique linguistic phenomena such as loans, calques, or switches, the situation of contact between two dialects of the same language also leads to particular linguistic outcomes. There are some important linguistic notions that inform the research of dialect contact and that form the theoretical framework of my study of dialect contact in Los Angeles. These are some of the main theories.

In accommodation theory, Giles and Coupland argued that people adjust their speech, gestures, and vocal patterns to accommodate to others. This framework explores the various reasons why individuals emphasize or minimize the social differences between themselves and their interlocutors through verbal and nonverbal communication. This theory addresses the links between language, context, and identity by exploring intergroup and interpersonal factors that lead to accommodating communication behaviors (Gallois, Ogay, and Giles). There are two main accommodation processes described by this theory: *convergence,* which refers to the strategies through which interlocutors adapt to each other's communicative behaviors, in order to reduce differences, and *divergence,* which refers to the instances in which individuals accentuate their speech and nonverbal differences. In the case of dialect contact, when speakers of different varieties of the same language interact continuously and inhabit the same spaces, we can expect that convergence, and, perhaps in some cases, divergence, will take place. It is also expected that the accommodation will gear toward the most prestigious or predominant dialect (Chicano Spanish in this case).

Dialect leveling refers to the assimilation of dialects by reducing the "variation between dialects of the same language in situations where speakers of these dialects are brought together" (Lefebvre 46). Dialect leveling is triggered by contact between dialects and has been observed in many parts of the world as a result of language standardization. As opposed to accommodation, which is a short-term approximation between speakers of different dialects in communication, dialect leveling is a long-term process that leads to convergence and the disappearance of distinct features in the precontact varieties.

Koinéization (Siegel) is the mixing of features of different dialects, which leads to a new dialect. It results from integration or unification of the speakers of the varieties in contact. A koiné is a structurally stabilized variety that is the product of heavy intermixture. According to Parodi ("El otro México"), Chicano Spanish is a koiné mainly derived from rural varieties of Spanish in Mexico and the predominant variety of Spanish in L.A.

Diglossia (Ferguson, Fishman "Bilingualism," Gumperz) refers to the specialization of use of two languages that are in contact within the same geographical area. Diglossic situations are also very common around the world. Usually one of the languages or varieties is considered *high* and is associated with official status (carries overt prestige), while the *low* variety is often relegated to less formal situations.

All of these theories—accommodation, dialect leveling, koinéization, and diglossia—are at play in the linguistic situation of Los Angeles, with Spanish and English having had intense contact for centuries, but also in more recent times with the contact among different varieties of Spanish.

In previous studies, Parodi ("Normatividad," "El otro México") proposed that Central Americans living in Los Angeles acquire EVLA (Chicano Spanish) regardless of their parents' vernacular variety. Parodi studied the Spanish of Central Americans (mostly Salvadorians) in L.A. She divided her population into two groups: those born in L.A. or who arrived before eight years of age[1] and those who came as adults in their twenties and beyond. Parodi examined various linguistic features including morphological, phonological, and lexical traits, which are different between Mexican and Central American Spanish (see Table 2): for instance, the use of *vos* in Central America for the second-person singular instead of *tú* in Mexico (and EVLA). She found that typical Central American words and morphosyntactic features such as *vos* are not produced by Central Americans born and raised in L.A. Thus, Parodi concludes, there is evidence of dialect leveling resulting in a koiné that is mainly characterized by features of the most numerous, oldest, or prestigious dialect (Chicano Spanish or EVLA, in this case).

In my own research (Sánchez-Muñoz "Los distintos dialectos") examining contact between Central Americans and Chicanos in Los Angeles, some of my data coincides with Parodi's results. While some speakers abandon the use of *vos* and tend to produce words and terms that are typical of Chicano Spanish, my research indicates a stronger tendency toward bidialectalism rather than a complete leveling or adoption of a koiné.

In my study of dialect contact between Central American and Chicano Spanish in L.A., I was interested in examining how much convergence, if any, first-generation Central American immigrants showed toward the predominant Chicano Spanish of Los Angeles. To this end, I collected data from first-generation Salvadorians and Guatemalans who had been residing in L.A. for over ten years. The data collection procedures included open-ended sociolinguistic interviews, which ranged between forty-five and seventy minutes and aimed at eliciting information related to the speakers' ethnic and linguistic identity and dialect awareness. Speakers also completed a picture-naming task to see whether they would produce the local Chicano word for a given image of an object or action or whether they would first produce their own vernacular version of the word. For instance, when presented with a picture of a kite, the speaker would first say *piscucha* (Central American) or *papalote* (Mexican). The picture-naming task contained seventy images of objects or actions

---

1. Eight years of age has been established as the approximate cut-off age for nativelike dialect acquisition (Chambers, Parodi "Contacto").

that are commonly referred to by different words or expressions in Mexican and Central American varieties.

Although the results are inconclusive at this point since I have only included data from ten participants so far for this project, there is a clear tendency toward bidialectalism. Most speakers produce first the Chicano word about 50 percent of the time (usually for common actions or objects such as *sucio* or *chanclas* instead of *shuco* for "dirty" or *yinas* for "flip-flops"), but right away also explain that they would say it differently in their places of origin. It seems that most speakers easily code-switch between varieties depending on the situation and interlocutor. Regarding the use of *vos* versus *tú*, my observations indicate that *vos* is only used with family members and close friends from the same place of origin (Salvador or Guatemala), whereas *tú* is used with everyone else (Chicano, Mexican, Spaniard, etc.) This diglossic use of Central American variants for some situations may indicate a negotiation not only of linguistic spaces but also of ethnocultural alliances. This is more clearly evidenced in the open-ended interviews, where we find comments such as "*soy latino aquí en Los Angeles y es bueno poder hablar mi idioma con mucha de la gente de aquí, pero soy chapín de corazón*" ("I am Latino here in Los Angeles and it's good to be able to speak my language with the majority of the people here, but I'm Guatemalan at heart."). I argue that just as code-switching between Spanish and English is a way of negotiating the multifaceted identities of Chicanos in Los Angeles, the code-switching between different dialects also evidences negotiations of different aspects of being Latino in which both convergence and divergence are at play: *Juntos pero no revueltos* (Together but not mixed).

TEMPTED BY THE WORDS OF ANOTHER? ETHNICITY, LANGUAGE, AND IDENTITY

Language is one of the most powerful tools to construct one's identity. Language serves more than a purely communicative function; it serves as a symbolic marker of identity that, among other things, enables a particular group to distinguish itself from others (Fishman "Language and Ethnicity," Bucholtz). The complexities of ethnic and cultural identities are mirrored in speech practices particularly evident in urban environments as diverse as the city of Los Angeles. In the case of Chicanos, an indigenous connection, a Spanish-linguistic heritage, and an Anglo-centric reality are intertwined in a unique sociolinguistic space. As I have argued here and elsewhere, *Spanglish* (namely, code-switching, code-mixing, borrowings, and other language-contact phenomena commonly employed by Chicana/o bilinguals) evidences how speakers move between various identity spaces. Some of these spaces are realized in English, some in Spanish, some as a mixture of both; essentially speakers are creating a unique linguistic space in which identity can be constructed and reconstructed by means of language.

Additionally, the contact between different varieties of Spanish in the city results in negotiations not only between languages but also more subtly within the same language. In the case of Central Americans in Los Angeles, previous studies (Parodi "Contacto," "Normatividad," "El otro México") demonstrated that those born and/or raised in L.A. acquire a Chicano koiné, EVLA, with the distinct flavor of rural Mexican Spanish. Yet, many speakers show a clear tendency toward bidialectalism (Sánchez-Muñoz "Los distintos dialectos"). In this case, the negotiation of distinct varieties of Spanish with salient differences especially in the lexicon can also be seen as a form of linguistic hybridization. In this view, bidialectalism mirrors bilingualism and offers a fluid linguistic space for speakers to converge in a common Latino identity or diverge as a distinct ethnic culture.

Chicanos and other Latinos in the United States live together with the dominant Anglo culture, which marks its power politically, socially, and economically. Yet, in the urban linguistic landscape of Los Angeles, language takes center stage. Power is linguistically enacted as speakers of different languages and varieties juggle cultures on a daily basis. Speakers are not merely *tempted by the words of another,* but through code-switching between languages and dialects, they make those words and codes their own. The creation of linguistic third spaces (such as *Spanglish*) allows for the freedom to converge, diverge, take on, and abandon those words and codes. Bilingualism and bidialectalism are thus linguistic resources to better express the fluidity and complexity of the multifaceted immigrant experience.

WORKS CITED

Anzaldúa, G. *Borderlands/La Frontera: The New Mestiza.* 4th ed. San Francisco: Aunt Lute Books, 2012. Print.

Bucholtz, M. "Why Be Normal? Language and Identity Practices in a Community of Nerd Girls." *Language in Society* 28.2 (1999): 203–25. Print.

Chambers, J. K. *Sociolinguistic Theory.* Blackwell, 1995. Print.

Dumitrescu, D. "Spanglish: An Ongoing Controversy." *Building Communities and Making Connections.* Ed. Susana Rivera-Mills and Juan Antonio Trujillo. Newcastle upon Tyne: Cambridge Scholars, 2010. 136–67. Print.

Ferguson, C. A. "Diglossia." *Word-Journal of the International Linguistic Association* 15.2 (1959): 325–40. Print.

Fishman, J. A. "Bilingualism With and Without Diglossia; Diglossia With and Without Bilingualism." *Journal of Social Issues* 23.2 (1967): 29–38. Print.

——. "Language and Ethnicity." *Language, Ethnicity and Intergroup Relations* 15 (1977): 25. Print.

Fought, C. *Chicano English in Context*. New York: Palgrave Macmillan, 2003. Print.

Gallois, C., T. Ogay, and H. Giles. "Communication Accommodation Theory: A Look Back and a Look Ahead." *Theorizing About Intercultural Communication*. Ed. W. B. Gudykunst. Thousand Oaks, CA: Sage, 2005. 121–48.

Giles, H., and N. Coupland. *Language: Contexts and Consequences*. Pacific Grove, CA: Brooks/Cole, 1991. Print.

Gumperz, J. J. "Types of Linguistic Communities." *Anthropological Linguistics* (1962): 28–40. Print.

Lefebvre, C. *Creole Genesis and the Acquisition of Grammar: The Case of Haitian Creole*. Cambridge: Cambridge UP, 1998. Print.

Lipski, J. M. *Varieties of Spanish in the United States*. Georgetown UP, 2008. Print.

Otheguy, R., and N. Stern. "On So-Called Spanglish." *International Journal of Bilingualism* 15.1 (2011): 85–100. Print.

Parodi, C. "Contacto de Dialectos en Los Ángeles. Español Chicano y Español Mexicano." *Séptimo Encuentro Internacional de Lingüística en el Noroeste* T2 (2004): 277–93. Print.

——. "Normatividad y Diglosia en Los Ángeles. Un Modelo de Contacto Lingüístico." *Normatividad y uso lingüístico*. Ed. F. Colombo and A. Soler. México: UNAM, 2009. 47–67. Print.

——. "El otro México: Español Chicano, Koineización y Diglosia en Los Ángeles, California." *Realismo en el análisis de corpus orales, Coloquio de cambio y variación*. Ed. P. Martín Butragueño. México: El Colegio de México, 2011. 217–43. Print.

——. "En torno a la koiné de Los Ángeles, California." *Espacio y discurso: perspectivas acerca de regiones literarias y lingüísticas*. Ed. E. Mendoza Guerrero, M. López Berríos, and I. E. Moreno Rojas. México: Universidad Autónoma de Sinaloa, 2012. 185–204. Print.

Penfield, J., and J. L. Ornstein-Galicia. *Chicano English: An Ethnic Contact Dialect*. Amsterdam; Philadelphia: John Benjamins, 1985. Print.

Sánchez-Muñoz, A. "Los distintos dialectos del español en Los Angeles: Convergencia y divergencia." *Primer Congreso de la Academia Norteamericana de la Lengua Española* (ANLE), Library of Congress, Washington, DC, 2014. Lecture.

——. "Identidad y confianza lingüística en jóvenes latinos en el Sur de California." *El Español En Los Estados Unidos: E Pluribus Unum? Enfoques Multidisciplinarios* Ed. D. Dumitrescu and G. Piña-Rosales. New York: Academia Norteamericana de la Lengua Española / North American Academy of the Spanish Language, 2013. 217–32. Print.

Siegel, J. "Dialect Contact and Koinéization." *International Journal of the Sociology of Language* 99 (1993): 105–21. Print.

Stavans, I. *Spanglish: The Making of a New American Language*. New York: Rayo, 2003. Print.

CHAPTER 5

The Cultural Border, Magic, and Oblivion in *Bless Me, Ultima* (2013), *Obaba* (2005), and *Un embrujo* (1998)

JUAN PABLO GIL-OSLE

THESE THREE FILMS originate from three regions of the Hispanic world with an important, albeit conflictive, history of linguistic and cultural politics: *Bless Me, Ultima* (*Bendíceme, Ultima*), by Carl Franklin (U.S., 2013), based on the 1972 novel by Rudolfo Anaya; *Obaba* (Spain, 2005), directed by Montxo Armendariz, based on Bernardo Atxaga's novel *Obabakoak* (1989); and *Un embrujo* (Mexico, 1998), directed by Carlos Carrera.[1] The three films, and the novels on which they are based, contain an evocative sensation of cultures in which the haggard flame of tradition wanes. The local linguistic expressions in the mountains of New Mexico, in the towns of Basque Country, and in the natural wells of Yucatan appear to fall into oblivion—or at least to transform themselves—behind a magic veil, in addition to being associated with certain social groups. In these films, there emerges a reality, not original by any means, but present, all the while fading away as a result of perennial transformations from social pacts, words, and desires. The last *curanderos*, or healers, disappear from the New Mexico of *Bless Me, Ultima* and the Yucatan of *Un embrujo,* carrying with them their language and part of their tradition—Hispanic or Maya— in *Obabakoak* the last narrator forgets the words—in Basque—at the end of the book. The narratives by these creators of discourses

---

1. I thank José Flores, affiliated with Arizona State University, for the work he put into the translation of this essay into English.

are obliterated in the cultural borders of the Hispanic world, and their words remain in the barren wasteland of the (de)political linguistics of nationalism.

In past decades, an increasingly decentralized cultural production has sustained the realities on the border with the Hispanic world. From profoundly divergent worlds like the United States, Mexico, and Spain, each with strongly centralized cultural traditions as a result of their national entertainment industry, alternative worlds and voices are produced. The spaces where these voices and images are composed rely significantly on persecuted and outlawed minority languages. As represented in these films and texts, these languages' vitality is admirable, considering that for centuries they've remained present in the complex structural frameworks of colonization, assimilation, and globalization.[2] In literary terms, the magic of the shaman and the magic of tradition that embody the words of the minority languages are an expression of this *maravilla* (wonder) for the senses, in the purest Baroque sense of the word.

The (non)curative magic that permeates the fictions of social anguish along the borders can be seen as a continuation of magical realism's identity formations, in the manner that Harvey describes in *Bless Me, Ultima*. It may, in fact, be a ploy by the weak as a way of living in a hostile world; according to Caro Baroja, with respect to the power of the healer—elder woman, marginalized, and disappointed—who fashions herself as a fearful image to salvage the limitations of a hypertrophy self (402–3). With their way of viewing the world and expressing it, healers could see themselves as expiatory victims, whereby their passing allows them to enter a different phase, extrapolating the ideas of René Girard about the relationship between social violence and sacred sacrifice (Girard 36–39). More so, the rupturing of the laws of physics in Hispanic border cultures, both internally and externally, is also accompanied by a linguistic factor that tends to be omitted or, at best, mentioned in passing. One of the foremost representations of violence is the annihilation of an entire culture, silencing its people and forcing them to contemplate their own decimated culture. It is thus argued here that the traditions of the past, marginalized by other central cultural forces, express themselves as a linguistic code that contradicts the history of the linguistic policies of a nation, and that these languages, with their magic, fade in the plots of the analyzed films,

---

2. The topic of multilingualism seems to be whisked away, and ignored, on occasion. For instance, with respect to *Un embrujo*, there is bewilderment regarding the little attention paid to the presence of Mayan culture in the film: "Revisé algunas reseñas en el internet y me llamó la atención que en todas las que encontré no se mencionara ni por casualidad la presencia de la cultura maya. Muchos personajes secundarios claves inclusive hablaban en maya y no en castellano," even though the beginning of the film portrays a shaman's ritual by the sea, and Lupita's reaction to Eliseo's indifference. Lupita, an indigenous girl, decides to employ the shaman's magic to allure Eliseo (Forns-Broggi 139).

all within the complex processes of atonement and prevention of cultural violence along the border.

Here it is referred to as (non)curative magic because nothing gets resolved; the vanishing of the shaman in the pools of the Yucatan, the last healer woman fading into the mountains of New Mexico, and the last word devoured by a lizard in Basque Country within the mind of a narrator of stories that sought the creation of a literary cannon in Basque. However, in the three films, there exists a nostalgia that resides in the magic of the language of a border identity: Mayan, Spanish, and Basque—or varieties of these. Languages are extremely stigmatized in many ways and in different contexts within the borders where their speakers reside. Yet, the nostalgia that the speaker may feel toward a marginalized language, seeing the representations of his culture in another, not only serves as a site of negotiation of cultural binaries or of bilingualism but may also operate as a convincing aspect and intermediate space in which the spectator can sympathize with the minority.[3]

Despite all the differences in *Bless Me, Ultima, Obada,* and *Un embrujo,* as these fictions come to a close, so do the language and the magic fade. Would this then mean a movement toward equilibrium? That is, toward a symbolic union of the mainstream culture and the spectator after the short-lived presence of Spanish, Basque, and a Mayan dialect, as if to enact a comfortable *code-switch* for the monolingualism operating in the nation, in a condescending gesture of the plurality of *ethnolinguists.* It is no coincidence that the core nationalism of a language and a territory appear to operate within the large groups in the three countries. These three fictions emerge from a system organized by a monolingual cultural identity that is reminiscent of Herder and with an incontestable geographic demarcation—the principle of Wilson or Stalin (Hobsbawm 132–33)—as an expression of cultural and linguistic borders that the reductionism of an agrarian and marginal *volk* has not completely dispossessed of its presence and continuity. Those languages of the borderland *volk* are accompanied in the three films of this study by a strong presence of magic, the atavistic, at the same time irrational and pure, products of the towns.

With respect to Girard's theory on scapegoats—the necessary public sacrifice for the preservation of a hegemonic society—there exists in these films an element of the magical and the marvelous that mirrors a cathartic ritual. In the three fictions, there is a sacrificial closing—Ultima dies, the Yucatan shaman descends to the subterranean caverns, the lizard devours the linguis-

---

3. This leads me to think about the existence of nostalgia—illness caused by the desire to return to one's country of origin—and sympathy—the capacity to feel hurt or suffer together—as effects of the same cause in these productions of the linguistic borderlands.

tic abilities of the narrator—and as a result, the scapegoat cleanses the threats that sympathy and nostalgia arouse in the spectator. All ends in a return to the comfort and security of the rationalism of modernity. Nothing is as destabilizing as the flight of transformations that Alejo Carpentier offers to his readers as the reaffirmation of the power of voodoo in *The Kingdom of This World* (*El reino de este mundo*) during the edification of Haiti onward from the colonial and dictatorial ashes, or the paradoxical linguistic cornucopia of Jorge Luis Borges's short story "Funes the Memorious."

The question, then, is how to interpret the reoccurrence of these rational nonmythical endings from the perspective of myth and language in conjunction with national linguistic policies. In the sixteenth and seventeenth centuries, there was a well-known effort to create a vernacular language that encompassed all branches of knowledge and that would be concomitantly comparable to prestigious languages, like Latin and Greek. These academic and aesthetic efforts emerged in conjunction with the creations of empires, nations, and, of course, immense groups of minorities. The expressions that manifested from these instruments of monolingual globalization reached the most remote places and genres. For instance, in recent academic texts, the role of biographies from members of convents has been discussed as aiding in the formation of a transatlantic and global reality.[4] The production of these hagiographies and biographies would have helped to create some global imitations of behavior.

During these centuries, those models that compose the behavior have been expressed, consumed, and discussed in Spanish within the Spanish-speaking world. In the last decades, however, the increasing emphasis on linguistic minorities in connection with postcolonial theories has generated local expressions that fracture these global constructions. As Serge Gruzinski indicated, occidentalization is a complex process; it "includes all tools of domination employed in the Americas by Renaissance Europe: the Catholic religion, market mechanisms, cannon, books, and images" (53).[5] Although occidental globalization is a reality that is dominated by the phenomenon of the market, in the legacy of both Hispanic worlds it is not unreasonable to think about the instruments of globalization and *mestizaje* set up during the sixteenth and seventeenth centuries. Four of these instruments of domination that the Iberian world set in motion in the creation of globalism are present in the

---

4. See Bilinkoff and Molina and Strasser.

5. Gruzinski works with this theme of occidentalization and globalization in various books. What interests him is the creation of a decentralized cultural history beyond the local historiographies, rhetoric of alterity, national historiographies, *World History,* European history, in short, that type of provincialism called Eurocentrism (Gruzinski, *Las cuatro* 40–43).

three films of this essay. As previous critical works have established, aspects of religion and magic are fundamental in the cultural dichotomies of *Bless Me, Ultima*,[6] and are obviously the attractive aspects of *Un embrujo*, as is the silence related to the nature of the lizard and childhood that make up *Obaba* and its image.[7] With regard to the texts, two films are based on foundational texts, one from the Chicano Movement of the 1960s and 1970s,[8] and the other from the "Basqueness" of democracy in the 1980s, literate and international. Ultimately, it is obvious that these three films are a visual product. For this reason, the three films are pluralingual products within a market accustomed to the consumption of products in the hegemonic languages in the history of globalization.

The three films are products that do not completely converge with nationalist essentialism, except with the fluidity of identity on the linguistic borderlands of our nations, which on occasions are omitted. Likewise, some critics observe that *Bless Me, Ultima, Obaba,* and *Un embrujo* share the characteristic of being asocial and ahistorical (Caminero-Santangelo 116, Lamadrid 496, Rodríguez).[9] There has been an academic discussion with respect to this because on many occasions there is an impression that their plots are woven into a fabric that could well be located in remote corners of the planet and in other time periods. However, when one reflects on the political-linguistic campaigns in the North American Southwest and in Basque Country, it is difficult to accept without a doubt that works of art that employ a minority language have an apolitical essence. For instance, with regard to the book *Obabakoak*, it was said to not be a political text, which in turn explained its success in Spain and abroad. Yet, linguistic policy and literary canons interlace with the endemic problems of the language; the language and tradition in which Atxaga writes (Gil-Osle). In fact, the use of Basque is a top concern in cultural production, not just for this author but for many Basque intellec-

---

6. See Lamadrid, Harvey, Martínez-Cruz, among others.

7. Elena Grau-Lleveria also mentions the imposed silences, by lizards or institutional dynamics. She says, "in *Bless me, Ultima* y *Felices días tío Sergio*, the plots present a peculiar structure in which there are a series of gaps that are suggested to be related to the historical silence imposed by the system of power" (72). *Obabakoak* concludes with the senseless babbling of the silenced narrator in the section titled "Azken hitza," "The Last Word."

8. "Rudolfo Anaya's *Bless Me, Ultima* is regarded as a classic of Chicano/Latino literature and even of ethnic American literature" (Caminero-Santangelo 115).

9. For example, Néstor E. Rodríguez, concerned with showing that Atxaga has not a political agenda but an exclusively artistic one in *Obabakoak*, writes a study about the implications of the Spanish translation of the book. He does this by way of the affirmations Atxaga makes in the epilogue of the Spanish translation, and comments: "I would like to propose that the gesture of Atxaga to make language the core of his literary project is a result of a dissuasive act that consists in deflecting the Spanish reader's attention from the ideological reading of the novel emphasizing on the contrary the literary project that has inspired it" (178, 183).

tuals. Atxaga describes in these words the barren land that the Basque island has become:

> Denbora batean lekhu hau delizios izan zen, eta egungo egunean, berriz, mortu dago, antzinako gauza gehienak bezalaxe. Hargatik iduritzen zaitzu hain eskas eta labor. Ordea egin izan balitz eskuaraz hanbat liburu nola egin baita frantsesez edo bertze erdara edo hizkuntzaz, hek bezain aberats eta konplitu izanen zen eskuara ere. (*Obabakoak* 331)

> There was a time when this place was delicious, while in the present, in turn, it is arid and lifeless. For this reason, the island appears to you as diminutive and limited. However, if there had been as many books written in Basque as there have been written in French or any other language, Basque too would be a rich and perfect language.

Nevertheless, the concern over a production in the Basque language is not only one of Basque art for art's sake, but the writing—including the quotidian use of the language in private and public—is today a political act, just as it was in the time of its prohibition, because it is a minority language in Basque Country, and is marginalized and stigmatized in other geographic and political spaces as well.

In *Bless Me, Ultima,* similar affirmations have been made that would explain its success beyond the market of Chicano readership in the United States. However, from the book's beginning it is noticeably clear to whom and where Spanish is spoken, as it is with English. It is a constant metalinguistic reference in which the narrator conveys that the characters live within two languages: "'Jason no está aquí,' (Jason is not here) she said. All of the older people spoke only in Spanish, and I myself understood only Spanish" (Anaya 9). In addition, in the beginning, the author establishes the Anglophone effect carried out in the schools that the community children attend (10). Schooling is the threshold of bilingualism and probably of the diglossia of literate Anglophones and illiterate Spanish-speakers:

> [Deborah] had been to school two years and now she spoke only English. She was teaching Theresa and half the time I didn't understand what they were saying. (9)

> I wished that I could always be near her, but that was impossible. The war had taken my brothers away, and so the school would take me away. "Ready, mama," Deborah called. She said that in school the teachers let them speak only in English I wondered how I would be able to speak to the teachers. (30)

In the movie, it would seem that the linguistic aspect is less relevant, except that Ultima speaks to her young *curandero* (healer) apprentice in Spanish, and all things in nature are specifically named in Spanish. The plants, the herbs, the places retain their Spanish names and some indigenous ones as Ultima gathers them in the fields (Anaya 45–48), a terminology that surreptitiously penetrates the spectator, as in the memories of the lost Basque words in the beginning of *Soinujoilearen Semea* (*The Accordionist's Son*) and in the closing of *Obabakoak*.

Without language there is no margin for identity; each lost word of the cultural heritage is like each one of those young girls who do not speak the language of their parents in *Bless Me, Ultima,* or like the synonym of the word butterfly, "tximeleta" in Basque, that in reality is never a synonym but more like a different variety of butterfly. This wealth begins to fade as the imperialist push for globalization and nationalism has for centuries undervalued the human cultural mosaic.

WORKS CITED

Anaya, Rudolfo. *Bless Me, Ultima.* 1972. Berkeley, CA: Tonatuih-Quinto Sol International, 1986. Print.

Atxaga, Bernardo. *Obabakoak.* Barcelona: Ediciones B, 1977. Print.

Baroja, Caro. *Las brujas y su mundo.* Madrid: Alianza, 1997. Print.

Bilinkoff, Jodi. *Related Lives: Confessors and Their Female Penitents, 1450–1750.* Ithaca: Cornell UP, 2005. Print.

Bless Me, Ultima. Dir. Carl Franklin. Sony Pictures Home Entertainment. 2013. Film.

Caminero-Santangelo, Marta. "'Jason's Indian': Mexican Americans and the Denial of Indigenous Ethnicity in Anaya's *Bless Me, Ultima.*" *Critique* 45.2 (2004): 115–28. Print.

Caro Baroja, Julio. *Las brujas y su mundo.* Madrid: Alianza, 1997. Print.

Carpentier, Ajejo. *El reino de este mundo.* Barcelona: Seix Barral, 1986. Print.

Forns-Broggi, Roberto. "Un embrujo by Carlos Carrera." *Chasqui* 28.1 (1999): 138–40. Print.

Gil-Osle, Juan Pablo. "Bernardo Atxaga: canon, plagio y euskera literario." *Bulletin of Spanish Studies: Hispanic Studies and Researches on Spain, Portugal and Latin America* 91 (2014): 869–87. Print.

Ginzburg, Carlo. *Ecstasies: Deciphering the Witches' Sabbath.* New York: Pantheon Books, 1991. Print.

Girard, René. *La violence et le sacré.* Paris: Hachette, 1990. Print.

Grau-Lleveria, Elena. "Historia e identidad nacional en dos autores latinoamericanos contemporáneos. Rudolfo Anaya y Magali García Ramis." *Neophilologus* 85 (2005): 71–78. Print.

Gruzinski, Serge. *Las cuatro partes del mundo: Historia de una mundialización.* México: Fondo de Cultura Económica, 2010. Print.

———. *The Mestizo Mind: The Intellectual Dynamics of Colonization and Globalization.* New York: Routledge, 2002. Print.

Harvey, Meredith. "The Archetypal Wise Woman in Postcolonial Works of Magical Realism of the Americas: An Examination of Rudolfo Anaya's *Bless Me, Ultima,* Toni Morrison's *Paradise,* and Gabriel García Márquez's *Cien años de soledad.*" Diss. Idaho State U, 2010. Print.

Hobsbawm, Eric. *Nation and Nationalism since 1780: Programme, Myth, Reality.* Cambridge: Cambridge UP, 1990. Print.

Lamadrid, Enrique R. "Myth as the Cognitive Process of Popular Culture in Rudolfo Anaya's *Bless Me, Ultima*: The Dialectics of Knowledge." *Hispania* 68 (1985): 496–501. Print.

Martínez-Cruz, Paloma. "Interpreting the (Me)xican Wise Woman: Convivial and Representation." Diss. Columbia University, 2004. Print.

Molina, J. Michelle, and Ulrike Strasser. "Missionary Men and the Global Currency of Female Sanctity." *Women, Religion and the Atlantic World (1600–1800).* Ed. Daniella Kostroun and Lisa Vollendorf. Toronto: U Toronto P, 2009. 156–70. Print.

Obaba. Dir. Montxo Armendariz. Megacom Film. 2005. Film.

Rodríguez, Néstor E. "La palabra está en otra parte: escritura e identidad en *Obabakoak.*" *Revista Hispánica Moderna* 54.1 (2001): 176–90. Print.

Un embrujo. Dir. Carlos Carrera. Salamandra Producciones. 1998. Film.

CHAPTER 6

El Malcriado (1964–1975)
La voz impresa del campesino y su impronta

VÍCTOR FUENTES

EN SU PRIMERA reunión organizativa, celebrada en Fresno en 1962, César Chávez y la Unión de Campesinos incluyeron el proyecto de la creación de un periódico propio que actuara como agitador y organizador colectivo de la organización.[1] Este periódico tuvo un antecedente del mismo nombre, *El Malcriado*, fundado en Los Angeles en 1923 por Daniel Venegas, autor de la tan lograda novela de la inmigración mexicana, *Las aventuras de don Chipote, o cuando los pericos mamen*.[2] Tal *Malcriado* se anunciaba como un semanario joco-serio de caricaturas.[3] En 1968, Antonio Orendain asocia este periódico a cierta prensa periódica mexicana de lucha social diciendo que su antecedente se encontraba en multitud de efímeros periódicos locales nacidos en México

---

1. Me valgo en mi estudio, además de los ejemplares que poseo, de la colección bastante completa de la edición en español de la biblioteca de la Universidad de California, en Santa Bárbara. Algunos de los primeros números en español y una muy completa colección de la edición en inglés se encuentran en la red en el *Farm Worker Movement Documentation Project*. En las citas y referencias me he limitado a señalar el número y la fecha del periódico al que aludo.

2. *El Heraldo*, 1928; Arte Público, 1999.

3. César Chávez, quien de pequeño vendió periódicos en las calles de Los Angeles, en una charla a los distribuidores de *El Malcriado* (16-2-1974), explica cómo surgió el nombre en la reunión en Fresno de 1962: "Ahí establecimos la idea de tener un periódico y hubo un concurso y pagamos veinticinco dólares al que se ganara el premio. Y un señor dijo; que se llame El M, y nos gustó y le pusimos "El M" (1). Este documento se conserva en la Oficina del Presidente en La Paz.

durante los años de la Revolución. Estos, destaca Orendain, eran como un relámpago que anunciaba una tormenta. De hecho, una sección de *El Malcriado* de Venegas se titularía "Relámpagos." Estos periódicos, por medio de sus "malcriados," pasaban la voz de pueblo en pueblo y de ciudad en ciudad.

El propósito de este ensayo es de presentar una síntesis del contenido temático de *El Malcriado*, periódico que surge en los 1960s con la lucha de los campesinos dirigidos por César Chávez. Me limito a una visión general de cómo *El Malcriado* va informando e involucrando a sus asociados y lectores en el devenir de la gesta histórica de los campesinos, entre 1964 y 1975, deslindando características y temas centrales en sus diversas etapas de existencia.

PRIMERA ETAPA (DICIEMBRE 1964–VERANO 1967): UN PRIMER AUGE PERIODÍSTICO

Desde diciembre de 1964 y hasta el número dieciséis, *El Malcriado* se publica quincenalmente y exclusivamente en español. Con limitadísimos medios de producción, y teniendo que hacer el viaje de Delano a Fresno para su impresión, y distribuyéndolo por tiendas de Delano a Merced, se trataba de una gestión ímproba. Desde sus comienzos se une como editor Bill Fisher, voluntario que trae consigo cierta experiencia periodística, aunque en el periódico no aparecieran su nombre o el de sus asistentes ya que *El Malcriado* representaba un trabajo colectivo que destacaba la "voz del campesino," como se subtitula a partir del número cuatro. Esta voz colectiva se expresaba en forma de poemas, corridos e historietas que documentan su lucha social.[4]

Dado que, en un principio, sus redactores y la mayoría de sus lectores eran campesinos de baja escolaridad, esta voz aparecía escrita en su forma hablada; en otras palabras, carecía de atención al uso del tilde, de acentos escritos o de la eñe. Igualmente, había poca atención a la puntuación y uso correcto de las letras *c, s, z*; *b* y *v*; *g* y *j*; el de escribir una palabra con *h* o sin *h*, entre otras faltas gramaticales.

De aquí, la valentía con que los editores se lanzan a hacer un periódico por encima de tales limitaciones, asumiéndolas, pero aspirando a que, en algún momento, se llegara a superarlas, como ocurriría en algunas de sus fases. Desde los primeros números, se muestran muy sensibles a las críticas que les hacen algunos lectores recriminándoles por no "escribir bien en español." Ya en el número tres, y, en la "Contestación a un lector que critica," el

---

4. Sería tema de un extenso ensayo o de una monografía recoger estas improvisaciones creadoras, poesía, cantos, cuentos y dichos, en su mayoría, de expresión y autoría popular que aparecen en *El Malcriado*. Por mi parte, lo dejo para otra ocasión.

editor comenta que un mexicano "que se afrenta de nosotros por el hecho de no saber explicarnos de la mejor forma del idioma castellano," escribe, muy aguda y hasta poéticamente:

> Que no se da cuenta de que no importa el saber, cuando el dolor nos alcanza se grita sin temor a la falta de educación. Que hubiese pasado si Francisco Villa y Emiliano Zapata hubiera decidido primero ir a educarse para luego luchar por un mejor ideal. Pedimos sueldos mejores para los no-educados para los que ganamos el pan con el sudor de nuestro rostro y no con el sudor de nuestra lengua.[5]

Escrito, más que con la tinta gramatical, con ese sudor, *El Malcriado* nace muy consciente de ser un instrumento fundamental en la lucha campesina. Tres armas tienen nuestra lucha—dirá César Chávez años más tarde—la huelga, el boicot y *El Malcriado*. De pequeña extensión (veintiocho centímetros de largo y veintiuno de ancho), en la portada del primer número aparece la caricatura de un campesino: "Don Sotaco" (como reza a su pie; la S sustituyendo a la Z de Zotaco) hombre de baja estatura, en la expresión sonorense y, en este caso, designando al tipo del campesino sin conciencia de clase y subordinado al patrón, aunque, en el fondo, nada tonto. Sin llevar fecha, este primer número es de diciembre de 1964. En el segundo número, aparece la figura de un mal encarado personaje con el rótulo de "Don Coyote." En números posteriores, se unirá la de otro facineroso, el gordiflón "Ranchero." Este trío, de tan irreverentes y cómicas caricaturas, "Don Sotaco," "Don Coyote" y el "Ranchero" (este último, sin Don) son creaciones de Andy Zermeño, sobresaliente artista gráfico de Los Angeles, California. Estos personajes estarán presentes a lo largo de varios años simbolizando el devenir de la lucha de los campesinos de la cual fue parte la familia de Zermeño también.

A partir del tercer número, *El Malcriado* vincula la lucha y la cultura del campesinado migrante, en su mayoría de origen mexicano, a la herencia de la Revolución Mexicana. Un nutrido grupo de portadas reproducen impresionantes grabados y dibujos del gran Taller de Gráfica popular mexicano, iniciado en 1937.[6] Entre ellas se destacan muestras artísticas de la vida revo-

---

5. En el editorial del número ocho leemos: "Si acaso usamos palabras vulgares o malas palabras, si hacemos ataques pesados, es únicamente porque la situación lo demanda. Cuando un contratista balacea a un campesino en sangre fría en el fil, lo menos que podemos decirle es que es un perro. Cuando los patrones aquí en California tienen a nuestra raza muerta de hambre, es nuestro deber decirles que son desgraciados. Cuando un campesino comienza a portarse como un moleta, es nuestro deber atacarle por vendido."

6. Se suceden, entre los números tres y diez las siguientes portadas-joyas, de tan reconocidos artistas: "Los hombres de la Revolución (3), "Protesta de una madre contra la guerra,"

lucionaria y rural de México, al igual que la iconografía de las dos figuras mítico-legendarias de la Revolución: Pancho Villa y Emiliano Zapata.

En el primer año del periódico se van dando a conocer las bases organizativas, el espíritu de lucha de la Unión, y los programas de beneficios para sus miembros. Es un tanto sorprendente ver que en el primer número de *El Malcriado*, el "Viva la Causa," se anuncia como el lema propuesto "para el movimiento de esta campaña" y se insiste en la dignidad del campesino y en el orgullo de su labor. En el número cuatro leemos: "Es una vergüenza que en el presente el 'oficio del campesino' sea como una maldición siendo que fue el primer oficio que existió"; y en la sección "Tinta y Papel," titulada "Limpiar el Oficio del Campesino," se propone: "Este periódico tratará de poner el 'oficio' del campesino en su respectivo lugar que le corresponde y limpiarlo del lodo que los rancheros han cubierto al trabajador." También se afirma el derecho que Dios ha dado al campesino y al pobre de "procurarse ellos y su familia una vida mejor." Tal declaración se refuerza, y ya desde el segundo número, con palabras de la Encíclica, *Rerun Novarun* (1891) del Papa León XIII; citas que, con otras bíblicas, se reiteran diseminadas a través de la historia del periódico.[7]

"La voz del campesino" es también la de muchos de sus lectores, como se refleja en la amplia sección, "Lo que la gente piensa. Cartas de los lectores," es la sección donde sus propias experiencias e ideas, recibiendo contestaciones elogiosas. En otras ocasiones, son los propios rancheros o simpatizantes quienes escriben su protesta sobre cómo son representados, a los cuales los editores contestan en burlonas respuestas. El tono del lenguaje de la edición en español aspira a ser como el que definiera César Chávez en una ocasión, contraponiendo el sistema anglosajón de la prensa, *reservado, profesional,* y el sistema latinoamericano, *calentito con chile y pimienta y que hierva un poquito la sangre* y que él adopta en sus charlas y discursos en español. Este estilo es el que, igualmente, se expresa en muchas de las cartas de los lectores criticando a los patrones y sus aliados.[8]

Andrea Gómez (4), "El volatín," Leopoldo Méndez (5), "El cortador de sisal," Alfredo Zalce (6), "Mujeres de espaldas con trenzas," Francisco Dosanante, "Descansando," María Yampolski (8), "Procesión revolucionaria" (10), Ignacio Aguirre.

7. El catolicismo social que anima a la lucha de la Unión y que propaga *El Malcriado*, tiene su gran antecedente en la Organización del *Catholic Worker*, con su periódico de tal nombre, fundado en 1933 por Dorothy Day, quien, en los años de la Huelga, fuera una ardiente defensora de la causa campesina.

8. Veamos este ejemplo: "Contra los esquiroles pelagatos, lombricientos, lambiscones, mequetrefes. A otros les dicen los 'bigotes' . . . ¡lástima de bigotes! Aunque para ellos es una gran ventaja porque dicen que los usan para sepillar las botas del patrón," firmando por Epifanio Camacho. McFarland.

En pro del tono picante, en el número cuatro se nos dice: "De vez en cuando en esta revista se publicarán selecciones de un famoso libro mexicano, llamado *Picardía mexicana* por A. Jiménez. Este libro se compone de chistes colorados y toda clase de picardías." Abundan, en este primer *El Malcriado*, tales picardías, con dichos (varios del tipo *como decía mi abuelita*, con la marca del propio César), refranes y chistes *colorados* gráficos y sacados de periódicos mexicanos o españoles.[9] Aún los trabuques entre la palabra pronunciada y la ortográfica, dan ocasión a juegos verbales. Por ejemplo, en el número dos, y tomando *sas* por *zas*, leemos: "Mi abuelita decía que el diablo fue el que hizo a los sastres de tres *sas*. Comenzo así sas, uno, sas, dos, y sas tres." O con-fundiendo el utensilio doméstico brasero con bracero, y deshumanizando a éste por prestarse a ser rompe-huelgas. Su "Diccionario enciclopédico," en el número once, ofrece esta definición: "Bracero: un objeto de barro o metal."

Al darse los primeros brotes de la Huelga, la editorial del número dieciséis se titula "Emiliano Zapata," destacándole como figura ejemplar para la victoria de los campesinos. En el diecinueve, cuando ya está en marcha la huelga, se define a la Asociación de Trabajadores Campesinos como un movimiento ("¿Qué es un movimiento? Un movimiento es bastante gente con una idea para que sus acciones sean como una gran ola de agua que nada ni nadie pueda pararla"). En el número veinte, ese oleaje plasma en la portada que anuncia HUELGA GENERAL EN LA UVA, con César Chávez, micrófono en mano, ocupándola y profetizando lo que se lograría: "GANAREMOS." En el veintiuno, la portada la llena la figura de Dolores Huerta alzando la pancarta "HUELGA."

Esta gloriosa página de la historia, donde las víctimas alcanzan su victoria, es llevada al lector por un equipo de fotógrafos voluntarios que presentan impactantes imágenes visuales de la lucha. Dado el irrefrenable empuje, para el segundo año de la Huelga, *El Malcriado* cuenta con la colaboración de un grupo de intelectuales y artistas orgánicos,[10] dándole al periódico una impronta renovadora cultural entre los números cuarenta y seis y cincuenta y seis. A tono con esto, en el número cincuenta y dos (29-12-66), un breve artículo nombra a "El Quijote, símbolo de *El Malcriado*," ilustrándose con el

---

9. En uno de ellos aparece una dama abriéndole la puerta al esposo y esperándolo: "Vienes sin pelos en la chaqueta, ¿Has estado con una mujer calva?"

10. En esto del intelectual y artista orgánico, me valgo de la definición de Antonio Gramsci quien nos dijera: "que todo grupo social que nace en el terreno de una función esencial en el mundo de la producción económica, crea, dentro de sí, orgánicamente un estrato de intelectuales orgánicos que dan al grupo su homogeneidad y conciencia de su propia función en el terreno económico, en el político-social y en el cultural" (21) *La función de los intelectuales*. México: Grijalbo, 1967.

dibujo del hidalgo castellano llevando el botón de la Unión y en su escudo el águila negra de la bandera. Al mismo tiempo una nota anuncia que *El Malcriado* se propone aumentar su circulación de los actuales quince mil ejemplares a cien mil de modo que se pueda alcanzar o cubrir todo el escenario laboral del país. Sumariamente, cito algunas de las nuevas aportaciones y secciones. En el número cuarenta y siete se publica el ensayo de Luis Valdez, "El alma de la raza," identificada ésta con el de la lucha laboral campesina; en los cuarenta y ocho y cuarenta y nueve se presenta la sección "La presencia de la mujer" con fotos de bellas jóvenes militantes; en el cincuenta y uno, que sale a color y aumentado en número de páginas, en la "Página de la mujer" se inaugura un consultorio femenino titulado "Señorita Alma, consejos." En el cincuenta y dos, junto a una foto de Joan Báez cantando con su guitarra, se publica un bello poema de elogio para ella firmado por Leopoldo V. Meza. En el cincuenta y dos, y dentro del nuevo aliciente cultural, literario y artístico, plasmado en la creada "Editorial del Campesino," se anuncia un "Club de lectores de habla hispana," algo bastante portentoso viniendo de donde viene y que muestra que la causa campesina va más allá de sus reivindicaciones socio-económicas, y donde expresa el llamado de "¡Piense en el futuro! y "Para el campesino que se instruye. ¡El porvenir está en sus manos!"[11]

Junto a una serie de poemas, la mayoría enviado por lectores y en forma de corrido, aparecen una serie de cuentos y relatos de Gene Nelson, de Agustín Lira y de Bill Esher; también dos relatos sobre Villa bajo el título general, "La causa del pobre." En el cincuenta y dos se introduce la historieta de *comics*, *La dolce vita in the North,* iniciada por Andrés Zermeño y Daniel de los Reyes y continuada, al regresarse estos periodistas a México, por Luis Valdez. Igualmente, entre los números cincuenta y dos y cincuenta y seis se publica un "Suplemento" con ensayos de Bob Dudnik sobre huelgas y momentos claves de la historia laboral del país. En varias contraportadas se anuncia el popular disco, "Viva la Causa." En estos números, entre el cuarenta y seis y el cincuenta y seis, y por primera, y casi única vez, aparecen los nombres de los autores/as de las colaboraciones. En el cincuenta y cuatro y cincuenta y cinco, se dan los de quienes confeccionaban el periódico.[12] Se trata de un equipo que de haberse

---

11. Se escribe que con solo veinticinco centavos uno puede inscribirse en el Club de Lectores, y se anuncia que la "Farm Workers Press Inc., (Las Editorial del Campesino) ha decido formar el CLUB DE LECTORES de habla hispana, para cuyos socios se publicarán ediciones especiales en español para serles vendidos también los libros a un precio especial." Se trata de uno de los logros de la Unión, tan favorecido por César Chávez, asiduo lector, y tan promotor de la educación y de la cultura, algo que apenas tratan quienes escriben libros en inglés sobre él.

12. Bill Esher, director general, Daniel de los Reyes, editor asociado, Andrés Zermeño, director artístico, Emmon Clarke, director asociado, Manuel Zapiens, jefe de circulación, Mary

podido mantener hubiera hecho de *El Malcriado*, además de un periódico laboral nacional en español, uno de relevante presencia literaria y artística de la comunidad hispano parlante de los Estados Unidos.

A partir del número cincuenta y seis, ya no se publica el Directorio y amenguan las colaboraciones literarias y artísticas. En el sesenta (10-5-1967) en lo que podría ser como reacción a alguna crítica expresadas en las Cartas de los lectores (de que el periódico se estaba alejando de la problemática campesina) se informa que la sección editorial será escrita por los campesinos. No obstante, este primer *Malcriado* abruptamente deja de existir en el verano del 1967, pero no sin antes dejarnos en uno de sus últimos números (el sesenta y dos, del siete de junio de 1967), los entrañables y conmovedores "Recuerdos de una vieja," la obrera campesina que participó en la sangrienta huelga algodonera de Corcoran de 1932. Ella comparte que recuerda con mucha lucidez que la huelga de algodón fue una huelga violenta donde hubo muchos huelguistas mal heridos. Firma su testimonio como Helen Flores de Handford, California.

REAPARICIÓN CON MIRAS MÁS CONCENTRADAS EN LOS OBJETIVOS DE LA LUCHA, CAUSA LABORAL, Y COMO PARTE OFICIAL DE LA UNIÓN (FEBRERO 1968–JUNIO 1970)

Lo dicho arriba lo evoca Doug Adair, a quien Dolores Huerta le comunicó, en diciembre de 1967, que la junta directiva quería reanudar la publicación de *El Malcriado* pero que César Chávez lo quería como parte oficial de la Unión y le invitaban a que él se hiciera cargo del periódico. También nos da cuenta del grupo editorial de esta etapa[13] y apunta que, en este nuevo ciclo, el periódico se concentrara más en promover el boicot de las uvas en la edición en inglés que en organizar a los campesinos a través de la edición en español.

Oportunamente, se relanza durante las fechas en que César vive su sacrificado ayuno de veinticinco días. Lleva fecha del veintiuno de febrero, pero se distribuye a principio de marzo, volviendo al formato anterior a su renovación y ampliación en el número cincuenta y uno y más mermado en páginas y corrección ortográfica. En el segundo número, del domingo diez de marzo, se anuncia triunfantemente "¡10,000 se unen al fin del ayuno!" con un artículo donde se describe el acto con la multitudinaria misa y fiesta de celebración

---

Murphy, Marcia B. Sánchez y Donna Haber, personal de redacción (de aquí, tal "presencia de la mujer") y Pablo Carriles y Bob Dunick, colaboradores.

13. Junto a él, colaboran David Fishlow, periodista profesional, Rudy Reyes y Marcia Brook Sánchez, redactores en la etapa anterior, y Jaime Reyes, quien trabajara con Fishlow en las traducciones de artículos en inglés al español.

con la participación—y la memorable foto—de Robert F. Kennedy sentado junto a César Chávez tras haber recibido ambos el pan de la Comunión (a menos de un mes del fin de este ayuno por la no-violencia, el cuatro de abril caía abatido criminalmente Martin Luther King, Jr.). La portada del número cuatro de este volumen de *El Malcriado* (15-4-1968) reproduce su rostro con el titular: "Asesinado ayudando a un sindicato." En el Editorial, "El hombre que mataron," se afirma el vínculo entre la lucha de los trabajadores campesinos de California y el difunto Dr. Martin Luther King, "un vínculo de amor y de liderazgo que no se va a poder quebrar con una bala." *El Malcriado* del primero de junio publicaba toda una página llamando al voto por el senador Robert F. Kennedy y quince días después, la portada del número cuatro, la ocupa una reproducción de un sonriente Robert F. Kennedy ante un micrófono, foto alusiva a su gran triunfo en las elecciones primarias de California el seis de junio. Sin embargo, lo que leemos en la página que abre el número es la noticia de su asesinato, "En Paz Descanse Nuestro Amigo," mitigado el dolor por el conmovedor artículo firmado por Antonio Orendain[14] y el siguiente, "El Triunfo y la tragedia," donde se da cuenta de la procesión en memoria y honor del "gran amigo" en Delano, el domingo diez de junio. El número nueve (1-7-1968) informa que unos vándalos han profanado la cruz cristiana erecta a la entrada de los cuarenta acres, serrándola y queriéndola quemar. El propio César, y tras su ayuno-pasión, empezó a recibir amenazas de muerte.

En la portada del número doce (15-8-1968), una mano empuña un afilado destornillador con la etiqueta "Consumers Boycott" que atraviesa al ranchero por su gordinflón vientre. El brazo que asesta el golpe lleva—tatuados en inglés—los nombres de quienes lo dan: "Big City Mayors, Housewives, NAACP, Teachers, Civil Rights Groups, Presidential Candidates, Political Organizations, Religious Leaders." La del número dieciséis (15-10-1968), muestra a Nixon atiborrándose de uvas tomadas de una caja que con su nombre le ofrece el ranchero y de cuyos racimos se desprenden los huelguistas. Nixon está en un barril y con sus "pezuñas," en lugar de aplastar las uvas, pisotea a figuras diminutas de los campesinos con sus pancartas. El título del dibujo es "¡Pare a Nixon! ¡Raza!"

En el número del quince de julio, 1968, se publica una nota, "Los periódicos chicanos," donde da los nombres y direcciones de diez de ellos a través de todo el país y se nos dice que *El Malcriado* se ha unido a la "Asociación de la Prensa Chicana (Chicano Press Association en inglés). El editorial del quince de noviembre, "Dice *El Malcriado*," trata de la elección de Nixon a la presidencia. Tras expresar "profunda tristeza" por lo sucedido y uniendo a

---

14. En el número doce, se nos dice que este artículo aparecerá en el libro *A Tribute to Robert F. Kennedy*, que publicará Doubleday en octubre de ese año.

Nixon con Reagan afirma que ninguno de los dos podrá acabar con la Unión, pues ésta es parte de todo un "movimiento" multirracial en los Estados Unidos. Vemos que ya la Unión anuncia y hace suya la "Rainbow Coalition" que posteriormente encabezará el reverendo Jesse Jackson. También *El Malcriado* se asocia al movimiento en contra de la guerra de Vietnam. Un emotivo y enternecedor caso relacionado con esto lo encontramos en el número trece (1-9-1968) cuyo editorial es "Contra la violencia en Convención de Chicago." Se trata de una carta del padre Ton Totole, de la iglesia "All Saints Church" de Denver, Colorado. Un soldado chicano en Vietnam, sabiendo que él hablaba "la singular lengua de la frontera," le pasó una copia de *El Malcriado* recibida de su pueblo natal, Bakersfield y ambos conversaron sobre su contenido y de los problemas "at home." Murió el soldado en combate y la copia quedó como parte de sus papeles. Dio con ella el clérigo y le hizo recordar el orgullo del caído porque "his people were doing something."[15]

Otro tema que aparece en *El Malcriado*, en 1968 y 1969, será el de los venenos pesticidas en los "files" y asociado, también, a una sensibilidad ecológica y de defensa del medio ambiente en unas fechas en que esta sensibilidad apenas se iniciaba en el país. En la edición del primero del primer día de septiembre de 1968 hay un artículo, "Contra los pesticidas," donde se trata de que los rancheros ocultan los usos de tales venenos y que el abogado de la Unión, Jerry Cohen, ha iniciado la investigación. Meses después, el número veintidós (15-1-1969), presenta la portada con el grabado de Guadalupe Posada de la calavera insecto empuñando otras calaveritas y huesos con el título "Venenos en el fil." Se reporta una "reunión especial sobre pesticidas" en Delano a la que acudieron 250 personas y donde César declaró que el problema de los pesticidas era el más importante en las discusiones con los rancheros.

A partir del primero de marzo de 1969, se inicia el tomo tres, número uno sin algún cambio sustancial de formato o contenido, pero ahora con Doug Adair de editor reemplazando a Fishlow. No obstante, la edición en español concluye en el número cuatro con apenas una modesta hoja disculpatoria por no seguir imprimiendo *El Malcriado* en esta lengua debido, principalmente, a que su personal se desplaza a la huelga y al boicot. Se anuncia que pasado este período se comenzará a imprimir un periódico que será el orgullo de todos.[16] La edición en inglés continúa hasta febrero de 1971 cuando, igualmente, con-

---

15. De aquí que ofrezca su ayuda. La copia que tiene es el número cuarenta y seis (con la portada de la bella activista chicana con el águila de la Unión, que contemplaría el joven soldado en Vietnam con placer), pide una suscripción y añade: "My resources are yours; the spark that ignited the light that shone so frecuently in his eyes must not be extinguished."

16. Como indica Doug Adair, siendo él editor, la edición conjunta llegó a tener una circulación de diez mil ejemplares por tirada, la mayoría los de la edición en inglés, y con un gasto

cluye. Curiosa y desafortunadamente, en los meses en que la Unión se acerca y logra su gran triunfo, no contamos con su expresión periodística en español lo cual corrobora los limitados medios materiales con que contaba.

ETAPA DE APOGEO (1972-1974)

El Malcriado surge de nuevo, en ambas ediciones (español e inglés), como volumen cuatro, el veinticuatro de marzo de 1972 y como la "Voz Oficial de la Unión de Trabajadores Campesinos." Este año es boyante y de optimismo para la Unión. La membresía ha ascendido a decenas de miles afiliados y se subrayan las nuevas perspectivas que se abren. La fuerza motriz es "estar siempre pegado al pueblo. El momento que te apartas del pueblo, te pierdes." De ahí, la importancia que da a *El Malcriado* este nuevo relanzamiento: "El arma de la prensa es un arma tremenda... qué el pueblo lo aprecie y lo use como arma." En el número del 9-6-1972, la portada aparece con el símbolo del águila. En el centro de ella se emiten rayos lumínicos, usándose por primera vez, el titular "¡Sí Se Puede!," en relación a la campaña de revocación del gobernador de Arizona. Se trata de un momento cumbre del movimiento y del periódico.[17]

El Malcriado del veintitrés de julio está dedicado al final del segundo ayuno de César Chávez en Arizona. En una de las fotos, aparece el senador George McGovern, candidato demócrata a la presidencia, junto a Dolores Huerta, comentando que César Chávez es un hombre "consagrado para traerles las buenas nuevas a los pobres." En otra página leemos que Coretta King y Joan Báez visitan a Chávez. Báez declara que "César Chávez es un alma maravillosa." Un alma que se expresa en sus declaraciones sobre el ayuno con unas palabras que podemos considerar como la suma de una entrega total de César Chávez a la causa campesina y de los pobres:

> La tragedia mayor para cualquier persona—no es el morir—es el haber vivido y morir sin llegar a conocer la satisfacción de entregar su vida por los demás. La mayor tragedia es nacer y no gozar de la vida por temor a perder algo de seguridad o porque tememos amar y dar de nosotros mismos a los demás.

---

de veinte mil dólares llegaron a ingresar cuarenta mil, en gran parte debido a la venta de los materiales del Taller Gráfico: libros, carteles, calendarios, postales y medallas de la Unión.

17. Por estas fechas, es cuando, y durante más de un año, me integré de voluntario a la redacción de *El Malcriado*, yendo los fines de semana, cada quince días, a colaborar en corrección y redacción de la edición en español y haciendo algunas entrevistas y reportajes. Y en aquel verano del setenta y dos, pasé una temporada viviendo en La Paz, Baja California.

En el número seis, del cuatro de agosto, leemos que en la convención del partido demócrata se respalda el boicot y que el senador Edward Kennedy les habló a cuarenta millones de norteamericanos tratándolos de "Compañeros boicoteros de lechuga." Se nos dice también que la distribución de *El Malcriado* ha subido a veinticinco mil, trece mil en español y doce mil de la edición inglesa. En el número siete, del dieciocho de agosto, se vuelve a la tradición de *El Malcriado* de traer el arte y la poesía a sus páginas. Se reproduce un grabado de Leopoldo Méndez, "Despojo de la tierra de los yaquis" a cargo del ejército de Porfirio Díaz, y otro de Arturo García Bustos, "El peón encasillado." En las mismas páginas se incluye una serie de poemas, entre ellos "El corrido de César Chávez" de Alfredo Vásquez; el de los "Boicoteros" de Margarito Cabello y poemas de Francisco Núñez Gómez, autor del "Brindis campesino." Se resalta también el triunfo artístico de las Fiestas Campesinas en San José, del treinta de junio y del uno y dos de julio, con conciertos musicales de los renombrados Taj Mahal, Luis Gasca y el gran Carlos Santana.

Los números de *El Malcriado* del otoño cubren amplia información sobre las dos grandes campañas políticas en las que se vuelca la Unión: la de la revocación del gobernador de Arizona y la de en contra de la proposición veintidós, lanzada por la Farm Bureau ("Farm Burro," en el lenguaje campesino) y los rancheros, para lograr ilegalizar el boicoteo. *El Malcriado* del veintinueve de septiembre marca uno de los mayores momentos de apogeo del triunfo de la Unión. La portada, bajo el titular "El campesino en marcha," está ilustrada por las fotos del acto-asamblea celebrando el "séptimo Aniversario de la Huelga Liberadora de la Uva en Delano." Las páginas centrales reproducen varios discursos de los dirigentes, culminando con el de Chávez, dirigido a los campesinos con el que se cerró tal triunfalista manifestación. Expuso los logros y beneficios alcanzados en esos siete años, destacando a los campesinos como los grandes protagonistas de lo logrado y lo que queda por alcanzar. En el editorial del número doce, del veintisiete de octubre, "*El Malcriado* se une a la lucha contra Proposición 22," se anuncia que su personal deja la redacción y la imprenta para unirse a la campaña y se suspende la publicación hasta después del día siete de noviembre. Cuando reaparece, el primero de diciembre, su número trece del volumen cuatro es para celebrar el gran triunfo que los votantes californianos han dado a los campesinos, derrotando la Proposición 22 por un gran margen. Con el "espíritu de sacrificio y comunidad," que se manifiesta en el editorial del número catorce, *El Malcriado* se despide de 1972.

El volumen seis, número uno, del año nuevo, toda la portada la ocupa el titular, en grandes letras, "1973 AÑO DEL BOICOTEO," expresando la esperanza de que en ese año se repita el triunfo de junio de 1970. No obstante, ya en estos primeros meses de 1973, *El Malcriado* empieza a dar noticias premonitorias de las fuerzas que se desencadenarán en el verano. El veintiséis de enero se da noticia de una bomba puesta en el garaje y en la gasolinera de la Unión en los cuarenta acres; el nueve de febrero de que la oficina en Terra Bella ha sido destruida; y el seis de abril que la de Caléxico ha sido vandalizada. Cumpliéndose las temidas premoniciones, el número nueve, el cuatro de mayo, la portada de *El Malcriado* la cubre el grito gráfico, tres veces repetido, de HUELGA, a la que salen los campesinos en Coachella. Se ha consumado la gran traición de rancheros, no renovando los contratos de la uva, y firmándolos con los *Teamsters*. La portada del quince de mayo anuncia: "¡Firmes en la Huelga!, En el piquete," pero casi toda ella la llena la foto de un campesino encorvado acosado por un policía. Número tras número, entre junio y septiembre, *El Malcriado* reporta los logros del boicoteo por muchas ciudades del país. *El Malcriado* del veintiuno de septiembre es toda una expresión gráfica y fotográfica del gran duelo que embarga a los huelguistas tras los asesinatos de Nagi Mohsia Daifullah y Juan Cruz, dos mártires de la Unión y de su campaña de la no-violencia.

Pese a las adversidades, el apoyo a la Unión sigue siendo muy fuerte y en el periódico del cinco de octubre se habla de la primera Convención de la Unión en Fresno que tomó lugar del veintiuno al veintitrés de septiembre. Se nos dice que 325 delegados asisten a la convención, representando a cerca de sesenta mil personas. De ser este número el real, indicaría la fuerza que había logrado la Unión. En noviembre y diciembre, el periódico sigue manteniendo su exultante espíritu de lucha, denunciando las maniobras siniestras de los *Teamsters* (sus luchas internas, los lazos con la mafia, y contubernio con la administración de Nixon). A pesar de los logros, el último número de 1973, el del veintiocho de diciembre, es un llamado a la solidaridad y al apoyo. También trasluce lo que ha afectado a la Unión, los duros golpes sufridos en el verano de 1973. Una niña ocupa toda la contraportada de este número de fin de año. Con su conmovedora llamada de boicoteadora ha logrado que cuarenta y cinco personas den el "Sí" a no comprar lechugas, pero espera que las próximas Navidades las pueda pasar en casa, y no en la fría orilla de la calle pidiendo el socorro público para La Causa.

Las páginas centrales de *El Malcriado*, del número del dieciocho de enero de 1974 titulado, "1973–1974: *El Malcriado* arma del campesinado," presenta una reflexión de lo logrado y sobre qué hacer para que el periódico sea un arma todavía más eficaz. Por ejemplo, se menciona el duro trabajo de publicarlo y distribuirlo cada dos semanas. Se agradece que muchos voluntarios—trabajadores, estudiantes, profesores, periodistas y artistas—pasaran los fines de semana en La Paz trabajando en la producción del periódico. No cabe duda de que con esta ayuda, *El Malcriado*, entre 1972 y 1974, llegó a ser un periódico laboral, progresista/radical, informativo y educativo con un tiraje regular. Sin embargo, aunque en su versión en español intentará mantenerse fiel a la voz del campesino, al lograr hacerla ortográficamente correcta se perdió mucho de aquel estilo "calentito con chile y pimenta y que hierva un poquito la sangre," del que hablara César Chávez en su primera etapa.

Con la pérdida de miles de afiliados, el mayor apoyo que tiene la Unión lo encuentra en la AFL-CIO y en los otros sindicatos agrupados en esta gran federación laboral. De aquí que el periódico, aunque volviera a añadir al título, "La voz del campesino," se ajusta ahora a ser un periódico sindicalista, centrándose en el apoyo que los campesinos siguen dando a la Unión y en los esporádicos logros que alcanza. En abril se renueva la huelga de la uva en Coachella que no tendrá el número de "piquetes" que acudieron a la del año anterior, ni el mismo apoyo monetario por parte de la AFL-CIO. Por estas fechas se da un gran cambio en *El Malcriado*. En mayo, Rubén Montoya, el artista gráfico quien venía montando el periódico desde 1971, dejó la Unión. Por las mismas fechas también lo hizo Venustiano Olguín quien dirigía la edición en español desde 1972. En el editorial del número del treinta y uno de julio se anuncia un "nuevo *Malcriado*," diciendo—y traduzco de la edición en inglés[18]—que "representa un renovado esfuerzo de la UFW de América, AFL-CIO, de publicar un nuevo periódico que exponga la miseria y explotación de los trabajadores campesinos y simultáneamente construir la unidad del movimiento laboral." También se nos dice que el nuevo editor es Carlos R. Calderón, activista del Movimiento Chicano desde 1968. Igualmente, se anuncia que en el nuevo personal se ha reclutado a algunos "talentos de primera fila" del Movimiento Chicano. Sin embargo, estas promesas no se materializan en el periódico. Encontramos algunos reportes de brutalidad policiaca contra chicanos en Los Angeles y un reportaje (en el número de septiembre) del Moratorio Chicano, del diecinueve de agosto en Los Angeles y de la muerte del reconocido periodista Rubén Salazar por la policía.[19]

A partir del treinta y uno de julio, el renovado *Malcriado* aparece con un nuevo encabezamiento. Contra un fondo rojo vemos el águila negra con sus dos alas extendidas. En el ala derecha se inscribe UFW y en la izquierda AFL-CIO. El contenido del periódico se enfoca más en cuestiones laborales. Vinculado a este sindicalismo obrero, nacional y bastante chovinista, en este

---

18. Me valgo ahora de números de la edición en inglés, pues no he conseguido ejemplares en español. Posiblemente, en algunos meses dejará de aparecer. Sólo he logrado uno del que me ocupo más adelante, el de diciembre.

19. Se nos dice que fue el primer reportero en ocuparse de la Asociación Campesina, entrevistando a César Chávez en Delano, en 1962, y siguiendo, a través de los años, con reportajes sobre la Unión.

verano y otoño de 1974 *El Malcriado* se hizo amplio eco de la controversial campaña de la Unión para hacer frente al gran impedimento de ganar las huelgas emprendidas causada por masiva llegada de esquiroles procedentes de México. Contra esta afluencia, César Chávez impulsó una campaña nacional—muy aireada en *El Malcriado*—para que el Gobierno, las autoridades de Inmigración y la Migra detuvieran el flujo de "Illegal Aliens."[20] No obstante, esta campaña tuvo poco eco entre los militantes y simpatizantes de la Unión.[21] El mismo *El Malcriado* deja de dar cuenta de ella en sus dos números de diciembre y, posteriormente, César Chávez y la Unión se desdecirán de ella. En estos números se resalta algo que sí tuvo bastante éxito; el boicot contra la gran corporación vinatera, "Gallo Wines," afectando hasta el 25 porciento de sus grandiosas ventas. Por estas fechas, en varios periódicos y programas de la televisión nacionales se empiezan a dar por muerta a la Unión frente al ataque del colosal sindicato de los *Teamsters* y de los poderosos conglomerados agrícolas. *El Malcriado* sale al paso a tales agoreros pronósticos y aseveraciones. El editorial del dieciséis de diciembre, que reaparece en español, "Triunfa el boicoteo. Vencerá la Unión," está escrito "contestando a los periodistas destrampados que han escrito el obituario de la Unión," y en tono muy militante habla de "liberación" y del "empuje del movimiento campesino chavista en lucha contra los monopolistas agrarios norteamericanos." En tono más mesurado, en la edición en inglés del dieciocho de noviembre, Wayne C. Hartmire también sale al contra ataque en el tema del obituario de la Unión y de César Chávez. En su artículo, "The Facts Behind the Myth: is Chavez Dead?," señala hábilmente las cartas que la Unión sigue teniendo a su favor. Por su parte, Jacques E. Levy habla del viaje que César Chávez hiciera en octubre por Europa, entrevistándose con destacados líderes sindicalistas en Suecia, Inglaterra, Bél-

---

20. *El Malcriado* del veintiocho de septiembre, y me atengo a la edición en inglés, triunfalmente anuncia, lo que tanto pedía y necesitaba la Unión: "Meany reaffirms support for UFW. Lashed out at Teamsters-Grower Alliance." Sin embargo, la página en que se publica el discurso del presidente de la AFL-CIO, reafirmando-tal apoyo, devienen las más bochornosas de la historia del periódico, pues Meany carga contra los indocumentados en forma desaforada. Sostiene que 600 mil han sido aprehendidos en el Suroeste, pero que eso equivale a muy poco ya que (y lo dejo en su idioma) "as the estimate of the number who remained at large take jobs away for U. S. workers run into millions. These millions of illegals could be stopped, could be returned to their own country" (7). A la luz de dichas palabras, resulta más reprobable otro titular de este número, "Chavez Assails Scabbing by 'Illegals.'" Este número, por su parte, solo tiene ocho páginas anunciando ya el próximo fin de *El Malcriado*.

21. Un ejemplo de esto lo encontramos en la carta de un simpatizante que publica *El Malcriado* (18-10-1974), en la que reprocha a la UFW de haber caído en el viejo juego de "dividir y reinarás," con el nombre de "Legal/Ilegal": "No hay tal cosa como trabajador ilegal. Estos ilegales son sus hermanos y hermanas. Estos llamados 'foreños ilegales' son sus hermanos y hermanas. Son víctimas del mismo sistema del que son víctimas Uds . . . Viva la Causa." Lo firma Thomas J. Morgan, desde Milwaukee.

gica y Francia que dieron su apoyo al Boicot y de la visita privada que se tuvo con el Papa Pío VI. Se reprime en la misma página once, la "Declaración del Papa," los esfuerzos de la Unión y, con sus saludos "especialmente afectuosos," a la comunidad méxico-americana en los Estados Unidos.

El primer, único y final número de *El Malcriado* de 1975, lleva la fecha de enero-febrero. Se publica con dos secciones. En la primera aparece el artículo que ya tratamos en el capítulo anterior de tono optimista y confiando tanto en el boicot: "Chavez Speaks on UFW Fight. 'Reports of Our Death Have Been Greatly Exaggerated.'" Pero la segunda sección es una desoladora despedida del más amplio y sostenido, *El Malcriado,* iniciado en 1972. En su casi totalidad, y salvo algún corto artículo como el de "UFW Wins: Jobless Aid for Farworkers," son páginas tras páginas con multitud de esquelas de solidaridad con la Unión, la casi totalidad de organizaciones y oficinas locales laborales a través del país, testimonio de lo que la Unión vino a significar dentro del sindicalismo obrero nacional, y que, igualmente, ilustran la gran dependencia de la solidaridad laboral que vivía la UFW en la situación límite que atravesaba en dichas fechas.

EL REBROTE DE *EL MALCRIADITO*

Y, sin embargo, como tantas veces a través de la historia de la Unión y de su periódico, pronto nos encontramos con una nueva sorpresa de rebote y rebote. El quince de marzo, en Los Angeles, aparece un pequeño periodiquito, mensual, de cuatro páginas que, con sus nueve números, durará hasta diciembre de 1975. Este periódico es editado en la oficina del boicot de Los Angeles y publicado solamente en inglés.[22] Hay en este hijo de *El Malcriado*— una tan activa y entusiasta elaboración hecha por un pequeño grupo de activistas y voluntarios urbanos—algo que nos recuerda a *El Malcriado* de sus comienzos, once años antes. En el primer *Malcriadito* se nos anuncia que: "*El Malcriado,* the regular UFW newspaper has ceased publication temporarily because of lack of funds."[23] Y este periodiquito viene a llenar su hueco y también a testimoniar que la Unión "sigue viva y coleando."

---

22. Aunque en su presentación nos dicen que, en sus publicaciones futuras, piensan hacer también en español. El Farmworker Movement Documentation Project transcribe, en la red de Internet, los nueve números de *El Malcriadito*.

23. Pero sí volvió a resurgir, con un solo número en noviembre de 1972, cuatro o cinco en 1982, y como revista de pequeño formato, entre 1984 y 1990 o 1991, no he podido fijar con certeza la fecha de su última desaparición. Me ocupo de este *Malcriado* en el último capítulo de mi libro: *César Chávez y la Unión: una historia victoriosa de los de abajo*.

De él, y para terminar este ensayo, solo destacaré que en sus nueve números de 1975, con entusiasmo exaltante, se publican buenas noticias del activismo y nuevos logros de la Unión y del boicot, principalmente en el área de Los Angeles. En el número siete de septiembre se da el cómputo de los resultados obtenidos hasta entonces: más de nueve mil votos para la UFW, casi seis mil para los *Teamsters* y casi tres mil por no sindicalizarse. En el de octubre-noviembre, número ocho, se nos da uno más completo. Se anuncia que para el treinta de octubre, la Unión ha ganado una mayoría de elecciones, 152 de 290, representando a cerca de veintidós mil trabajadores, mientras que los *Teamsters* han ganado en noventa y una elecciones, con alrededor de once mil. También se anuncia que el "Harris Poll Reports: Millions Back Boycott," y que el miembro de la Junta Directiva, Mack Lyons, declara una nueva victoria: la renovación de un nuevo contrato con la Coca-Cola, por tres años y cubriendo a más de mil trabajadores campesinos, casi todos afroamericanos. No obstante, su activismo y buenas noticias, con su número nueve, de diciembre, *El Malcriadito,* también deja de existir. De su grupo editorial y corresponsales, solo mencionaré dos nombres centrales, el de su editora, Linda García, y el de un asiduo corresponsal, el reconocido periodista laboral y comentarista radial, Sam Kushner, autor del valioso libro *Long Road to Delano.* Dándonos su testimonio de los triunfos logrados en 1975, este *Malcriadito* enarboló en alto la antorcha de la libertad, dignidad y de las esperanzas de los trabajadores campesinos.

OBRAS CITADAS

Fuentes, Víctor. *César Chávez y la Unión: una historia victoriosa de los de abajo*. Moorpark, CA: Floricanto Press, 2015. Print.

Gramsci, Antonio. *La formación de los intelectuales*. México: Grijalbo, 1967. Print.

Jiménez. A. *Picardía Mexicana*. México, D.F: Cost-Amic, 1960. Print.

Kushner, Sam. *Long Road to Delano*. New York: International Publisher, 1975. Print.

Venegas, Daniel. *Las aventuras de don Chipote, o cuando los pericos mamen*. Houston: Arte Público Press, 1999. Print.

PART II

SPANISH PERSPECTIVES *DE ALLÁ*

CHAPTER 7

Tendiendo puentes, compartiendo conocimientos

The International Conference on Chicano Literature in Spain (1998–2016)

JULIO CAÑERO

UNTIL NOT long ago, for the vast majority of the Spanish population, Latin America began in Patagonia and ended at the border cities of Ciudad Juárez, Tijuana, or (Heroica) Nogales. Many were unaware that crossing the Río Grande (the Río Bravo in Mexico), in the "sister" cities across the border, El Paso, San Diego, or Nogales (Arizona), Latino culture stretched and lavished through what, to our misunderstanding, was a monolingual English-speaking territory. Spaniards, perhaps from their anti-American animosity, had forgotten that this area, taken by the United States from Mexico or bought from Spain, had been part of our nation. Focusing on the study of the exploits of Viriato, El Gran Capitán, or Cortés, we were ignorant of other illustrious names like Vázquez de Coronado, De Soto, Cabeza de Vaca, or Junípero Serra: compatriots who once walked the land that eventually would turn into the United States, building, therefore, a shared history.

The situation has reverted in recent decades considerably. Our rulers, starting with King Felipe VI, have dedicated countless efforts to spread the knowledge of a Hispanic United States past on both sides of the Atlantic. But before our politicians realized that common history or paid attention to the Latino population in the United States, Spanish academics had begun to scrutinize them from different analytical angles, most of them focused on literature and culture. Numerous dissertations, research papers, publications, seminars, and conferences have been devoted to the study of the fastest growing group in the United States. Among the members of this heterogeneous community labeled as Latinos, Mexican Americans or Chicanos have deserved special attention by Spanish researchers. In this essay, I present the studies about Chicanos that have been carried out in Spain, both by Spaniards and by researchers from other nationalities who reside permanently in Spain, or those analyses developed by Spanish scholars outside our borders.

While spending the summer of 2014 conducting research at the University of California in Santa Barbara, I was contacted by Professor Jesús Rosales to participate in his new academic project. He was compiling articles by Spanish scholars working on both sides of the Atlantic and whose major research interest was Chicano literature. I must confess that Rosales's first and logical thought, as I will explain shortly, was of Dr. José Antonio Gurpegui, Professor of American Studies at the Universidad de Alcalá. However, since Gurpegui was about to begin a much-deserved sabbatical, we both decided that I should occupy Gurpegui's place in the book. Nonetheless, had the topic suggested by Rosales been literary, I would have had to regretfully decline his interesting proposal, as over the years my research interests have derived from aspects related to U.S. culture, society, and politics, rather than literature.

In other words, I would have not been comfortable dealing with an exclusively literary topic. But the idea that he had in mind, and which I develop in the following pages, seduced me: to narrate the story behind the ten conferences on Chicano literature that have taken place in Spain biennially since 1998, and their contribution to the diffusion of Chicano works in my country. In short, I was asked to become a chronicler, like Villagrá or Cabeza de Vaca, of a journey that began in the beautiful city of Granada and whose latest stop was the *Villa y Corte* of Madrid. With the exception of 2004 and 2014, I have attended all. I can say, then, that I know quite well the ins and outs of these meetings. Scrutinizing and rereading their programs and publications has brought to my mind many anecdotes that, for obvious reasons, I do not share here. I instead focus on the academic contribution of Spanish scholars in Spain to the spread of Chicano studies as a result of these conferences.

The interest for Latinos in the United States did not begin in the Spanish academic world with the first conference in Granada. However, until the last decade of the last century, the majority of the Spanish population remained oblivious to the rich cultural reality of the Hispanic minority in the United States. As a worthy exception, the reputed scholar Manuel Alvar (1992) was interested in the maintenance of Cervantes's language among the Hispanic communities of the American Southwest. In any case, the interest of the Spanish university did not go beyond the use of Spanish by those groups in their battle against the hegemony of the English language. Everything related to Hispanic or Latino cultural expressions—literature or artistic creations—had no place in our university departments.

It is difficult to believe the lack of curiosity that we had in Spain for the fastest growing community in the United States. Today the recovery of a common past, a shared heritage with the Hispanic population of the United States, is of the utmost importance for the Spanish government.[1] Twenty years ago, however, this relevance was not contemplated within the academic world, to say nothing of the interest of Spanish society more generally. The departments of Spanish restricted themselves to what happened south of the Rio Bravo, wholly ignoring the artistic creations north of the river. In English departments, the picture was also bleak; in those departments, American literature was looked down upon compared with English literature (see Rodríguez Jiménez). If Whitman or Faulkner were considered secondary literary figures, little could be done to vindicate the study of Latino authors in general, and Chicano in particular.

Despite the insensibility in the Spanish departments and the disdain of the "Brits" in the English ones, there was someone who was not content to follow the dictates of the majority when regarding the study of Chicanos. That someone was José Antonio Gurpegui. I have said on other occasions that Gurpegui is, without a doubt, the "trailblazer" of Chicano studies in my country (Cañero "Dos décadas" 8–9). I would not dare to say that without Gurpegui Chicano studies would never have arrived to Spain; however, I am certain that without him this discipline would not occupy the important position it currently enjoys in Spanish universities. I will offer an example: since the organization of the "Quinto Congreso Internacional de Culturas hispanas de los Estados Unidos de América," held at the Universidad de Alcalá in 1992, with the title "El Poder Hispano," no other similar forum was organized. It is thanks to José Antonio Gurpegui's tenacity in promoting these studies that ten international conferences have successfully been organized since 1998.

If José Antonio was the impetus on this side of the Atlantic, also incontestable is the interest from Chicano and Chicana authors and critics in promoting an academic rapprochement with the old Hispania. Although the term *Hispanic* has been rejected by many Chicanos, it is undeniable that we share a common history, a universal culture known as *Hispana*. It was only a matter of time before the re-encounter between Spaniards and Chicanos would develop into a series of conferences, as Chicano literary critics shared Gurpegui's desire to organize these transatlantic meetings. I do not wish to offend

---

1. For more information, see http://www.lamoncloa.gob.es/espana/eh14/exterior/Paginas/index.aspx.

anyone by unconsciously omitting their names, but, to name a few, professors such as Francisco Lomelí, María Herrera-Sobek, Antonio and Teresa Márquez, and Alejandro Morales also were responsible for increasing interest in Chicano culture throughout Spain. Their persistence, along with many Spanish researchers, was the real germ of the two decades of Chicano conferences in Spain that are presented in the following pages.

THE FIRST INTERNATIONAL CONFERENCE ON CHICANO LANGUAGE AND LITERATURE
Universidad de Granada (April 1–3, 1998)

Professor Manuel Villar Raso was the organizer of the first conference on Chicano literature. Villar Raso, a writer himself, had first heard of the legendary region of Aztlán while visiting the University of Arizona. This unexpected discovery brought him to procure the works of what could be considered the canonical Chicano writers: Miguel Méndez, Rolando Hinojosa, José Antonio Villarreal, Aristeo Brito, and Rudolfo Anaya. As he read and studied the artistic value of these books, he realized that had these authors been Latin Americans, their recognition and success in Spain would have been tremendous (qtd. in Arias). However, Chicano writers mostly were unknown to the Spanish public, and only a small group of scholars were interested in their work. Villar Raso decided to set up, along with the collaboration of Gurpegui, a conference on Chicano literature, for, he stated, Chicanos were creating a literature "que era urgente dar a conocer en España" (2).

More than twenty Chicano artists came to this first conference in Granada. We were lucky—and I include myself, for this was one of the first conferences in which I participated as a PhD candidate—to listen firsthand to Rudolfo Anaya, Miguel Méndez, Alicia Gaspar de Alba, Erlinda Gonzales-Berry, Alejandro Morales, and many more. Also, the *flor y nata* (crème de la crème), as we say in Spanish, of Chicano literary critics attended this intense first meeting. The Spanish counterpoint was given by reputed professors such as José A. Gurpegui, Juan Antonio Perles Rochel, Federico Eguíluz, and José Miguel Santamaría, the first generation of the *de allá* Spanish scholars. Together with these well-established Spanish critics, the conference was attended by a group of (then) young academics who were, for different reasons and from different perspectives, interested in Chicano studies. I am referring to Rosa Morillas, Imelda Martín-Junquera, María Henríquez, María Antònia Oliver, and the author of this brief *relación,* (chronicle) Julio Cañero; in other words, those who would make the second generation of Spanish researchers on Chicano studies.

That first conference made Granada for three days the cultural capital of Aztlán. I will not comment on the academic significance of the papers presented by that second generation of critics *de allá,* which, for the most part, was significant. Nonetheless, we were young and had limited access to sources in addition to being far from the cores of Chicano literature. To the Chicano literary critics, our presentations were probably conventional and too canonical. I do not wish to upset any of my friends and colleagues of that second generation should they read these lines, so allow me to take myself as an example of the generalizations that we used to make. My paper, entitled "La comunidad chicana y la colonia interna estadounidense: breves apuntes teóricos," tried to prove that Chicanos were an internally colonized minority, basing my assertions on the works of Tomás Almaguer, Rodolfo Acuña, and Mario Barrera. Today I would not claim such a thing—at least from the nineties onward—but the analysis I presented, with all its simplifications, and along with those of my colleagues, demonstrated a newly acquired interest for Chicano studies in Spain. It was almost mandatory for us to call for another symposium.

THE SECOND INTERNATIONAL CONFERENCE ON CHICANO LITERATURE
Universidad del País Vasco (April 5–7, 2000)

In 2000, the conference moved to Vitoria, in the Basque Country, and was organized by professors Federico Eguíluz and Amaia Ibarrarán Vigalondo, both of the English Department of the Universidad del País Vasco. As I posed in the introduction, the interest in Chicano literature in Spain has always been located in English departments, not in the Spanish ones, and this designation has been a constant issue in the organization of these conferences. Federico and Amaia did a wonderful job, not only because of the value of the academic meeting *per se,* but also due to the political situation in the Basque Country at the time. A mere two months before the inauguration of the conference, Fernando Buesa, a socialist politician and a professor at the Universidad del País Vasco, was assassinated by ETA on campus, near the symposium venue. Moreover, during the conference, several panels were interrupted by extreme left-wing radicals who protested for education in the Basque language. José Antonio Gurpegui still recalls how he, Federico, and Amaia had to talk to the radical leaders to explain that Chicanos were a subjugated minority whose voice deserved and needed to be heard.

The academic value of the presentations by Spanish participants was *in crescendo*, and their papers "[daban] a conocer de forma científica el rico mundo de la cultura chicana" (Eguíluz 10). First-generation and second-generation Spanish scholars discussed less general issues and placed more interest on new Chicano authors and approaches. I would like to mention here three recurrent participants who, in spite of not being Spanish-born, had developed their academic life in Spain. The first is Nathalie Bléser, who has closely studied Rudolfo Anaya's work. The second is Russell Dinapoli, whose interests mostly deal with Chicano poetry. Last, but not least, is Klaus Zilles, probably the *Spaniard* who has best approached Rolando Hinojosa's literary corpus. These three are good examples of how Chicano literature was acquiring more significant academic attention in Spain.

THE THIRD INTERNATIONAL CONFERENCE ON CHICANO LITERATURE: PERSPECTIVAS TRANSATLÁNTICAS EN LA LITERATURA CHICANA
Universidad de Málaga (May 24–29, 2002)

Juan Antonio Perles Rochel, whose PhD dissertation was the first on Chicano literature presented in Spain, surprised us all with the venue of the third conference. All sessions were held at Málaga's Diocesan Seminar, a place for retirement and study which proved fertile both for the quality of the panels and for the informal conversations it enabled. Professor Perles recalled that the topics presented by Spanish scholars showed "un altísimo interés en desentrañar y comprender la excepcionalidad chicana" (11). Additionally, in Málaga "quedó claro que la interacción entre España, Europa y Aztlán puede aportar un espacio de diálogo en el que se desarrollen estrategias comunes de subversión en un mundo globalizado" (12). Spanish scholars, burdened by a past of conquest, did not approach Chicano culture as an act of "constriction" or expiation of guilt (11). Rather, their presentations began to offer innovative analytic perspectives on Chicano creations, opening new spaces for academic dialogue between Spain and the United States.

The following cases are clear examples of the new spaces revealed by Spanish scholars. Departing from Luce Irigaray's philosophical principles on feminism, Esther Alvarez explored the figure of Doña Marina in some of Cherríe Moraga's works, evidencing how Moraga turned La Malinche into a "model of defiance, independence and survival" ("Daughters" 59). Also on Moraga, Carmen González explored the poetics of fragmentation in the Chicana author through the myth of Coyolxauhqui, which González identified with the dismembering of womanhood; a necessary step, González affirmed, towards "a reconstruction process leading to self fulfillment [sic]" (137). Finally, Alejandro Martín examined how rap music was a tool used by Chicanos to denounce their subordinated position in the United States (199). At this conference, even constructs from Chicano popular culture caught the attention of Spanish researchers. New academic bridges were being constructed.

THE FOURTH INTERNATIONAL CONFERENCE ON CHICANO LITERATURE
Universidad de Sevilla (May 12–14, 2004)

I have no personal memories of this conference for, as I mentioned earlier, I was unable to attend it. My *relación* (chronicle) of this conference must therefore be indirect and comes from the book edited by, among others, Juan Ignacio (Nacho) Guijarro. I assume that, as at former conferences, this publication is composed of a selection of the presented papers. According to the editor, the resulting compilation scrutinized Chicano artistic creation from a wide range of viewpoints:

> There are articles that examine from feminist, comparative and close-reading approaches specific authors and literary texts, others discuss more general ideological and cultural issues like folklore, ethnicity, identity, sexuality or stereotypes, while some contributions focus on Chicano films and murals. (Lerate and Guijarro 11)

Allow me to comment on three works by Spanish authors in order to give the reader an idea of the originality of their analyses. Manuel Brito presented a paper in which he studied the experimental poet, playwright, and labor activist Rodrigo Toscano. For Brito, Toscano's poetry was "much closer to the experimental tendencies of contemporary American poetry in the late twentieth century than to the usual claims of Chicano cultural identity" (52), making Toscano's topics universal. In "Refining the Father Figure in Contemporary Chicana Literature," Antonia Domínguez suggested that "a new and challenging concept of fatherhood is being proposed by Chicano/a writers" (88), and she exemplified it by considering paternity in authors like Denise Chávez,

Helena María Viramontes, and Arturo Islas. The last example is devoted to the exploration of the transformations made by Alicia Gaspar de Alba from the 1987 Spanish version to the 1993 English version of her story "They're Just Silly Rabbits." In the words of María A. Toda, these changes responded to "una serie de exigencias ideológicas procedentes de ciertas políticas de identidad" (253) (a series of ideological exigencies that came from certain identity policies, editors translation) which, she affirms, were detrimental to the complexity and humor of the earlier version of the story. I believe these three works provide an innovative critical approach to Chicano literary criticism.

THE FIFTH INTERNATIONAL CONFERENCE ON CHICANO LITERATURE: INTERPRETING THE NEW MILENIO
Universidad de Alcalá (May 22–25, 2006)

Finally, the conference reached my home city, and its fifth edition was held at the Universidad de Alcalá. This meeting represented a turning point in the organization of the biennial forum. Since then, the Instituto Franklin de la Universidad de Alcalá has provided the local committees with its full resources to coordinate the seminar. In other words, the Instituto Franklin's team has worked *codo con codo* (side by side) to help other universities organize a successful event. It is only natural that the first direct involvement of the Instituto Franklin was held at the Universidad de Alcalá. This research center, of which I am currently director, is the only higher education organization devoted to the investigation and promotion of North American culture in Spain. Additionally, one of our priority lines of research is the Latino community in the United States—especially Chicanos. In Europe, and as a result of the research conducted at the Instituto Franklin, the Universidad de Alcalá is a recognized research center on Chicanos and Latinos.

A third generation of Spanish researchers presented its academic credentials at this conference. As most of those from the second generation were attaining tenure or about to be promoted, young researchers were unveiling their own critical voice. I am referring specifically to Aishih Wehbe-Herrera, María Jesús Castro Dopacio, and Eva Fernández de Pinedo. Wehbe-Herrera, departing from scarce referential sources, focused on some major concepts that affect the construction of Chicano masculinity(ies) such as *machismo* and hegemonic/subordinate masculinities (80). Castro Dopacio presented a very illustrative paper on the connections between Chicana and Puerto Riqueña literature, studying the more traditional representations of the Virgen of

Guadalupe—as an example of motherhood and housewifery—and the revisiting of those representations to attribute new characteristics to the Virgen which are closer to modern-day Chicanas and Riqueñas (116). Eva Fernández approached the rewriting of mainstream fairy tales by Chicana writer Silvia González. In her paper, Fernández verified the two obstacles U.S.-born children of Mexican descent must face while approaching their roots: "the nostalgic and biased vision of the homeland passed on by their parents and the commodified imagines of their minority propagated by the mainstream" (198). Needless to say, and I hope you excuse this slight dose of *chovinismo* (chauvinism), Alcalá's conference was one of the best.

THE SIXTH INTERNATIONAL CONFERENCE ON CHICANO LITERATURE: NEW CHALLENGES FOR THE NEW MILENIO
Universidad de Alicante (May 22–24, 2008)

After a decade of encounters, it was clear that the interest in Chicano artistic expression—the conferences began with literature, but the spectrum was soon expanded to include other arts—had grown considerably on both sides of the Atlantic. Along with the *trendsetters* of Chicano literary criticism, younger critics came to Spain to share their work with Spanish scholars. Here, Spanish researchers continued to contribute with their papers to provide different interpretations, at times informed by their personal experiences with Chicano literature. This was the case of plenary speaker Isabel Durán, whose presentation, "Teaching Chicana/o Literature Abroad: The Use of Autobiography for Comparative Purposes," was centered on instructing this type of literature outside the United States. I must confess that Isabel's speech at the Universidad de Alicante is one of the best I have attended on the topic of Chicano studies.

Through a succession of vicissitudes, I came to be the editor of the volume that compiled some of the papers presented at the sixth conference. The book, entitled *Nuevas reflexiones en torno a la literatura y cultura chicana*, was selected in 2010 by *El Portal del Hispanismo*, the Instituto Cervantes, and the Spanish Ministry of Education as "book of the week."[2] One of the young Spanish contributors, Olvido Andújar, dealt with the representation of Latinos in American TV shows. She used the example of *Desperate Housewives* to study how Gabrielle Solis's identity was built in a *mainstream* screening. Ana Díaz López scrutinized Ana Castillo's *So Far from God*'s main character, Sofi, as if she were the protagonist of what Díaz López called the first "telenovela

---

2. For more information, see http://hispanismo.cervantes.es/libros.asp?DOCN=436.

chicana" (49). Contrary to the archetypical construction of female identities in *telenovelas* (soap operas), this novel, Díaz López said, "subvierte el ideal femenino que encontramos en televisión . . . Sofi deconstruye la teoría del cautiverio femenino que promulgan las telenovelas erigiéndose en una figura extraordinariamente feminista" (50). Both Andújar and Díaz López representented new directions taken by young Spanish researchers dedicated to Chicano studies.

THE SEVENTH INTERNATIONAL CONFERENCE ON CHICANO LITERATURE: WRITING THE LANDSCAPE/ LANDSCAPES OF WRITING
Universidad de León (May 27–29, 2010)

The topic of this conference was very much interconnected with the research interest of the organizer, Dr. Imelda Martín-Junquera. Martín-Junquera, a renowned Spanish scholar of ecofeminist literary criticism, expressed that the selection of participants was an attempt "to portray the different types of physical, ideological, symbolical, and spiritual landscapes that have been present in Chicano Literature throughout its existence" ("Introduction" 1). All papers presented, either by American or by European scholars, shared a common denominator: "the recurrent focus on nature and culture as two intertwined subject matters and the relationships established between them" (ibid.).

Among the different contributions made by Spanish scholars, three of the topics, in particular, caught my attention. Two discussed the use of Spanish in Chicano literature, and the other the translation into Spanish of works written in English by Chicano authors. The paper by José Antonio Gurpegui, "'In Spanish, Mi Hermano, in Spanish': Is Good to Speak in Español in USA," focused on the relation between the use of Spanish and the socioeconomic position of the people who speak it in the United States today. Gurpegui's contribution, although questioning the linguistic influence of Spanish in English, foresaw a strength in the use of this language in the United States due to the demographic growth of its speakers (191). In "Writing on the Border: English y español también," Cecilia Montes-Alcalá scrutinized the use of Spanish and code-switching in Chicano bilingual literature. Following a sociopragmatic approach, Montes-Alcalá concluded that the use of code-switching was by no means arbitrary or marginal, but a valid aesthetic device (227).

Finally, in her paper "(Too) Changing Landscapes: The Translation of US Hispanic Literature into Spanish," María López Pons showed the relation between the translation of Chicano authors' works into Spanish and the lack of success of those translated works in the Iberian market. The reason, she said, was the translator's need to understand deeply the literary landscapes in which Chicano writers place their work. Without that knowledge, Lopéz Pons pointed out, a translated Chicano work ended up being "an extremely neutralizing translation or a bizarre amalgam of translating techniques that leaves readers puzzled" (209). The best example of a novel translated into Spanish was, according to her, *Caramelo,* by Sandra Cisneros. The novel, López Pons affirmed, proved that cooperation between the translator, in this case Liliana Valenzuela, and the author was a guarantor of success.

THE EIGHTH INTERNATIONAL CONFERENCE ON CHICANO LITERATURE: CROSSING THE BORDERS OF IMAGINATION
Universidad de Castilla-La Mancha (May 24–26, 2012)

Toledo, the Imperial City, was the site of the eighth conference, and Mar Ramón Torrijos was our host. Perhaps as a result of its proximity to Madrid, Toledo's conference was attended by many scholars from both sides of the Atlantic (Ramón Torrijos 12). One of the attendees, Armando Miguélez, a Spanish critic from *de acá,* who eventually returned to Spain, was one of the first Spaniards to work on Chicano literature in the United States. His PhD dissertation, supervised by Justo S. Alarcón and presented in 1981, dealt with "cuentos literarios chicanos" from 1877 to 1950. I met Armando in 1998 at a conference in Cáceres and found his presentation groundbreaking. On a personal note, it was wonderful to see him again in Toledo and to hear his talk about one of the first Chicano writers, Adolfo Carrillo.

Along with Miguélez, I would like to devote some lines to someone I consider one of the finest Spanish literary critics on Chicano literature and culture: Maria Antònia Oliver. She has presented at most of the conferences, and the quality of her papers and publications confirms my assertion. In Toledo, Maria Antònia discussed the search for ethnic difference in Stephanie Elizondo Griest's *Mexican Enough.* I highly recommend the reading of her prolific critical works, for they are a good example of Spanish scholars' quality, an analytic excellence that is also evident in Esther Alvarez, to whom I referred before. In Toledo, Esther Alvarez was acclaimed during the conference for offering the Universidad de Oviedo as the next venue for the symposium. The conference would move, once again, from South to North.

THE NINTH INTERNATIONAL CONFERENCE ON CHICANO LITERATURE AND LATINO STUDIES: CITYSCAPES: URBAN AND HUMAN CARTOGRAPHIES
Universidad de Oviedo (May 28–30, 2014)

As in 2004, I was unable to attend this conference. However, as said before, I was personally involved in its organization. For instance, and as an *appetizer*, I arranged a roundtable at the Casa de América in Madrid in which notable Chicano and Chicana literary critics and writers gave their opinion on the current status of Chicano literature. Additionally, the team at the Instituto Franklin worked closely with that of the Universidad de Oviedo to organize the conference. Nonetheless, and as will be the case with future conferences, the leading role was assumed by the HispaUSA Association,[3] created to stimulate and encourage the conjunct study of Latinos in the United States by American and Spanish researchers. Thanks no doubt in part to these collaborations, the conference was a resounding success. Acclaimed Chicano literary critics and writers from the States came yet again to share with their Spanish colleagues their analysis. Promising young researchers such as Noelia de Gregorio and Laura Vázquez, both *de allá* researchers, gave an outstanding response to the challenges proposed by the American critics. The results of this conference already have been disseminated in a recently published book edited by Professor Esther Alvarez (*Geographies*).

THE 10TH INTERNATIONAL CONFERENCE ON CHICANO LITERATURE AND LATINO STUDIES: CULTURA Y HERENCIA HISPANA: CONSTRUYENDO UNA IDENTIDAD
Universidad Complutense de Madrid (May 30–June 1, 2016)

The latest, as of this writing, meeting on Chicano literature and Latino studies in Spain was held at the Universidad Complutense de Madrid. The Conference was organized by Asociación HispaUSA, and by Complutense professors Isabel Durán, Carmen M. Méndez, and Eusebio de Lorenzo. Scholars from many different geographical areas, which implies that these Spanish seminars have become a reference in the study of Chicanas/os Latinas/os outside the United States, pondered how literature has served to preserve culture and heritage within the Chicano and Latino community, something that, by extension,

---

3. See the HipaUSA website: http://www.hispausa.com/.

has helped to build a distinctive, but multifaceted identity.[4] As in the previous gatherings, the academic level was outstanding. Plenary lectures, panels, roundtables, and book presentations showed the good health that this academic area has enjoyed all over the world.

I would like to focus on the three plenary speakers of this conference. Given the political situation of the United States, creative writing professor and author Reyna Grande dissertated on a currently high controversial topic: immigration and its influence in the construction of Chicana/o literary identity in the United States. Our admired Gary Francisco Keller, professor and founder of Bilingual Review Press, discussed the existence of a transcendent Chicana/o biculturalism through art, the use of language and everyday life. Finally, the acclaimed Spanish author María Dueñas described her experience as a visiting scholar at the University of California, Santa Barbara—hosted by my dearest friend, Professor Francisco Lomelí. María Dueñas explained how this enriching stay helped her prepare her successful novel *Misión Olvido* (2012). In this novel, Dueñas sketches the historical links between Spain and the United States and the importance of the *herencia Hispana* (Hispanic heritage) through the main character's search of a forgotten Franciscan site within the California Missions Trail.

CONCLUSION

In the former pages I have attempted to summarize almost two decades of Chicano studies in Spain. As we have seen, this discipline had a difficult beginning in Spain, as it was virtually nonexistent in Spanish departments and irrelevant for the English ones. Even so, Spanish professors such as José Antonio Gurpegui, Manuel Villar, and Juan Antonio Perles believed that the situation could, and should, be reversed. Thanks to them and many Chicano authors and critics, Spain now convenes the most important seminar on the topic outside the United States. With preparations underway for its eleventh meeting, we can conclude that the conferences have been a success. However, that success is not measured merely by the biennial celebration of an international academic conference, though the meetings have served to *tender puentes* (build bridges) and *compartir conocimientos* (share knowledge) through which Spaniards have learned a great deal from the critics of Aztlán. I truly believe that the input of Spanish critics has been instrumental in developing

---

4. The full program of this tenth conference can be viewed at http://hispausa.com/Congresos/.

Chicano studies in the United States as well; their particular analytic contributions have had a critical impact on both sides of the Atlantic.

In Spain, the inspiration of those Spanish critics is notable. Because of their work, there are now university courses solely devoted to the study of Chicano literature, and I am referring not only to North American Literature syllabi, in which Chicano writers and critics are already included, but to MA and PhD courses as well. Thanks to them, young scholars have had qualified directors for their doctoral dissertations on Chicano literature. New scholars have been incorporated in the pool of Spanish critics whose research interests are focused on Chicano studies (it would be interesting for an article, in the near future, to track the publications and contributions made by newer generations), and numerous publicly funded research projects have been developed to explore Chicano literature's singularity.

Their effort has permitted the Instituto Franklin, the institution I have the honor to head, to take an active role in promoting Chicano studies. We publish an indexed research journal, *Camino Real*, whose articles exclusively deal with Latinos in the United States; promote Chicano writers by publishing the translation of some of their works into Spanish with the goal of making them accessible to the Spanish public; offer the opportunity to Chicano scholars to spend a month at our university to work on both fictional or critical texts; and, finally, continuously support the celebration of the Chicano literature conference in Spain.

I conclude with the hope that this small contribution helps to continue building bridges and sharing knowledge between scholars from both sides of the Atlantic. By the time this book is published, the 11th Conference on Chicano Literature and Latino Studies (2018), to be held at the historical Universidad de Salamanca and hosted by Professor Román Alvarez, will have its Call for Papers almost ready. I hope you are as ready as we are to begin this next stage of Chicano studies in Spain.

WORKS CITED

Alvar, Manuel. "El español de Estados Unidos: diacronía y sincronía." *Revista de Filología Española* 72.3–4 (1992): 469–90. Print.

Alvarez, Esther, ed. "The Daughters of La Malinche: Examining the Effects of the Myth in Cherríe Moraga's Work." *Perspectivas Transatlánticas en la Literatura Chicana. Ensayos y Creatividad.* Ed. María Herrera-Sobek et al. Málaga: Servicio de Publicaciones de la Universidad de Málaga, 2002. 51–60. Print.

———. *Geographies of Identity: Mapping, Crossing, and Transgressing Urban and Human Boundaries.* Biblioteca Benjamin Franklin. Arre, Navarra: Servicio de Publicaciones de la Universidad de Alcalá, 2016. Print.

Andújar Molina, Olvido. 2010. "La representación del personaje hispano en la nueva ficción televisiva norteamericana. El caso de *Desperate Housewives*." *Nuevas reflexiones en torno a la literatura y cultura chicana*. Ed. Julio Cañero. Biblioteca Benjamin Franklin. Arre, Navarra: Servicio de Publicaciones de la Universidad de Alcalá, 2010. 101–22. Print.

Arias, Jesús. 1998. "Escritores Chicanos piden desde Granada que se respeten los rasgos propios del 'Spanglish.'" *El País.com. El País*, 3 Apr. 1998. Web. 10 Feb. 2015.

Bléser, Nathalie. "Historia de un secuestro o cómo apresar al duende de una tierra encantada: Nuevo México en la obra de Anaya." *Aztlán. Ensayos sobre literatura chicana*. Ed. Federico Eguíluz Otero de Latierro et al. Zarautz, Guipuzkoa: Servicio Editorial de la Universidad del País Vasco, 2001. 11–24. Print.

Brito, Manuel. "Language Working to Uncover the Social and the Cultural: The Example of Rodrigo Toscano." *Critical Essays on Chicano Studies*. Ed. Ramón Espejo et al. Bern: Peter Lang, 2007. 51–64. Print.

Cañero, Julio. "La comunidad chicana y la colonia interna estadounidense: breves apuntes teóricos." *Literatura Chicana. Reflexiones y ensayos críticos*. Ed. Rosa Morillas Sánchez and Manuel Villar Raso. Granada: Editorial Comares, 2000. 79–90. Print.

———. "Dos décadas de estudios en España sobre la población hispana de los Estados Unidos: el Instituto Franklin y la presente edición como ejemplos." *Nuevas reflexiones en torno a la literatura y cultura chicana*. Ed. Julio Cañero. Biblioteca Benjamin Franklin. Arre, Navarra: Servicio de Publicaciones de la Universidad de Alcalá, 2010. 7–13. Print.

———, ed. *Nuevas reflexiones en torno a la literatura y cultura chicana*. Biblioteca Benjamin Franklin. Arre, Navarra: Servicio de Publicaciones de la Universidad de Alcalá, 2010. Print.

Castro Dopacio, María Jesús. "La Virgen de Guadalupe ante la frontera de género: Confluencias narrativas 'chicano-riqueñas.'" *Interpreting the New Milenio*. Ed. José Antonio Gurpegui. Newcastle: Cambridge Scholars, 2008. 113–19. Print.

Díaz López, Ana. "Sofi, 'la héroe' de la (*tele*)novela *So Far from God*." *Nuevas reflexiones en torno a la literatura y cultura chicana*. Ed. Julio Cañero. Biblioteca Benjamin Franklin. Arre, Navarra: Servicio de Publicaciones de la Universidad de Alcalá, 2010. 49–56. Print.

Dinapoli, Russell. "Creatively Depicting Disarticulation and Rearticulation in Contemporary Chicano Discourse." *Aztlán. Ensayos sobre literatura chicana*. Ed. Federico Eguíluz Otero de Latierro et al. Zarautz, Guipuzkoa: Servicio Editorial de la Universidad del País Vasco, 2001. 25–32. Print.

Domínguez Miguela, Antonia. "Redefining the Father Figure in Contemporary Chicana Literature." *Critical Essays on Chicano Studies*. Ed. Ramón Espejo et al. Bern: Peter Lang, 2007. 77–90. Print.

Durán, Isabel. "Teaching Chicana/o Literature Abroad: The Use of Autobiography for Comparative Purposes." 6th International Conference on Chicano Literature. New Challenges for the New Milenio. Universidad de Alicante, Alicante. 24 May 2008. Lecture.

Eguíluz Ortíz de Latierro, Federico. Prólogo. *Aztlán. Ensayos sobre literatura chicana*. Ed. Federico Eguíluz Otero de Latierro et al. Zarautz, Guipuzkoa: Servicio Editorial de la Universidad del País Vasco, 2001. 9–10. Print.

Eguíluz Ortíz de Latierro, Federico et al., eds. *Aztlán. Ensayos sobre literatura chicana*. Zarautz, Guipuzkoa: Servicio Editorial de la Universidad del País Vasco, 2001. Print.

Espejo, Ramón et al., eds. *Critical Essays on Chicano Studies*. Bern: Peter Lang, 2007. Print.

Fernández de Pinedo, Eva. "There Is No Place Like Mexico: Re-Interpreting *The Wizard Of Oz* in a Play by Silvia Gonzalez." *Interpreting the New Milenio*. Ed. José Antonio Gurpegui. Newcastle: Cambridge Scholars, 2008. 196–205. Print.

González Ramos, Carmen. "Re-membering Coyolxauhqui: The Poetics of Fragmentation in Cherríe Moraga's Work." *Perspectivas Transatlánticas en la Literatura Chicana. Ensayos y Creatividad*. Ed. María Herrera Sobek et al. Málaga: Servicio de Publicaciones de la Universidad de Málaga, 2002. 137–46. Print.

Gurpegui, José Antonio. "'In Spanish, Mi Hermano, in Spanish': Is Good to Speak in Español in USA." *Landscapes of Writing in Chicano Literature*. Ed. Imelda Martín-Junquera. New York: Palgrave Macmillan, 2013. 189–200. Print.

———, ed. *Interpreting the New Milenio*. Newcastle: Cambridge Scholars, 2008. Print.

Herrera-Sobek, María et al., eds. *Perspectivas Transatlánticas en la Literatura Chicana. Ensayos y Creatividad*. Málaga: Servicio de Publicaciones de la Universidad de Málaga, 2002. Print.

HispaUSA. Instituto Franklin, n.d. Web. 10 Feb. 2015.

La Moncloa. Gobierno de España, 31 Dec. 2014. Web. 15 Mar. 2015.

Lerate, Jesús, and Juan I. Guijarro. "Introduction." *Critical Essays on Chicano Studies*. Ed. Ramón Espejo et al. Bern: Peter Lang, 2007. 11–18. Print.

López Pons, María. "(Too) Changing Landscapes: The Translation of US Hispanic Literature into Spanish." *Landscapes of Writing in Chicano Literature*. Ed. Imelda Martín-Junquera. New York: Palgrave Macmillan, 2013. 201–12. Print.

Martín-Junquera, Imelda. "Introduction." *Landscapes of Writing in Chicano Literature*. Ed. Imelda Martín Junquera. New York: Palgrave Macmillan, 2013. 1–12. Print.

———, ed. *Landscapes of Writing in Chicano Literature*. New York: Palgrave Macmillan, 2013. Print.

Martín Pareja, Alejandro. "Nuevos medios, nuevas voces: Rap y la tradición cultural chicana." *Perspectivas Transatlánticas en la Literatura Chicana. Ensayos y Creatividad*. Ed. María Herrera Sobek et al. Málaga: Servicio de Publicaciones de la Universidad de Málaga, 2002. 199–210. Print.

Miguélez, Armando. "Los artículos de Adolfo Carrillo: El modernismo como estilo." *8th International Conference on Chicano Literature. Crossing the Borders of Imagination*. Universidad de Castilla-La Mancha, Toledo. 24 May 2012. Lecture.

Montes-Alcalá, Cecilia. "Writing on the Border: English y español también." *Landscapes of Writing in Chicano Literature*. Ed. Imelda Martín-Junquera. New York: Palgrave Macmillan, 2013. 213–29. Print.

Morillas Sánchez, Rosa, and Manuel Villar Raso, eds. *Literatura Chicana. Reflexiones y ensayos críticos*. Granada: Editorial Comares, 2000. Print.

Oliver Rotger, Maria Antònia. "Tourism from the 'Third Space': Mexico and the Search for Ethnic Difference in Stephanie Elizondo Griest's *Mexican Enough*." *8th International Conference on Chicano Literature*. Universidad de Castilla-La Mancha, Toledo. 25 May 2012. Lecture.

Perles Rochel, Juan Antonio. "Introducción." *Perspectivas Transatlánticas en la Literatura Chicana. Ensayos y Creatividad*. Ed. María Herrera Sobek et al. Málaga: Servicio de Publicaciones de la Universidad de Málaga, 2002. 11–18. Print.

Portal del Hispanismo. Instituto Cervantes, n.d. Web. 15 Mar. 2015.

Ramón Torrijos, María del Mar. "Introduction." *Crossing the Borders of Imagination*. Ed. Ramón Torrijos. Biblioteca Benjamin Franklin. Arre, Navarra: Servicio de Publicaciones de la Universidad de Alcalá, 2014. Print.

Rodríguez Jiménez, Francisco. *¿Antídoto contra el antiamericanismo? American Studies en España, 1945-1969*. Biblioteca Javier Coy D'Estudis Nord-Americans. Valencia: Publicacions de la Universitat de València, 2010. Print.

Toda Iglesia, María Ángeles. "¿Cuántas cervezas? Dos versiones de un cuento de Alicia Gaspar de Alba." *Critical Essays on Chicano Studies*. Ed. Ramón Espejo et al. Bern: Peter Lang, 2007. 245-54. Print.

Villar Raso, Manuel. Prólogo. *Literatura Chicana. Reflexiones y ensayos críticos*. Ed. Rosa Morillas Sánchez and Manuel Villar Raso. Granada: Editorial Comares, 2000. 1-2. Print.

Wehbe Herrera, M. Aishih. "¿Y qué ha pasado con los hombres? Chicano Men and the Construction of Masculinity(ies)." *Interpreting the New Milenio*. Ed. José Antonio Gurpegui. Newcastle: Cambridge Scholars, 2008. 80-86. Print.

Zilles, Klaus. "Microstructure and Macrostructure in Rolando Hinojosa's *Klail City Death Trip Series*: The Case of the *Rafe Buenrostro Mysteries*." *Aztlán. Ensayos sobre literatura chicana*. Ed. Federico Eguíluz Otero de Latierro et al. Zarautz, Guipuzkoa: Servicio Editorial de la Universidad del País Vasco, 2001. 257-67. Print.

CHAPTER 8

Women's Literary Gardens as Eco-Spaces
Word Gathering with Anzaldúa and Hurston

CAROLINA NÚÑEZ-PUENTE

THIS CHAPTER puts forth a cross-cultural and cross-genre comparison between "*sus plumas al viento,*" a poem by Gloria Anzaldúa (1987), and "Sweat," a story by Zora Neale Hurston (1926). On one hand, even though the prose of *Borderlands* is well known, its poetry has received little critical response (e.g., Garber, Saldívar-Hull). On the other hand, although Hurston's "Sweat" has been extensively discussed, my critique probably is the first written from an ecofeminist viewpoint. In line with Alice Walker, I read Anzaldúa's and Hurston's works in search of both our mothers' literary gardens and the outdoor gardens represented in the texts. In the title of this essay, the prefix eco- refers to the ecology, economy, and language features or echoes, which will be examined in the close readings. Therein, the essay further revolves around the privilege that entails being able to play symbolically with the notion of water, a vital element for ecology. In Anzaldúa and Hurston, whereas the imagery of water—such as cash flow or flow of words—is generally the privilege of the upper classes, the literal water-derivatives—such as sweat, spit, pee, and blood—appear as the only possibility available to the workers. In brief, my comparative essay wishes to promote dialogue between cultures stemming from their literatures.

ECOFEMINISM IN CHICANO AND AFRICAN AMERICAN CULTURES

It is necessary to add a few words on ecofeminism, a movement that has at least two facets: one as the offshoot of ecology and feminism, and another as the offshoot of ecocriticism and feminism.[1] Broadly speaking, Greta Gaard and Lori Gruen define ecofeminism as a way of thinking and acting that "grows out of dialogue and focuses . . . on commonality while at the same time respecting difference . . . building coalitions . . . [in] solidarity . . . to achieve global justice and planetary health" (287). The interest of Chicanos/as and African Americans in ecofeminism is to be expected considering their historical fight for survival.

Chicana ecofeminist activists have reported that they are completely uninterested in separating themselves from men. Hence, "they frame their activism, as women, in class and race-conscious ways" (Kirk 187) in order to "transform relationships among people and between people and the nonhuman world, so that there is the possibility that our children's children will inherit a healthier planet" (191). As we will see later on, the lack of dialogue between women and men is unfortunately present in Anzaldúa's and Hurston's texts. Jorge Marcone and Priscilla Solís Ybarra argue that Mexican and Chicano literary productions are representative of environmental literature. Both these literatures, they contend, "engage a social-justice agenda, the legacy of the Mexican Revolution, and the political ecology of dispossession" (93). Therein, to foundational definitions of environmental literature, Marcone and Solís Ybarra add a few features that are crucial to Mexican and Chicana/o authors: their imbrications in nonenvironmental problems; the shaking of certain conceptions related to creation and tradition in the world; and the dialogue with indigenous and pre-Columbian traditions (94). Curiously, as I will show, these characteristics can be found in both Anzaldúa's and Hurston's writings.

Similarly to Chicano/a critics, Jeffrey Myers protests that African American writing has been ignored by environmental literature canons. From his point of view, this exclusion is due to the following reasons: a narrow conception of the genre of nature writing as nonfiction; "a reluctance to think of urban space as 'natural' space" (185); "a subordination of environmental justice issues to concerns over wildlife and wilderness preservation" (185); and the history of slavery. For his part, Michael Bennett locates a main current of antipastoralism that has taken place from slave narratives to Toni Morrison. According to Bennett: "Slavery created a system whereby those of European

---

1. As to its literary facet, ecofeminism asks among other things the following questions: "What previously unnoticed elements of a literary text are made visible . . . when one reads from an ecofeminist perspective? Can this perspective tell literary critics anything new about a text . . . in terms of the traditional elements of . . . form and content? How might an ecofeminist perspective enhance explorations of connections and differences among 'characters' in a text—between humans and animals . . . and among human differences of race, class, and sexual orientation—connections and differences that affect our relationships with nature and with each other?" (Gaard and Murphy 7).

descent controlled a pastoral landscape that included those of African descent as part of their property" (205–6). Given African Americans' exodus to the city, many critics find surprising that Hurston repeatedly places her characters in Eatonville (FL), the rural South. Eatonville is supposed to be the first all-Black community in the United States; perhaps Hurston wanted to claim the rights of African Americans to enjoy a space they had made themselves. Correcting and expanding upon previous genres, I will argue that "Sweat" can be read as ecofeminist pastoral literature.

GARDENS IN CHICANO AND AFRICAN AMERICAN COMMUNITIES

The garden is a focal element in both Anzaldúa's and Hurston's texts; hence, it seems fair to consider its function in Chicano and African American communities. The practice of gardening has been viewed from different perspectives, ranging from those who consider it an art to those who include it within agriculture. Growing gardens is extremely satisfying for human beings, who feel it enriches their lives and provides a reward for their labor. This has been perfectly understood by promoters of community gardens, whose work has led community members to develop a greater sense of connection, and to experience less crime and vandalism (Schukoske). Gardening, of course, has a very long history.

From Nahuatl *chināmitl*, a chinampa is a square made of canes surrounded on three or four sides by canals. Chinampas are supposed to have emerged in the "Early Aztec/Middle Postclassic period (ad 1150–1350)" (Popper). According to Virginia Popper: "This type of construction . . . help[s] overcome the main limits to agriculture in the Basin of Mexico . . . [Since the] proximity of the . . . water . . . provides adequate soil moisture for crops." Nowadays, the Floating Gardens of Xochimilco (located in Mexico City) celebrate their Aztec past and attract tourists from all over the world. Nowadays too, according to Jos Stephens, "Latinos are prolific gardeners, especially in places where community gardens are accessible, and they use temporary farmers markets as community gathering places." Jonna McKone further notes that Latino courtyards are often used for social gatherings, encouraging conversation. Both scholars praise the work of James Rojas for placing Latinos/as at the front of U.S. American urbanism, especially in their use of public space. As Rojas explains, Latinos/as build fences around their front yards, which results in an extension of the threshold from the house to the street; this transforms the front yard into a *plaza*, a kind of public square that is typical of European-influenced design. Consequently, Latino/a "residents and pedestrians can participate in this street/plaza dialogue from the comfort and security of their enclosed front yards" (Rojas).

Africa is a vast continent with different traditions of gardening. Today, the gardens of Morocco, Uganda, and South Africa are famous for being among the most beautiful of the world, but it has not always been like this. Colonization destroyed many species of African flora, while it introduced not only European species but also pesticides. Thanks to initiatives such as the Greenbelt Movement, reforestation has been possible in Africa (Maathai). Regarding traditional African American gardens, their design and spiritual meanings can be traced to the time of slavery and even African heritage (Sills and Als). Therein, African American garden arrangements symbolize the divine in everyday life and the cycles of nature, among other issues. Though at first gardening was "associated . . . with slavery" (Tortorello 3), after the Civil War Blacks started to own land and continued the tradition of their ancestors. Dianne D. Glave puts forward that, customarily, low-income African American "women grew vegetable gardens primarily to sustain their families" (40); nevertheless, their gardens tend to express "values, aesthetic preferences, and spiritual beliefs" (Westmacott 1). Moreover, African Americans are very aware of the importance of community building through gardening. As an example, Black Urban Growers is an organization of Black farmers and urban gardeners "committed to building networks and community support for growers in both urban and rural settings."

CLOSELY READING ANZALDÚA'S AND HURSTON'S LITERARY GARDENS

As said, "*sus plumas el viento*" (1987) and "Sweat" (1926) deal with gardens; furthermore, in both pieces watering seems metaphorically interchangeable with writing. I need to pinpoint that Anzaldúa's and Hurston's ecofeminism stems from a class-conscious basis; accordingly, the authors use water imagery to show the economic hierarchy between whites and people of color, which results in the racialization of class (Johnson). Faithful to their publication chronology, I comment on Hurston's text first.

A title such as "Sweat" corresponds to the water-derivative that is most often associated with the working class. The title foreshadows the female protagonist's bitterest thoughts about her life: "Sweat, sweat, sweat! Work and sweat, cry and sweat, pray and sweat!" (Hurston 71). Delia Jones works as a washerwoman, which means that she also earns a living through water. More specifically, she is a Black woman, who sweats when sorting her white clients' clothes "according to color" every Sunday night (73). Although Hurston has been criticized for not "explor[ing] interracial themes" very often (Wall, "Zora" 77), the racial segregation of work is quite evident in this text. From here we could argue that, as E. P. Thompson states, class is not a category or a thing; it is a relationship characterized by a binary opposition: boss/worker, rich/proletarian.

Having a "sweaty" job is not the only matter Delia has to reckon with, as she is also a victim of gender abuse. Sykes Jones's aggressive behavior was evident only two months after the wedding, when he gave her "the first brutal beating" (76). From the village men sitting on the porch we learn that Delia used to be really "pritty" in her youth (77). Unfortunately, after fifteen years of marriage, her looks have changed dramatically; as the porch men say: "Too much knockin' will ruin *any* 'oman" (77). The porch men, however, do not try to help Delia, which could be Hurston's way of criticizing social passivity toward gender violence. Fortunately, and despite the "salty stream" of her tears that has drowned the "flowers" of her marriage (75), Delia has a garden that is "her little home. . . . It was lovely to her, lovely" (76). Besides her religious faith, her garden is Delia's source of beauty and hope. Planning ahead for the future, she "had built it for her old days, and planted one by one the trees and flowers there" (76). In this way, while Sykes's abuse hurts every being around him—including his wife's horse, which he likes whipping about (73–74)—Delia's ecofeminist ethic appears to follow the rhythm of nature.

Delia is not only physically but also psychologically abused by her husband, who seizes every opportunity to insult her. The hot steamy weather of Florida, which is powerful enough to "collapse" people's conversations (72), offers no help. Sykes especially likes mocking his wife's religious beliefs by calling her a "hypocrite," since she starts to do her work on Sundays "after taking sacrament at the church house" (74). One night, Sykes's accusations and brute behavior lead Delia to talk back smartly to him: "Mah tub of suds is filled yo' belly with vittles more times than yo' hands is filled it. Mah sweat is done paid for this house and Ah reckon Ah kin keep sweatin' in it" (75). Delia's flow of words, which even contains water imagery, denotes the starting point of her new speaking subjectivity. In his response, her amazed husband does "not strike her" as he usually does.[2]

---

2. While she is doing the talking, Delia is holding the "iron skillet" in a "defensive pose" (75). As a Bakhtinian feminist, I am far from overestimating the power of flowing words; only after overcoming the patriarchal, colonial, and class-based system in which we currently live, will we be able to enjoy radical dialogics—for more information, see Núñez-Puente *Feminism*.

Later in the story, Sykes brings home a snake, with the excuse of keeping it as a pet, but having actually plotted to murder his wife with it (79). Although Delia is terrified of snakes, she pulls herself together and tells him: "Ah hates you, Sykes. . . . Ah hates you tuh de same degree dat Ah useter love yuh" (81). Interestingly enough, Delia's bold, honest, and unpleasing speaking manner is not characteristic of either the white or Black women of the 1920s (Wall, "Introduction" 8). Therefore, our protagonist learns to speak in a feminist way not from any of her contemporaries but, perhaps, from an African ancestor, as I argue below.

Apart from having a flow of words, Delia is the breadwinner and owns the cash flow. Robert Hemenway has interpreted that Sykes looks for phallic symbols, such as the whip and the snake, in order to compensate for his emasculation (149). Contrary to Sykes's plan, at the end of the story, the snake bites and kills him; given this turning point, one could say Delia ends up having all the phallic features. In terms of her name's etymology, "Delia" is a feminine variant of Delos: the legendary birthplace of Artemis, a female, and Apollo, a male (*Behind the Name*). With her job, her smart talk, her name, and her thin muscular figure, Delia embodies the androgynous kind that can balance gender oppositions. This king of phallic feminine is represented in African mythology by the goddess Osun—a beautiful and intelligent mother, lover, worker, guardian and warrior—in which the essence of Alice Walker's "womanist concept is grounded" (Badejo 27). Osun is the African feminist ancestor of Delia I referred to above: she is Delia's speech instructor. Osun is "a river goddess" too (29), which helps me to swim into the tragic ending of "Sweat," which includes a couple of rivers.

After attending a "love feast" in church (Hurston 82), Delia drives back in her cart singing a Black spiritual song: "Jurden water, black an' col' / Chills the body, not the soul / An' Ah wantah cross Jurden in uh calm time." Her joyful feeling finishes abruptly when she arrives home to find that the snake has got into her laundry basket. Having jumped "up and down in . . . fear" (83), she leaves the house and hides in the upper hay barn. Early the next morning, after hearing that Sykes is in the house, Delia comes down from the barn and crouches outside the bedroom window. Inside the house, hierarchies such as human/animal and speech/sound are reversed by a very peculiar flow of words: "The snake is a ventriloquist. His whirr sounds . . . everywhere but where it is" (84), while Sykes's "cry" is that of "a maddened chimpanzee, a stricken gorilla . . . without a recognizable human sound" (84–85). At the same time, Delia experiences a curious symbiosis with nature. Feeling "ill" from the snake/man duel, she creeps "over to the four-o'clocks and [stretches] herself on the cool earth to recover," and when she goes to "her flower-bed," her legs suddenly stop "mov[ing]." That is, Delia's garden protects her as if giving her back the love with which she had looked after it; this contributes to the ecofeminism of the story by showing us that nature is on her side.

Delia finally enters the house, where she finds Sykes in a river of blood, only to go out immediately: "She could scarcely reach the Chinaberry tree, where she waited . . . while . . . she knew the cold river was creeping up and up to extinguish that eye which must know by now that she knew" (85). First, the plays on words—eye-I, Jordan River–river of blood, know-now-knew—add up to the text's lyricism somehow ironically. Second, "Sweat" appears to rewrite the Garden of Eden in a Black ecofeminist working-class fashion: we have a Black washerwoman, a Black man, a snake, a garden, a tree, and—as Billie Holiday used to sing—the "Strange Fruit" of racism. Unlike in the biblical garden, the Tree of Knowledge is replanted here as a chinaberry tree. With its ironic and racial overtones, Hurston's tree provides a knowledge that only guarantees female survival. The fact that Delia does not help her husband-abuser in his agony has provoked controversy among critics. Kathryn Seidel solves the problem as simply as follows: "She can save his life or she can save her own" (180). For her part, Cheryl Wall wonders: afterwards, "how will Delia, good Christian though she has tried to be, ever cross Jordan in a calm time?" ("Introduction" 12–13). Faithful to the dialogical spirit of "Sweat," I leave you this question to think about.[3]

If the protagonist of "Sweat" finds shelter in a garden owned by herself, Anzaldúa's poem "*sus plumas el viento*" (her feathers the wind) tells a different story. "*sus plumas*" is dedicated to the author's mother, Amalia, a Chicana farmworker from Texas. The poem gathers her daily labor and relationship with her co-workers, as well as her frustrations and aspirations. The farm (not the garden) where Amalia has to work is owned by white people. The line "White heat no water no place to pee" entails a criticism of the exploitation of the people of color working on U.S. American soil (Anzaldúa 117); in this way, "water" and "pee" refer to the water-derivatives attributed to the working classes. Honoring the bilingual echoes of Chicano language, the physical hardship of Amalia's labor is manifested both as her "*sudor*" (repeated twice 116, 117) and as her "sweat drying on top of old sweat" (116). As happened to Delia, "washing" is one of Amalia's many duties (118). However, instead of a puddle of water, we get a puddle of shit, "*charco de mierda*" (117), and her "feet soaking in cold puddles" in "110 degree heat" (118). Unlike Delia's name, Amalia's complicated etymology confirms her difficult fate: from Germanic *amal* or

---

3. I have given my own answer to Wall's question. Based on the religious syncretism taking place in the Caribbean and Gulf of Mexico areas, I interpret that the river goddess Osun will help Delia to go across Jordan when the time comes—see Núñez-Puente "Reading".

"work," Greek *amalós*, which means "tender, weak," and a more obscure and hopeful origin which is "energetic, active" (*Behind the Name*). Unlike Delia, Amalia seems unable to produce a powerful flow of words, and she just "flicks her tongue over upper lip / where the salt stings her cracked mouth" (116).

In addition, the stanzas of "*sus plumas*" almost flow off the page, since margins are being constantly moved, as if Amalia wanted to escape perhaps to a garden of her own. Since "stanza" is also the Italian word for "room," she could thus be looking for *a stanza of her own* in the Woolfian manner. Fortunately, the *plumas* (read as feathers) that Amalia, the mother, wishes to have are for Gloria, the daughter, the *plumas* (read as quills) with which she and her peer authors can write. In the prose of *Borderlands,* we read: "I look at my fingers, see plumes growing there. From the fingers, my feathers, black and red ink drips across the page" (71). Anzaldúa's words give us hope that Chicano/a literature can denounce and even overcome situations like Amalia's.[4]

"*sus plumas el viento*" is included in the poetry section of *Borderlands* called "La Pérdida" (The Loss), which could respond to Juan Bruce-Novoa's interpretation of Chicano poetry as an elegy and a response to chaos. An elegy presupposes a loss and is used "to soothe the pain" in order to survive the loss (9). I would like to take a closer look at the loss not only of Chicanos/as but also of Mexicans. First, after crossing the waters of Río Grande, Mexican immigrants are reified as body parts or "wetbacks." Second, Mexican and Chicano/a workers are turned into animals by being forced to work "*Como una mula*" (Like a mule, Anzaldúa 118). Third, a worker who is unable to speak English fluently is completely deprived of his/her humanity. Fourth, female fieldworkers can even suffer a blurring of their sex by turning into kinds of shattered men: "*Manos hinchadas,* quebradas, (Swollen and broken hands) / thick and calloused like a man's" (117).[5] Fifth, Anzaldúa's mother has lost something else and moans: "*las chuparrosas de los jardines / ¿en dónde están de su mamagrande?*" (117) ("Where were the hummingbirds from her grandmother's gardens?" [119]). Like Alice Walker, Amalia is in search of her grandmother's garden or the mythical Aztlán, the original territory where Chicanos/as come from. Therefore, the longed-for garden uncovers a past and a present of two colonizations (by the Spaniards and the Anglos), and their subsequent socioeconomic injustices.

---

4. Amalia's plea appears in different versions: "*Que le de sus plumas el viento*" (that the wind gives her its feathers), "*Si el viento le diera sus plumas*" (If the wind would give her feathers for fingers) (116–17). It must not go without noticing that in some varieties of Spanish the word *pluma* can also refer to a queer sexuality, which matches Anzaldúa's.

5. If readers are interested in Anzaldúa's poems that criticize the exploitation of Mexican and Chicano/a workers, I recommend "*Mar de repollos,*" "*sobre piedras con lagartijos,*" "*El sonavabitche,*" and "A Sea of Cabbages," which are in *Borderlands*.

Despite everything, Amalia keeps asking the wind to give her feathers in order to fly free: "*Pero el viento sur le tiró su saliva / pa' 'trás en la cara*" (118) ("But the wind threw her spit back in her face" [119]). Even more tragically, she looks ahead only to find that "the obsidian wind / cut tassels of blood / from the hummingbird's throat" (repeated twice 117, 118). Herein, "spit" and "blood" stand for the water-derivatives that are available to the working classes; taken metaphorically, they remind us of the violence used against both nature and workers of color in the United States. Thus, the poem includes the story of Pepita, one of Amalia's co-workers, who is sexually assaulted by "*un bolillo,*" her white boss (116). The hidden place where the rape occurs, "*entre las matas de maíz*" (among the stalks of corn) at "the irrigation ditch" (116) oozes with symbolism. The corn grains (read as semen) and the ditch (read as vagina) account for the native women raped during colonization—including La Malinche, who should be called *La Chingada,* according to some (e.g., Paz).

Unquestionably, the description of Pepita's rape while her boss is "landing on her, digging in, sucking" (116), conveys an ecofeminist criticism. Ecofeminists insist that the violation of the land and the rape of women emerged from the same patriarchal colonial mind-set (Mies and Shiva). In *Borderlands,* the criticism that most efficiently joins ecofeminism and (post)colonialism, but which is not generally read as such, is the following: "The U.S.-Mexican border *es una herida abierta* where the Third World grates against the first and bleeds" (Anzaldúa 3). The image of an open wound, impossible to be healed due to constant grating, is graphic enough to suggest rape in all its dimensions. As I expect to show, Anzaldúa's *plumas,* her queer feminist quill and flow of words, help her mother's flowing with the wind.

Apart from flying, hummingbirds sing and so does Chula, another of Amalia's co-workers: "singing *corridos* / making up *los versos* [the verses] as she / plants down the rows / hoes down the rows / picks down the rows" (116). Although Amalia is unable to sing, according to the lyrical voice, this happens because of "all those books" she has been reading (117). Therein, the poem denounces the lack of dialogue between popular and academic cultures. Singing with other people strengthens their resilience and sense of union, as happened to African slaves, and even to Hurston's Delia while being in church. Another connection with "Sweat" lies in Anzaldúa's interest in serpents, due not only to Earth goddess Coatlicue or Serpent Skirt, but also to her wish to "have my serpent's tongue [and] . . . overcome the tradition of silence" (59). Second, the hummingbird leads us to the myth of Philomela. Ovid tells us that Philomela was deprived of the power of speech by her rapist, who tore out her tongue to avoid being accused; afterwards, Philomela turned into a bird in order to sing her story. In the case of Chicanos/as, Anzaldúa accuses: "*El*

Anglo con cara de inocente nos arrancó la lengua (The Anglo with an innocent face tore out our tongues). Wild tongues can't be tamed, they can only be cut out" (54). As a result, Chicana intellectuals are *deslenguadas* (from *des-*, "without," and *lengua,* "tongue") only because they lack a domesticated tongue.

"*sus plumas*" goes on to show the hierarchy between intellectual and manual work that rules our world: "You're respected if you can use your head / instead of your back" (118), and even if you work "in air-conditioned offices." Like Hurston, Anzaldúa denounces an ongoing racialization of work (Johnson), in which the whites take the best jobs and the others do all the rest. Amalia's "palm(s)," "hands," and "*manos*" are mentioned seven times, the biblical number; the seven references emphasize her manual labor while "cutting (. . .) washing (. . .) weighing (. . .) packaging" (118; ellipses hers). Furthermore, the blank left on the page is evocative of the slow, heavy rhythm of agricultural work and highlights the socioeconomic criticism. The poem ends with an ecofeminist statement according to which "the hummingbird's shadow / becomes the navel of the Earth," or its most important constituent. These lines remind us that looking after nature is the most sensible of all human tasks. Finally, Anzaldúa's poem warns us that we must learn to take care of nature and practice ethics, if we want our existence to be as worthy as the hummingbird's.

CODA

Both outdoor and literary gardens should be considered forms of artistic expression. Beyond literature, experience tells us that to put gardens in our communities guarantees our physical, mental, and social well-being. For Anzaldúa and Hurston, the garden functions as a liberating space, which further links the protagonists to their ancestors. Whether in Aztlán or Africa, the gardens alluded to in the texts provide Chicanas and African American women with the imaginary domain (Cornell), that is, a space for human beings to imagine truly ethical ways of life with the hope one day of putting them into practice. It appears that the writings of women of color celebrate people's dialogues with outer (green) and inner (hopeful) nature as eco-spaces. However, neither Amalia nor Delia is able to enter into a dialogue with other people, something that severely curtails their dialogic or even human potential.

As suggested above, my comparative essay attempts to promote dialogue across cultures as well as across genres or, as Bakhtin would put it, different ways of thinking (Núñez-Puente *Feminism* 20). Pioneering scholars such as

Gonzálo Aguirre Beltrán and, more recently, Alejandro Hernández, George Lipsitz, and Micaela Sánchez have pointed out the vibrant links between Mexicans, Chicanos/as, and African Americans with regard to family, music, dance, and so on. It is thus not surprising that Anzaldúa worships *Yemayá* (*Borderlands* 3), who is an African and Afro-Caribbean deity par excellence. In *Borderlands* too, Anzaldúa makes a call to go beyond the "Latinoist movement" since having "Chicanos, Puerto Ricans, Cubans, and other Spanish-speaking people working together . . . is . . . not enough" (87); therefore, she appeals to the "Chicano, *indio,* American Indian, *mexicano,* immigrant Latino, Anglo in power, working-class Anglo, Black, Asian" to join her transformative project toward global dialogue.

Is it utopian to dream about an eco-space where people gather to share worlds by means of words? As implied throughout, this kind of dialogical relationship will only be possible when we rid ourselves of patriarchal and colonial ways of being. Perhaps the first step must be taken by scholars by proposing intercultural comparative studies as a way to clear the path toward such a garden. Above all, it is my wish that literary studies cherish the dialogue with women of color, and other women and men within different genres.

WORKS CITED

Aguirre Beltrán, Gonzálo. *Cuijla. Esbozo etnográfico de un pueblo negro.* México D. F.: Fondo de Cultura Económica, 1958. Print.

Anzaldúa, Gloria E. *Borderlands/La Frontera: The New Mestiza.* San Francisco: Aunt Lute Books, 1987. Print.

Badejo, Dierdre. "The Goddess Osun as a Paradigm for African Feminist Criticism." *Sage* 6.1 (Summer 1989): 27–31. Print.

Behind the Name. The Etymology and History of First Names. 1996. Web. 21 Nov. 2014.

Bennett, Michael. "Anti-Pastoralism, Frederick Douglass, and the Nature of Slavery." *Beyond Nature Writing: Expanding the Boundaries of Ecocriticism.* Ed. Karla Armbruster and Kathleen R. Wallace. Charlottesville: UP of Virginia, 2001. 195–210. Print.

Black Urban Growers. Black Farmers & Urban Gardeners. 2013. Web. 21 Nov. 2014.

Bruce-Novoa, Juan. *Chicano Poetry: A Response to Chaos.* Austin: U of Texas P, 1982. Print.

Christensen, Laird et al., eds. *Teaching North American Environmental Literature.* New York: MLA, 2008. Print.

Cornell, Drucilla. *The Imaginary Domain: Abortion, Pornography & Sexual Harassment.* New York: Routledge, 1995. Print.

Gaard, Greta, and Lori Gruen. "Ecofeminism: Toward Global Justice and Planetary Health." *Environmental Ethics: An Anthology.* Ed. Andrew Light and Holmes Rouston III. Oxford: Blackwell, 2003. 276–87. Print.

Gaard, Greta, and Patrick Murphy, eds. *Ecofeminist Literary Criticism: Theory, Interpretation, Pedagogy*. Urbana: U of Illinois P, 1998. Print.

Garber, Linda. "Spirit, Culture, Sex: Elements of the Creative Process in Anzaldúa's Poetry." *Entre Mundos / Among Worlds: New Perspectives on Gloria E. Anzaldúa*. Ed. AnaLouise Keating. New York: Palgrave, 2005. 213–26. Print.

Glave, Dianne D. "Rural African American Women, Gardening, and Progressive Reform." *"To Love the Wind and the Rain": African Americans and Environmental History*. Ed. Dianne D. Glave and Mark Stoll. Pittsburgh: U of Pittsburgh P, 2006. Print.

Hemenway, Robert. "From *Zora Neale Hurston: A Literary Bibliography*." Wall *Sweat*. 149–52. Print.

Holiday, Billie. "Strange Fruit." *YouTube*. 2009. Web. 21 Nov. 2014.

Hurston, Zora Neale. "Sweat." *Zora Neale Hurston: The Complete Stories*. Ed. Henry Louis Gates Jr. and Sieglinde Lemke. New York: Harper, 1995. Print.

Johnson, Barbara. *A World of Difference*. Baltimore: Johns Hopkins UP, 1987. Print.

Kirk, Gwyn. "Ecofeminism and Chicano Environmental Struggles: Bridges Across Gender and Race." *Chicano Culture, Ecology, Politics: Subversive Kin*. Ed. Devon Peña. Tucson: U of Arizona P, 1998. 177–200. Print.

Lipsitz, George. *Footsteps in the Dark: The Hidden Histories of Popular Music*. U of Minnesota P, 2007. Print.

Maathai, Wangari. *Unbowed: A Memoir*. New York: Alfred A. Knopf, 2006. Print.

Marcone, Jorge, and Priscilla Solís Ybarra. "Mexican and Chicana/o Environmental Writing: Unearthing and Inhabiting." Christensen et al. 93–111. Print.

McKone, Jonna. "Cities in Flux: Latino New Urbanism." *The City Fix*. 2 Nov. 2010. Web. 21 Nov. 2014.

Mies, Maria, and Vandana Shiva. *Ecofeminism*. London: Zed, 1993. Print.

Myers, Jeffrey. "Ready to Come Home: Teaching African American Literature as Environmental Literature." Christensen et al. 185–93. Print.

Núñez-Puente, Carolina. *Feminism and Dialogics: Charlotte Perkins Gilman, Meridel Le Sueur, Mikhail M. Bakhtin*. Valencia: Biblioteca Javier Coy, 2006. Print.

———. "Reading (from) the Afro-Caribbean in Hurston's 'Sweat': An Ecowomanist Voyage." *Transatlantic Vistas: Cultural Exchanges between the USA and Europe (Miradas transatlánticas: Intercambios culturales entre Estados Unidos y Europa)*. Ed. Isabel Durán Giménez-Rico, Carmen Méndez García, and Jaime de Salas Ortueta. Madrid: Fundamentos, 2016. 113–27. Print.

Paz, Octavio. *El laberinto de la soledad*. México D. F.: Cuadernos Americanos, 1950. Print.

Popper, Virginia. "Investigating Chinampa Farming." *Backdirt*. Cotsen Institute of Archaeology. (Fall/Winter 2000). Web. 21 Nov. 2014.

Rojas, James. "Latino Urbanism: Transforming the Suburbs." *Buildipedia*. 15 July 2013. Web. 21 Nov. 2014.

Saldívar-Hull, Sonia. "Introduction to the Second Edition." *Borderlands/La Frontera: The New Mestiza*. San Francisco: Aunt Lute Books, 2007. 1–15. Print.

Sánchez, Micaela, and Alejandro D. Hernández. "The *Son Jarocho* as Afro-Mexican Resistance Music." *The Journal of Pan African Studies* 6.1 (July 2013): 187–209. Web. 21 Nov. 2014. PDF file.

Seidel, Kathryn. "The Artist in the Kitchen: The Economics of Creativity in Hurston's 'Sweat.'" *Sweat*. Zora Neale Hurtson. Ed. Cheryl A. Wall. 169–82. Print.

Schukoske, Jane E. "Community Development through Gardening: State and Local Policies Transforming Urban Open Space." *Legislation and Public Policy* 3.351 (2000): 351–92. Print.

Sills, Vaughn, and Hilton Als. *Places for the Spirit: Traditional African American Gardens*. San Antonio: Trinity UP, 2010. Print.

Stephens, Jos. "Out of the Enclave: Latinos Adapt, and Adapt to, the American City." *Planetizen*. 22 Sept. 2008. Web. 21 Nov. 2014.

Thompson, E. P. *The Making of the English Working Class*. Harmondsworth: Penguin, 1978. Print.

Tortorello, Michael. "Juneteenth Gardens: Planting the Seeds of Survival." *The New York Times*. 13 (June 2012) 1–4. Web. 21 Nov. 2014.

Walker, Alice. *In Search of Our Mothers' Gardens: Womanist Prose*. San Diego: Harcourt Brace Jovanovich, 1983. Print.

Wall, Cheryl. "Introduction." *Sweat*. Zora Neale Hurston. New Brunswick: Rutgers UP, 1997. 3–20. Print.

———, ed. *Sweat*. Zora Neale Hurston. New Brunswick: Rutgers UP, 1997. Print.

———. "Zora Neale Hurston: Changing Her Own Words." *Zora Neale Hurston: Critical Perspectives Past and Present*. Ed. Henry Louis Gates Jr. and K. A. Appiah. New York: Amistad, 1993. 77–97. Print.

Westmacott, Richard. *African-American Gardens and Yards in the Rural South*. Knoxville: U of Tennessee P, 1992. Print.

CHAPTER 9

La Tierra

Sense of Place in Contemporary Chicano Literature

CARMEN LYDIA FLYS JUNQUERA

> The landscape changes man, and the man becomes landscape.
> —RUDOLFO ANAYA

THE IMPORTANCE of the land in Chicano literature cannot be overestimated. A sense of place is a key factor in both personal and cultural identity, as well as being a cornerstone in current environmental rhetoric. Being anchored in the local seems to be the first essential step to a more planetary appreciation of nature and environmental understanding. Yet this is one of the crucial and destabilizing elements of modernity, where rootedness seems to give way to alienation in nonplaces. Although there is debate around what a new concept of sense of place might be that would respond to our current more cosmopolitan character,[1] it seems that Chicano identity is still firmly rooted in the land. This essay explores this sense of place in three Chicano authors: Rudolfo Anaya, Ana Castillo, and Jimmy Santiago Baca.[2]

The first consideration is to evaluate the meaning of sense of place, and precisely the bilingual condition of Chicanos makes this concept more fluid. Even in English, the expression "sense of place" is deceptively simple. For geographer Yi-Fu Tuan, place can be defined as a "center of felt value" (*Space and Place* 4). According to Edward Relph, sense of place is a conscious, cognitive process, "a learned skill for critical environmental awareness that is used

---

1. See Heise, Plumwood, Thomashow, Tuan *Cosmos and Hearth*, and Flys Junquera "Wild Cosmopolitan Gardens."
2. The research for this essay was funded by the project "CLYMA" Ref. 2011-009 of the Franklin Institute.

to grasp what the world is like and how it is changing" (208). In Setha Low's anthropological understanding, "place attachment" is "the symbolic relationship formed by people giving culturally shared emotional/affective meanings to a particular space or piece of land that provides the basis for the individual's and group's understanding of and relation to the environment" (2). Sociologist David Hummon emphasizes the subjectivity of sense of place, being

> people's subjective perceptions of their environments and their more or less conscious feelings about those environments. Sense of place is inevitably dual in nature, involving both an interpretive perspective *on* the environment and an emotional reaction *to* the environment. . . . Sense of place involves a personal *orientation* toward place, in which ones' understanding of place and one's feelings about place become fused in the context of environmental meaning. (6; emphasis in the original)

As we see in these diverse definitions, sense of place entails the relationship to the land itself as well as to the community; yet, depending on the definition, one or the other is privileged. In the question of language, English seems to privilege the aspect referring to the physical place. Yet the expression "sense of place" does not translate well into Spanish. In Spanish the closest term would be *sentido de arraigo,* emphasizing rootedness and belonging to a community over the physical land. For Rudolfo Anaya, the relational quality of sense of place is what the Spanish term *la tierra* underscores. He argues that the term *la tierra*

> conveys a deeper relationship between man and his place, and it is this kinship to the environment which creates the metaphor and the epiphany in landscape. On one pole of the metaphor stands man, on the other is the raw, majestic and awe-inspiring landscape of the southwest; the epiphany is the natural response to that landscape, a coming together of these two forces. ("Writer's Landscape" 98–99)

Moreover, according to Anaya, the Chicano worldview "was centered in community and its relationship to the earth" ("Aztlán" 234), and he traces the origin of this worldview to the Pueblo Indians, considering "the recognition of the Earth as mother (la sagrada tierra)" ("Aztlán" 239). So much as Anaya claims the Spanish word *la tierra* has deeper implications for the relationship of humans to the land, likewise the Spanish version of sense of place, or *arraigo,* also emphasizes the rootedness in both the land and the community, the close intertwining of landscape and the humans who inhabit it.

A chosen, albeit mythical, place lies at the heart of the creation of Chicano identity, Aztlán. This place is imbued with symbolic, interpretative, and emotional characteristics, as Low and Hummon mention in their understanding of sense of place. Thus, one could argue that much of Chicano identity is enacted in the relationship with both the mythical and physical land, and this becomes evident in some of the texts analyzed. This deep relationship also gives way to an environmental awareness in many cases, in particular in the texts of Anaya and Castillo seen here. However, there also seems to be a generational shift in the interpretation of that relationship, which will be further explored.

The relationship with the land and its meaning is highlighted in Jimmy Santiago Baca's title story "The Importance of a Piece of Paper." The story sets out with the inheritance of the land at the parents' death. One of the three siblings, Adan, wants to sell his part of the land but Pancho refuses to even talk about the issue because "It's everything we stand for. Mom and Dad, their parents, and back generations all said—never sell the land!" (53).[3] Adan realizes the effect his proposal will cause since he too knew that "it had always been understood that the land was never to be sold or broken up" (52), but he needed the money and felt he was entitled to do what he wanted with his share of the inheritance. This contrast of views creates a wall between Pancho and Adan, which Marisol tries to negotiate. Despite Pancho and Marisol's efforts to find money to buy Adan's share and thus keep the land in the family, Adan sells to an Anglo professor, deepening the rift.

The story also emphasizes the connection between the land and the community. As a result of Jaylen's neglect to close a gate, Pancho's prize racehorse, Zapata, runs out and gets killed in a storm. Pancho argues that the obligation of closing gates, stated in the charter of the land grant, makes Jaylen responsible. Jaylen contests the obligation, claiming that he has not seen the legal documents of the charter and that he only understands private property, underscoring once again the sharp contrast between cultural values: handed-down tradition versus modern written legal documents; communal property and the commons versus private property. Jaylen takes the issue to court, and since no one can find the papers, the whole community stands to lose their rights to the land. Despite the family rift, the community appeals to their tradition and asks Adan, a lawyer, to intervene. They will only accept one of their own and ask him, appealing to his sense of community. All the older women go to his office and tell stories of how they helped him as a child. "They didn't ask him, they didn't accuse him or make him feel bad or put him under duress to do something—each simply gave her story with a smile" (*Importance* 93).

---

3. When referring to the fictional works analyzed, the first word of the title of the novel or collection of short stories is indicated in a parenthetical note. Likewise for critical works.

Adan tells Marisol that he can't defend them because there is "a conflict of interest" (94), something she cannot understand. She tells him that it is about "the survival of the village. I don't understand how to fight them, law is confusing, it's not English or Spanish, it's a foreign language. And it's not about you or me anymore, but about all our relatives who came before us, and those who will come after" (94). Adan finally shows up for the community meeting, but only to give advice, clarifying what is at stake if they don't find the charter of the land grant:

> You'll probably have to file individual titles to your land. There'll be litigation in court . . . some people will say it's not your land, you won't be able to afford lawyers to prove that it is, those with money will win. . . . Developers will offer you money and some will sell. Land taxes will go up, you won't be able to afford them. Everything will change . . . (96; ellipses in the original)

The land means all to the community, and their history, lifestyle, and identity are linked to that land. As a result of the impending loss of the land, Mr. Torrez, the oldest man in the village, has a heart attack and dies. At the end of the story, tradition and community prevail. As tradition dictates, the family looked for Mr. Torrez's old suit to bury him in, and in the box they found the original land grant papers. The funeral turns into a celebration of life and tradition, while the judge dismisses the case.

Despite the victory, inevitably, the sense that things are changing is there. Marisol is conscious that once the papers are found, she needs to record the titles at the county office and adapt to modern times. The story highlights the breach between the individual rights that predominate in the Anglo tradition and community rights handed down from the land grants. Adan claims, "It's not a personal thing, not against you or anyone, I'm just selling what's mine in the will, what I inherited from our parents" (*Importance* 51). The cultural clash of communal versus private is similar to the attempts of "Americanizing" Native peoples with the Land Allotment Acts in the early twentieth century.

In the story we see that Marisol, who had left the farm to study, comes home at the death of her parents and finds herself emotionally tied to the land despite the difficulties: "The farm didn't yield much money, and with the hundred acres they had inherited and the little money their parents' insurance had left, they barely made it month to month" (*Importance* 48). Yet she rises early to sit in the apple orchard and watch "the morning sun slowly crest the Manzano peaks to the east" (47) and to hear "a flock of Canadian geese somewhere overhead. In the arroyo sage tree to her left, a red-tailed hawk swooped down and perched" (48). The detailed observation of nature and its presence presides over all her actions. Even her romance with Jaylen begins with their walks along the cottonwoods along the riverbank, and their hikes up the mesa. The peace felt in nature, "mesmerized by the river, whose tiny wavelets enfolded seamlessly into one another in a dance of oneness" (69), marks their relationship. Yet the clash of cultures underlies the whole story as Pancho disapproves of Marisol's relationship with Jaylen, just as his father would have: "The two cultures seldom mixed. Whether anyone admitted or talked about it openly, the ill feelings between Hispanics and gringos were real and present. The differences went deeper than mere cultural customs: there was long-standing, deep resentment toward Anglos for what they had done to Chicanos in the past" (71). At the heart of this resentment is the loss of the land, as is repeated in so many authors.

The threat of losing the land also figures in Ana Castillo's *So Far from God*. Sofia faces innumerable challenges with her four daughters and a husband who abandoned them and only returns when they are already grown. She works hard at her butcher's shop and eventually tries to improve things for the economically depressed community. Her efforts are directed to living off the land, as had their ancestors. Their tradition had been the land but that is changing: "All we have ever known is this life, living off our land, that just gets más smaller y smaller. You know that my familia once had three hundred acres to farm and now all I got left of my father's hard work—and his father's and his father's—is casi nada, just a measly ten acres now, nomás, comadre! Barely enough for my family to live on!" (*So Far* 139). The changes Adan had warned the villagers about in the previous story were taking place here. Anglos and people from other parts of the country were coming and

> buying up land that had belonged to original families, who were being forced to give it up because they just couldn't live off of it no more, and the taxes were too high, and the children went off to Albuquerque or even farther away to work, or out of state to college, or out of the country with the Army, instead of staying home to work on the rancherías. The truth was that most people had not been able to live off their land for the better part of the last fifty years. Outsiders in the past had overused the land so that in some cases it was no good for raising crops or grazing livestock no more. (139)

Among the different ideas for revitalizing the community, the one project that unites the neighbors is that of returning to the land. They agree on "starting a sheep-grazing wool-weaving enterprise" (146). Ana Castillo bases this on the actual initiative of many women's associations in the Southwest, which she briefly mentions in the acknowledgment to the novel. The whole community participates whether "skilled as ranchers or not, many began working in some way for the cooperative—by learning an aspect of the business of sheep grazing, wool scouring, weaving, administration, and selling the wool products" (147). A year later, the wool-weaving cooperative provided the needed outlet for the women: "as cooperative owners of their wool-weaving business they had paying jobs they could count on and were proud of and the mothers among them didn't worry so much about their babies and childcare because they could bring their 'jitos to work" (147). Also, the cooperative gave the women pride in their traditional arts, since the local college began to recognize their skills and award college credits for them. The business also taught them that there was "a growing demand for their hormone-free meat" (147), which encourages them to expand the business of the Carne Buena Meat Market that Sofia had sold to the cooperative. These successes inspire the local people to continue to respond to their traditions. "Above all, to stay on their land, to work it as their families had for many generations, was the desire of everyone who joined in and became everyone's dream" (148).

However, much of their dream is threatened by ACME International, which is hiring women as assemblers and offering a good salary with the possibility of pay increases. The company was subcontracted to chemically clean parts for high-technology weapons for the Pentagon. The women working there begin having nausea and miscarriages, although the company doesn't explain to them the risks of the job, nor does it give them adequate protection. The people of the area didn't understand what was happening but begin to question the industry when they find "dead cows in the pasture, or sick sheep, and that one week late in winter when people woke up each morning to find it raining starlings . . . that dropped dead in mid-flight" (*So Far* 172). And the "Land of Enchantment" of their ancestors becomes the "Land of Entrapment" (172) as their land increasingly fails to produce, given the toxic contamination. The impending loss of the quality of their habitat makes them feel physically and culturally threatened, and they "spoke on the so many things that were killing their land and turning the people of those lands into an endangered species" (241–42).

By the end of the novel, even Sofia loses her land. Years ago, Domingo had bet away the land her father had left her and so she told him to leave. And now that he had returned, he had "given up the deed to the house" (*So Far* 215). The little land she had left and "the house of mud and straw and stucco and in some places brick—which had been her mother's and father's and her grandparent's, for that matter, and in which she and her sister had been born and raised—that house had belonged to *her*. The law, however, based on 'community property,' stated that the house also belonged to her legal husband"

(215). She discovers that Domingo, once again, had caused her ruin and she "was notified by the bank that her home, along with one measly acre next to her property which she had not given up to the Tome collective so as to keep Loca's horses, was being transferred over to a certain Judge *Julano*" (215). After working so hard and losing her four daughters, she realizes that "when it came to retirement time for herself, Sofia would no longer even have the satisfaction of knowing that she would die in her own home. And that really was the final straw for her" (217). The Chicano tragedy has always been the loss of the land. As Comadre Rita commiserates with Sofia:

> You know that my great-great-grandparents were the direct grantees of a land grant from King Felipe II, the very land *I* grew up on as a child. Except that what I grew up on was barely enough to plant a little corn, some calabashes, chiles, nomás, and graze a few goats and sheep to keep us alive.
>
> First the gringos took most of our land away when they took over the territory from Mexico—right after Mexico had taken it from Spain and like my vis-abuelo used to say, 'Ni no' habiamo' dado cuenta,' it all happened so fast! Then, little by little, my familia had to give it up 'cause they couldn't afford it no more, losing business on their churros and cattle. (217)

The loss of the land also appears in Rudolfo Anaya's novels. This loss haunts Clemente in *Heart of Aztlán,* making him lose his identity and self-worth. He anticipates that "When I sell my land I will be cast adrift, there will be no place left to return to, no home to come back to. . . . His soul and his heart were in the earth, and he knew that when he signed he would be cutting the strings of that attachment. It was like setting adrift on an unknown, uncharted ocean" (*Heart* 3). When he signs the contract, he feels that "the roots of his soul pulled away and severed themselves from the earth which had nurtured his life" (3). Many of the townspeople had sold out of necessity, and it broke their souls. Although Clemente swears to return, he is reminded, "They all say that, Clemente, but they don't return. I bought Baca's rancho by the river and he moved to Santa Fe and drank himself to death, I hear" (4). In a later novel, *Alburquerque,* when Abrán meets Lucinda's father, Juan Oso reflects on the importance of the land and the betrayal of the Anglos. He still keeps a copy of the document that General Kearny read to the people of Las Vegas, New Mexico, when he took the city in 1846. In that document Kearny promises friendship, protection, and respect for their traditions:

> I shall not expect you to take up arms and follow me, to fight your own people who may oppose me. But I now tell you, that those who remain peace-

ably at home, attending to their crops and their herds, shall be protected by me, in their property, their persons, and their religion: not a pepper, not an onion, shall be disturbed or taken by my troops, without pay, or by the consent of the owner. (*Alburquerque* 173)

Yet, as Juan Oso adds: "Not an onion, huh. In a few years the Maxwells and Catrons would take most of our land. And it didn't stop there. Remember that onion when you think of our history, they promised not to take it, but they stripped it away, layer by layer, until all we have left is what you see here. El corazón, the core of the onion. They can't strip the heart, it's all we have left" (173). The loss of the land implies the death of the soul for many, unable to adjust to an uprooted life in the city. Others live in resignation or hate. The deep resentment between the Anglo and the Chicano community lies largely in the betrayal over the land.

For an older generation of Chicanos reflected in literature, not only working the land but a close relationship with nature is essential. In Jimmy Santiago Baca's story "Matilda's Garden," when the protagonist gets married, his most severe doubt is whether Matilda will love the land. As he describes the house he plans to build, he is "afraid she might be having reservations" (*Importance* 3), yet watching her he is "awed by the familiar sensation that she seemed more an extension of nature's trees, grasses, and wild flowers than the offspring of humble parents" (4). Matilda's lips tasted of "the fragrance of sage," and her "fingers smelled like wild honeysuckle vines" (4). Matilda shared his "same wonder and love for farm life, and he couldn't express in words the immense satisfaction that welled up in him when he was in the field with her, shovels in their hands, soil under their sneakers, sweat pouring down their brows and backs" (11). Fifty years later, he still cherishes her memory linked to nature. The "old adobe house creaked like an ancient, Mexican ornament, built more for flowers to inhabit than humans; the heady aroma of Matilda's gardens swaddled him in a blanket of heavy, humid sweetness. She was right, of course, she had made the whole farm her garden and nurtured him with her love" (5). As he remembers her last breath, it

> became wild purple lilac in his mind, their vines curling out everywhere, so real to him he was certain that one day the driveway would brim with them. Wild purple lilacs swinging in the wind, seeds blooming at the front door, tendrils shaking against the window glass, nestled in the crevices, purple petals cascading off the roof. Maybe it was her spiritual self working through these images, creating a bridge from her world to his. All he knew was that

somehow she was communicating with him in the way that she loved most, through flowers. (8)

As in all the previous cases, working the land is what grounds this protagonist, and his place is that real and emotional garden created by his wife. For this older generation, an intimate relationship to the land, developed as a result of working and depending on it, is central to their identity. Without the land they are uprooted, something that threatens their identity and self-worth, at many levels: individual, community, and culture.

In contrast, most of the younger characters portrayed by these authors are presented initially as uprooted and with no sense of place or *arraigo*. In fact, several of the stories, such as "The Valentine's Day Card," "Enemies," or "Runaway," in Jimmy Santiago Baca's collection *The Importance of a Piece of Paper* highlight the plight of orphans, having no ties to family or land and not knowing how to anchor themselves in any meaningful relationship. In the case of *So Far from God*, despite Sofia's attachment to the land, her daughters suffer different fates, all marked by gender violence, an essential theme of the novel. Esperanza adopts the Anglo values, becoming a professional journalist. Yet the only way she can progress is by accepting a position as an embedded war reporter during the First Gulf War, where she, together with the soldiers, is taken prisoner and dies. Her body is never found and so cannot return to her land, not even in death. The second daughter, Fe, also buys the "American Dream" wholesale and, in order to purchase her dream house and appliances, accepts a job at ACME, developing cancer and dying. Neither seems to show a deep sense of place. Caridad, after having been brutally attacked by men, does embrace nature, her horses in particular, and turns to herbal remedies. In the end, in a rather mysterious sequence, she does return to the land when she jumps off a cliff and at the bottom witnesses only find the "spirit deity Tsichtinako calling loudly with a voice like wind, guiding the two women back, not out toward the sun's rays or up to the clouds but down, deep within the soft, moist dark earth where Esmeralda and Caridad would be safe and live forever" (*So Far* 211). Sofia's fourth daughter, La Loca, is the only one who had always remained closer to the land and animals, shunning contact with humans. Yet, she dies of AIDS, leaving Sofia alone. The sense of place and community attachment so strong in Sofia is not passed on to her daughters, each of whom meets a negative and premature death.

However, the best illustration of the attempt to restore a sense of place to a younger generation is that of Rudolfo Anaya in his Sonny Baca detective series. Where in his previous work the traditional land-based lifestyle (or its loss) is dominant, in this series Anaya portrays a more contemporary society. In this series, Sonny Baca, a barrio homeboy, but urban nonetheless, has to learn the importance of the land. The four volumes of the series, centered on the four seasons, *Zia Summer, Rio Grande Fall, Shaman Winter,* and *Jemez Spring,* trace this learning process, one of valuing the relationship with land and nature as an integral part of one's identity.

The environmentalist Mitchell Thomashow analyzes the importance of developing a sense of place in this modern world. In *Bringing the Biosphere Home,* he argues that focusing on the local is the first step toward understanding the global: only by exercising a place-based perceptual ecological vision can we begin to understand or fully appreciate the whole biosphere; the global appears by making connections between daily lives and the global political economy (loc. 208).[4] He also argues the need to explore the cultural past with an eye to the landscape, to relate the living experience of the present to that past and to the concerns of the future (loc. 946). Thomashow considers that perceptual ecology entails the need to cultivate sensory awareness and that a sense of place implies considering home, community, ecology, history, landscapes, and ecosystems. Linking one's ideological identity to the lifecycles of community and biosphere is a necessary step (loc. 1036–40).

Similarly, the ecofeminist project of Val Plumwood also tries to articulate the possibility of a sense of place in the modern world. Plumwood strives to establish a "materialist spirituality of place," to describe a culture that would be place-sensitive. She acknowledges that although "mobility rules modernity," in order to understand the "language of the land," a deep acquaintance with some specific place is necessary (231). She advocates an ecological spirituality that would be materialist in that it is based on the material and ecological bases of life, and dialogical in that it would be "communicative, open to the play of more-than-human forces and attentive to the ancestral voices of place and of earth" (229). Plumwood suggests that in traveling, the trip be viewed as an end, not just as the means to another holiday or for professional purposes. She advocates orienting journeying as a project of multiple place encounters in a dialogical manner, as "a communicative project to explore the more-than-human as a source of wonder and wisdom in a revelatory framework of mutual discovery and disclosure" (233). By doing so, we can avoid the monological mode of perceiving the earth, and we can try to address the earth as an agent with a voice, a history, and power. Clearly Plumwood's ideas reflect the attitudes of Anaya's spiritual guides, Eliseo and Lorenza, in these novels.

---

4. "Loc." indicates the location in the e-book.

Thus, with these ideas in mind as ways to develop a sense of place in a modern world, one can read Anaya's series as the process of reconnecting with the land in different ways that would not entail necessarily working the land as the older generation of Chicanos, but finding a deep connection with multiple places. In Anaya's earlier works, the few characters from the "outside" were always misplaced, restless, and lost. In this series, the effort to reconnect is one of the most important aspects where Don Eliseo is teaching Sonny to develop a deep relationship with the land. Sonny Baca is well integrated into modernity but has a weak sense of place, and precisely one of his "lessons" is finding his roots in the land, not his own land but that of the whole region of New Mexico, in order to reinhabit it. The whole series continues with the issues of identity, personal and very significantly cultural, historical, and spiritual. Through his fiction Anaya illustrates what Neil Evernden affirms, that story, geography and self are inextricably bound together (102–3), much the same as Thomashow's insistence of sense of place being the confluence of history and habitat (loc. 2262). Thomashow asserts that the interpenetration of species, people, and landscapes is the basis of any local language and that thus the stories of inhabitation provide the necessary knowledge of habitat and history (loc. 2430), which ground us and shape our identity. Anaya, despite his hybridization of genres and modes, detective fiction, classical bildungsroman or personal essays, incorporates as an essential aspect the intense relationship of humans to nature, intertwining history, stories, and inhabitation. Anaya clearly stated his commitment to his home place in 1977:

> The landscape can always expand. At this point in time I can choose whether or not to expand my landscape. In many ways I already have, but I find that which is honest to me and therefore to my writing comes from my deepest felt experiences, so I choose to stay at the center of the place which is providing me energy, and whose energy is healing me because the exploration into my world is a process through which I come to know myself and my earth better. For the moment, I am content to continue with this exploration, and to convey to my reader the center of my universe. ("A Writer's Landscape" 102)

Anaya's feelings express the same thing as the abovementioned quote from Plumwood when she speaks of place being a source of mutual discovery and disclosure. Yet this deep feeling is not the same as that of Pancho and Marisol, nor Clemente and Sofia for their farm or family land grant. Anaya refers to New Mexico, a broader experience of land, and in this series Sonny learns to connect to this larger landscape. In the first novel, *Zia Summer*, the Zia sun and the summer solstice constitute the chronotope of the novel, a space responsive to history, land, and plot. The approach of the summer solstice has both real and symbolic meaning, both for the detection of the crime and for the learning and initiation of Sonny as a future brujo. Don Eliseo, Sonny's guide, teaches him to pray to the sun every morning. As Sonny prays to the sun, he feels its energy and, "if he learned the way of his abuelos, he was sure the light would enter his soul" (*Zia* 204). Precisely Sonny's increasing awareness of natural cycles and of the relationship of humans to nature and with it, of his Chicano heritage, constitutes the central theme of the novel, displacing the narrative plot of solving the murder mystery and preventing the sabotage.

Another nature motif interwoven into the novel and whose development is parallel to the criminal investigation is that of Don Eliseo's cottonwood tree. The novel begins with Sonny dreaming that his leg is being cut off, only to awaken and hear a chainsaw searing into the branches of the cottonwood that has been tagged dead and ordered to be cut down. The parallels are very clear. Don Eliseo is reluctant to cut it and decides to nurse it back to health, "his ear pressed against the tree, like a doctor to the heartbeat of a patient" (*Zia* 5). Eliseo feels "like that old tree . . . dry, but still alive" (66), and he points out to Sonny that "the raices, Sonny, beneath the earth the roots of all these trees stretch far, connecting to other trees, until the entire valley is connected. You can't kill a tree and not kill the past. The trees are like the gente of the valley, sooner or later we're all related. . . . How can I cut down my history?" (75). This clearly illustrates that sense of *arraigo* as place and community attachment as well as Thomashow's confluence of habitat and history. At the end of the novel, as Sonny returns home to tell Eliseo that he has defeated the criminal Raven and solved Gloria's murder, Eliseo runs out crying "My alamo! A branch put out leaves. Little green leaves, moist and tender. . . . It's a miracle! The tree is alive!" (383). Both victories take place on the summer solstice, but in case a distracted reader forgets what is more important, the murder or the tree, Anaya ends saying that that summer might be remembered as that of Gloria's cult murder, "But the viejecitos of the valley would remember it was the summer when Don Eliseo's tree recovered miraculously and offered forth its green leaves" (386).

In the second novel, *Rio Grande Fall,* nature comes alive, and the spirit world lying within nature provides the clues both to Sonny's past, his values, and to the detection of the new murder he is confronted with. The process of learning that takes place in this novel is precisely one of identifying with his nagual, his animal spirit—part of the Pueblo Indian cosmology—and thus being able to not only attain harmony with nature but also be a part of it. Lorenza, his guide together with Eliseo, tells him that nature is the key to the past, to one's heritage and identity, the "world of nature is our world. . . . Our nature is linked to that of our ancestors, to their beliefs" (*Rio* 121). In his dream-visions he learns to enter that world through a lake and to meet the coyote, his nagual. In these visions, he seems to become a coyote; "their energy flowed to him, filling him with lightness, exuberation. He was running, close to the ground, close to the scents of other animals, running with the coyotes, free, flying" (129). Identification with the coyote is essential, as he must learn its trickster ways in order to defeat Raven, another trickster figure that changes guises but represents evil. The sacredness of the land and the earth is made explicit: it is "full of ancient spirits. Full of knowledge" (26). It "was the meeting ground of spiritual ways. Hispanos and Mexicanos had learned the Pueblo ways" (124). Once again, the intimate relationship between nature, land, history, roots, community, and identity is made patent. Moreover, throughout the series Anaya also stresses the importance of community attachment. In this sense he subverts the generic formula of detective fiction with the lone individualist detective. In all the novels, Sonny clearly enlists the help of the community to solve each murder. To a degree, one could suggest that it is the community who solves the crimes in the present as an effort to redress the crimes of the past, something made evident in the third novel.

Shaman Winter deepens the relationship between history and habitat. The novel, despite the detective plot, delves into more typical Anaya concerns and literary modes such as the rewriting of history and a magical real play of time and alternative realities. In this novel, precisely the awareness of the past and its effects, both cultural and ecological, on the present permeate the plot. Thus Anaya highlights four significant historical periods, the Spanish conquest and Oñate's incursion into New Mexico in 1598, the American conquest of New Mexico by General Kearny in 1846, the lifestyle of the Wild West with Billy the Kid and Sonny's grandfather, and law enforcer Elfego Baca with the present. These moments symbolize Sonny's bloodlines, through his imagined foremothers, tying his present together with that of the community, represented by the four kidnapped girls. Although this novel has this significant aspect of rewriting history in a magical realism mode, the past episodes he links to his present survival have to do not only with political conquest but, rather, with the conquest of the land and the displacement and oppression of indigenous peoples, a kind of ecological imperialism, to use Alfred Crosby's term. Therefore, both the cultural and the ecological aspects of the past are made patent and Anaya forces his characters, and readers, into this awareness, precisely one of the challenges that Thomashow pointed out for attaining a place-based perceptual ecology, necessary for understanding the biosphere. For Sonny, to solve the kidnappings of the present he needs to understand the history of the land and the power relationships inscribed upon it.

The Rio Grande valley could be viewed as the central chronotope of all of Anaya's fiction. The whole valley is viewed as a special, sacred land—a motif repeated throughout the different novels of the series—but it also figures prominently as part of the local economy, and of the tourist and bohemian attraction of New Mexico. In the last of the series, *Jemez Spring,* water takes on special relevance. Anaya continuously portrays the river as inspired, having eyes, voices, faces, moods, and soul: "at each turn the river put on a different face" (*Jemez* 70), but he also comments on the environmental issues connected to the river. The environmentalists, in real life and in the novel, are concerned about the extinction of the silvery minnow in the Rio Grande and how the lack of flooding has negatively affected the cottonwood *bosque,* a habitat for a number of species. The paradoxical effects of the Cochiti Dam and reservoir are discussed, as are the historic water rights of the local people. Before the dam, the floods used to arrive like "the herd of brave bulls, a thundering whoosh of hooves roaring down the streambed to fertilize the cities with lifegiving waters" (44), but no longer. The "river was the alchemist of the valley. The water was the gold rush that swept away the compost," but "now the river was dying. Too many cities siphoning off the water. Too many needs for too little water" (45). This novel clearly takes the step advocated by Thomashow of perceiving the global from the local. Anaya ties the specific problems of the Rio Grande valley to global disputes over water. "It's all about water. Without water our fields die, we die. We become the West Bank Palestinians" (133). Sonny's mentor Eliseo, now a spirit, tells Sonny:

> Future wars will be fought over water, not oil. Sure, the GIs beat Saddam's ill-equipped army, and the first thing they took were the oil fields. But just wait till Turkey says it can build dams on the Euphrates. Then you'll see a real fight. Same on the Jordan, in Africa, and here on the Rio Grande. Wherever a river or an aquifer crosses borders, that equals war. Every nation has to feed its people. Corn, soy, and wheat need water. (177)

Thus, Sonny's sense of place, anchored in the local, allows him to link to a more global perception and concern for the biosphere. And with Sonny's awareness comes that of the reader, who inadvertently learns from the novel.

Different characters in the series have the impulse to try to reinhabit their home place—not always successfully—some of them flounder in a faux new age, while others try to go back to indigenous traditions and lifestyles. Sonny, the protagonist, continues his discovery of his deep rootedness in his home place and traditions, nevertheless trying to balance them with contemporary lifestyles. For Anaya, valuing place, of both the human and the more-than-human-world and their mutual dependence, is a constant feature. He also shares in the freeing of the self from excessive rationalism, similar to Plumwood's materialist (as in the physical, tangible world) spirituality. His magical real strategies attest to a spiritual world and alternative belief systems, which are anchored in nature, particularly in the characters of Lorenza and Eliseo. Sonny Baca begins to enlarge his ethics of proximity to imagining a greater community, one of the whole world, particularly in *Jemez Spring*. Although he does not travel and his dialogic project of communication with multiple places is limited to New Mexico, he does engage in a place-based perceptual ecology like that espoused by Thomashow, a way to value a sense of place without necessarily having to work the land.

In conclusion, *la tierra* and a sense of place are essential components in Chicano identity and traditions. While this rootedness was clear in older generations who worked the land, a change is necessary for contemporary Chicanos, most of whom no longer work the land. As Kate Rigby argues, perhaps we need to conceive of dwelling as "an achievement, something which we have to learn again and again, something which involves conscious commitment" (11), and Anaya's strategy in this series addresses this idea. Sonny clearly learns to reconnect with the land. Anaya himself has expressed his deep sense of place in New Mexico without working the land. In a similar way, urban Chicanos, and indeed all human beings, could learn to listen to their traditions and the voices of the land in order to cultivate a meaningful relationship with the earth that would ground them, personally and culturally, and enable them to attain a place-based perceptual ecology, linking their local reality to our globalized planet. Our identity, humanity, and survival lie in recognizing our embeddedness in the lifecycles of history, community, and habitat. In that sense, as the epigraph of the essay states, we are indeed one with the landscape.

WORKS CITED

Anaya, Rudolfo. *Alburquerque*. New York: Warner Books, 1992. Print.

———. "Aztlán: A Homeland without Boundaries." *Aztlán: Essays on the Chicano Homeland*. Ed. Rudolfo Anaya and Francisco Lomelí. Albuquerque: U of New Mexico P, 1991. 230–41. Print.

———. *Heart of Aztlán*. Albuquerque: U of New Mexico P, 1988. Print.

———. *Jemez Spring*. Albuquerque: U of New Mexico P, 2005. Print.

———. *Río Grande Fall*. New York: Time Warner, 1996. Print.

———. *Shaman Winter*. New York: Time Warner, 1999. Print.

———. "The Writer's Landscape: Epiphany in Landscape." *Latin American Literary Review* 5.10 (Spring–Summer 1997): 98–102. Print.

———. *Zia Summer*. New York: Time Warner, 1995. Print.

Anaya, Rudolfo, and Francisco Lomelí, eds. *Aztlán: Essays on the Chicano Homeland*. Albuquerque: U of New Mexico P, 1991. Print.

Baca, Jimmy Santiago. *The Importance of a Piece of Paper*. New York: Grove, 2004. Print.

Castillo, Ana. *So Far from God*. London: Women's Press, 1994. Print.

Crosby, Alfred. *Ecological Imperialism: The Biological Expansion of Europe, 900–1900*. Cambridge: Cambridge UP, 1986. Print.

Evernden, Neil. "Beyond Ecology: Self, Place, and the Pathetic Fallacy." *The Ecocriticism Reader: Landmarks in Literary Ecology*. Ed. Cheryll Glotfelty and Harold Fromm. Athens: U of Georgia P, 1996, 92–104. Print.

Flys Junquera, Carmen. "Wild Cosmopolitan Gardens: Some Notes towards a Cosmopolitan Sense of Place." *Tamkang Review* 42.1 (December 2011): 3–26. Print.

Heise, Ursula K. *Sense of Place and Sense of Planet: The Environmental Imagination of the Global*. New York: Oxford UP, 2008. Print.

Hummon, David. "Community Attachment: Local Sentiment and Sense of Place." *Place Attachment*. Ed. I. Altman and Setha Low. New York: Plenum, 1992, 253–78. Print.

Low, Setha, and I. Altman. "Introduction." *Place Attachment*. Ed. Altman and Low. New York: Plenum, 1992, 1–12. Print.

Plumwood, Val. *Environmental Culture: The Ecological Crisis of Reason*. London: Routledge, 2002. Print.

Relph, Edward. *Place and Placelessness*. London: Pion, 1976. Print.

Rigby, Kate. *Topographies of the Sacred: The Poetics of Place in European Romanticism*. Charlottesville: U of Virginia P, 2004. Print.

Thomashow, Mitchell. *Bringing the Biosphere Home: Learning to Perceive Global Environmental Change*. Boston: MIT Press, 2001. Kindle e-book.

Tuan, Yi-Fu. *Cosmos and Hearth: A Cosmopolite's Viewpoint*. Minneapolis: U of Minnesota P, 1996. Print.

———. *Space and Place: The Perspective of Experience*. Minneapolis: U of Minnesota P, 1977. Print.

CHAPTER 10

La narración de los linchamientos de los méxicoamericanos en el suroeste de los EEUU en el siglo XIX y principios del XX

ARMANDO MIGUÉLEZ

ESTE ENSAYO trata de la narración de los linchamientos de los méxicoamericanos en el suroeste de los Estados Unidos en el siglo XIX y principios del siglo XX. Se consideran tres tipos de linchamiento en sentido lato: 1) los espontáneos o repentinos, como en el caso de los linchamientos de Antonio Ruiz/William W. Jenkins, Carlos Murrieta y Ramón Cortés; 2) los perpetrados por las masas dirigidas por grupos de vigilantes que se toman la justicia por su mano: el caso de El Monte, la familia Berreyesa, Pancho Daniel, Miguel Soto y los crímenes del condado Amador, California; y 3) los crímenes de estado. El propósito de este trabajo es el de ofrecer algunos ejemplos de estos acontecimientos bajo los periódicos de la época que documentan estos actos inhumanos y execrables; esta vez, bajo la voz de la víctima. Son los textos sobre estas atrocidades que los intelectuales y el pueblo victimizados escribieron como una manera no sólo de producir un documento objetivo sino de crear un texto donde la fuerza expresiva de la palabra pudiera describir también, a nivel simbólico, un acontecimiento tan trágico como los linchamientos.

La conquista del Norte de México por parte de los EEUU en el siglo XIX, fue una guerra expansionista y con tintes religiosos en la que subyacían percepciones de que era una guerra justa, una guerra que debía realizarse porque el otro, el conquistado, era inferior, y, por lo tanto, era el deber del conquistador someterlo a un orden superior. Con esta premisa todas las acciones llevadas a cabo por el usurpador van encaminadas a aniquilar al vasallo moral y físicamente. Ken González-Day ha documentado 352 linchamientos, la mayoría ejercidos contra mexicanos, en el oeste americano de 1850 a 1935. Sólo de 1855 a 1859 en California se produjeron cuarenta y siete linchamientos de los llamados masivos.[1] Con los últimos estudios sobre el tema ya se habla de la identificación de cerca de 700 linchamientos de méxicoamericanos en los EEUU de 1848 a los años de 1930. Y sin identificar, la cifra puede rondar los 2000.

Si a éstos les añadimos los ajusticiamientos y sentencias de muerte individuales cometidos por agentes de la *justicia* o por *kangaroo courts*[2] sin ninguna garantía legal para el acusado, las cifras adquieren proporciones de genocidio. California era una completa anarquía desde 1848 hasta finales del siglo XIX. La ley la imponían las Juntas de Vigilantes que hacían reuniones y decidían quién era bueno y quien era malo, o quién se podía quedar en la ciudad y quién no. En 1855, en el condado de Amador, una de estas Juntas resolvió, según nos dice *El Clamor Público* (28-VIII-1855), expulsar a "toda población española-mexicana-chilena" del Condado. Después que fueron ahorcados los tres mexicanos en Ranchería, sólo por sospecha de que habían tenido parte en los asesinatos que se habían cometido recientemente, se convocó una junta de los ciudadanos americanos, que como era de moda en estos casos, adoptaron un número de resoluciones; entre las más interesantes se incluyen las siguientes:

> RESUELTO: Que nosotros, ciudadanos del condado del Amador, reunidos en convención, creyendo que es necesario para nuestra protección y seguridad, estamos a favor de expeler a toda la población española o mexicana de nuestro condado, a lo menos que puedan dar evidencia satisfactoria de su buen carácter moral, y produzcan testimonio de los medios como obtienen su subsistencia.

> RESUELTO: Que esta Convención recomienda a los ciudadanos de cada precinto examinar el carácter de la población mexicana o chilena en sus distritos respectivos, que la decisión de seis americanos blancos y respetables decidirán quienes serán permitidos quedarse, y su decisión

---

1. Ver Gonzales-Day. *Lynching in the West*, 2006; Carrigan and Webb. *Forgotten Dead*, 2013.

2. *El Clamor Público* de Los Angeles, California publicó en español y francés (dos y veintitres de agosto de 1856) el juicio contra William W. Jenkins, sheriff que mató a Antonio Ruiz por unas deudas. La mera narración de los procedimientos, el jurado (sacado de una lista de cuarenta y ocho, que el periódico enumera) y las declaraciones son una prueba más de la ausencia de garantías y de un estado de derecho que no tenía más que las formalidades que se ven en los westerns.

en todos los casos será definitiva, cuando sea tocante a mexicanos y chilenos.

RESUELTO: Que todo chileno o mexicano que sea expulsado como se requiere por la anterior resolución, se le concederá un tiempo razonable para realizar sus bienes.[3]

Y así sucedía por todos los territorios del ocupado Norte de México.[4] De esta manera las muertes extrajudiciales estaban a la orden del día. Había un plan de exterminio y de exclusión absoluta del que había sido dueño de esa tierra y había pasado a ser subyugado y vencido. El estado de anarquía era tal que Manuel Retes propuso crear un estado Anfisciónico a la manera de las ciudades-estado griegas en las que los ciudadanos del Estado de California fueran puestos bajo la tutela de los cónsules de sus respetivos países ya que las autoridades de California y el gobierno federal de los Estados Unidos eran incapaces de proteger a los ciudadanos que estaban a merced del más fuerte en una verdadera ley de la selva.[5]

La información más exhaustiva sobre esta situación y sobre las atrocidades fortuitas cometidas contra las personas del tronco cultural hispano en los EEUU, con una crítica contundente y veraz, se contiene en la prensa en español por todos los Estados del Suroeste de los EEUU. Si no fuera por estos periódicos, hoy creeríamos que el Oeste Norteamericano fue lo que las películas del oeste nos dicen que era: unos lugares en que sí se violaban las leyes pero para eso estaba el brazo justiciero del sheriff: para impartir y restablecer el orden. Sin embargo, la prensa en español (y también en francés e italiano) de todos estos lugares cuenta y comenta otra historia diferente.

Me voy a referir a solo media docena de periódicos (de más de medio millar existentes): *El Eco del Pacífico* y *El Nuevo* Mundo, publicados en el siglo XIX en San Francisco, California; *El Clamor Público* y *Regeneración*, publicados en el siglo XIX y en las primeras décadas del XX, en Los Angeles, California; y *El Ranchero* y *El Bejareño*, publicados en el siglo XIX en San Antonio, Texas.

---

3. "Muerte a los Españoles." *El Clamor Público*, Los Angeles, California, 28-VIII-1855.

4. Carey McWilliams en 1949 publica su libro *North from Mexico: The Spanish-Speaking People of the United States*. (segunda edición en Greenwood Press, 1968 y traducción *Al Norte de México: el conflicto entre "anglos" e "hispanos"* (México D. F., Siglo XXI,1968) popularizando la denominación de "norte de México" para "el Suroeste de los EEUU" como era habitual nombrar a esta región de los EEUU en la historiografía clásica norteamericana.

5. Manuel Retes, "Expresión simultánea del pueblo de California." *El Clamor Público*, Los Angeles, California, 24-VII-1858.

EL ECO DEL PACÍFICO (1852–1857)

El Eco del Pacífico fue uno de los dos periódicos que se publicaron en San Francisco a mediados del siglo XIX que tienen editoriales fortísimos sobre estas prácticas bárbaras. Por ejemplo, Javier Jofré, el editor de *El Eco del Pacífico,* escribe:

> Nada más gracioso que ver a parte de la prensa de esta ciudad hablar de la superioridad de la raza sajona, sobre todo cuando se trata de compararla con la nuestra. ¡Cómo se pondera su habilidad, su perfeccionamiento, su generosidad! Y en cambio, ¡cuán atraso, cuántos vicios, cuánta incapacidad para gobernarnos en nuestros pueblos y cuánta crueldad desplegamos para martirizar a sus libertadores, nosotros los pícaros, que tenemos el pecado de defender de sus garras nuestros países, nuestros recuerdos, nuestras creencias, nuestra historia, en fin!
>
> Tal es en resumen el resultado de las comparaciones que no una, sino muchas veces, hemos visto establecerse directa o indirectamente por los escritores parciales de este país; pero ¿por qué no ser alguna vez imparciales? les preguntaremos, y se responderá que, exigir semejante cosa es pedir peras al olmo. Se nos responderá, "la Unión Americana es hoy muy grande, y extenderá cada día su área de la libertad sobre la América, debiendo nosotros, que somos de una pobre raza imperfecta, ceder el puesto al pueblo libre por excelencia." Mal que pese a los que así piensan, nosotros diremos que absolutamente no conocen nuestros pueblos. ¡No el ejemplo que hoy presenta Nicaragua, ni esas glorias postizas obtenidas sobre México, serán jamás suficiente fundamento para probar que los pueblos españoles han de sucumbir a un supuesto destino manifiesto, teoría inventada sólo para soplar a la vanidad de un pueblo a quien la fortuna o el capricho ha hecho ser feliz!
>
> Se calcula el atraso de nuestros pueblos por las desgracias por donde han atravesado, y se dice: "es una raza degenerada" ¡Miserable engaño! ¿Desde cuándo la desgracia, hija más bien de la juventud de estos pueblos que de otras causas, es un crimen? ¿A dónde está su degeneración? En esos pueblos más que en la afortunada Unión del Norte se encuentra entre sus individuos honradez y justicia; en esos pueblos no levanta el populacho cadalsos para sacrificar impunemente víctimas inocentes, y si en alguno de ellos se encuentran salteadores, aun no han llegado como aquí, a hacer de esta ocupación una profesión lucrativa. Los expedicionarios que a las órdenes de Walker invadieron la Baja California ¿qué otro nombre merecen? Las depredaciones y crímenes cometidos en aquel territorio aún vibran en nuestros oídos. Fue en la Alta California que se organizó aquella expedición a vista

y paciencia de las autoridades. Pues bien, en ningún país español se habría podido realizar impunemente tan semejante monstruosidad, y si es porque en ellos se respeta el honor y la justicia en sus relaciones externas, que se nos llama degenerados, con orgullo aceptamos desde luego, la tal calificación y dejamos con gusto al pueblo americano la gloria de no poseer estas virtudes.

Jamás haremos al pueblo americano el insulto de negar que no hay honradez entre muchos de sus individuos pero no debemos fijarnos en el pueblo—siempre el pueblo de todos los países es bueno—puede ser oprimido; pero nunca injusto. Es el gobierno a donde debemos fijar nuestra atención. Como nunca hemos visto en este país que se hayan castigado los crímenes cometidos por un populacho inmoral y corrompido, y por el contrario hemos visto que se ha hecho la vista gorda a las empresas ilegales que se han realizado, tenemos el derecho de concluir que, este tan decantado gobierno, o no es justo o es por su debilidad una pura farsa ridícula. Semejante monstruosidad nunca se ha vista en la América española. Resumamos.

Si hay crímenes en nuestros pueblos, ni son de tanta magnitud ni tan descarados como aquí. Si ha inmoralidad en nuestros gobiernos, lo cual no es exacto, pues muchos de ellos son venerados por su honradez y su justicia, han respetado por lo menos para no comprometer el honor de su patria. Ni nuestros pueblos ni nuestros gobiernos han manifestado jamás lo que se ha ostentado particularmente en California. Si *fructibus eorum cognacetis eos* ¿en cuál de las dos razas habrá más vileza y degeneración?[6]

EL NUEVO MUNDO (1864–1868)

El Nuevo Mundo de San Francisco fundado por José María Vigil, uno de los eruditos mexicanos más importantes del siglo XIX, y continuado después por Francisco P. Ramírez (1837–1908) y Felipe Fierro (1825–1881), ahonda también en el problema de la falta de justicia entre la población en general y la mexicana y otras minorías en particular, sin tener que decir que, al publicarse en plena Guerra de Secesión, criticara también la esclavitud como uno de los crímenes más ignominiosos que se pueden cometer entre los seres humanos. "La esclavitud, esa reliquia de la edad media, ese resto de barbarie e inhumanidad, quedará para siempre borrada del suelo de los Estados Unidos," nos dice en un editorial del 3-II-1865. Y el 26-VII-1864 publica el testimonio de un padre, Alejo Baldenebro, que al buscar a su hijo que no vuelve a casa, descubre que fue asesinado con un amigo en las inmediaciones de Virginia City en el

---

6. "Comparaciones," reproducido de *El Eco del Pacífico* de San Francisco en *El Clamor Público* de Los Angeles, California, del 15 de marzo de 1856.

estado de Nevada. El periódico reproduce un interrogatorio entre el intérprete Andrés Ortiz y los empleados de la oficina del fiscal y el fiscal mismo:

> ORTIZ: Señores empleados, ¿pueden Vdes. decir dónde están los cinco hombres que mataron a esos dos mejicanos?
>
> LOS EMPLEADOS: Se les formó un jurado y se fueron libres.
>
> ORTIZ: Y ¿quiénes fueron los testigos de este jurado?
>
> LOS EMPLEADOS: Pues fueron los mismo cinco que los mataron, porque allí no había nadie que viera el pleito sino los vivos matadores y los muertos, y como no hubo quién pidiera en favor de los muertos, se dejaron ir los vivos.
>
> ORTIZ: Cómo es eso señor fiscal, ¿V. no sabe que es pagado por las leyes o el Condado para hablar y defender a los muertos y perseguir a los criminales?
>
> ¿Podrán Vds. mostrarme la causa que tienen por escrito de lo que se ha versado en el jurado del que han sido testigos los malhechores de su mismo crimen y su propia causa?
>
> LOS EMPLEADOS: La enseñaron y la leyeron.
>
> ORTIZ: ¿Vieron Vdes. con qué armas han matado los cinco hombres a los dos mejicanos?
>
> LOS EMPLEADOS: Si, las vimos, los cinco tenían los unos rifles y pistolas de seis tiros (*double barrel shot gun*) y pistola.
>
> ORTIZ: ¿Y saben Vdes. que la raza española está al tanto de conocer lo mismo que cualquier otra gente, que los rifles alcanzan, ofenden y matan a más de 500 yardas, y las escopetas de dos tiros de más calibre que los rifles alcanzan también a más de 100 yardas, y que los dos mejicanos sólo aparece tenían una pistola cada uno de seis tiros?
>
> EL FISCAL (CON SEMBLANTE TACITURNO): Si, pero los dos mejicanos muertos, con sus pistolas comenzaron a tirar primero.
>
> ORTIZ: ¿Encontraron Vdes. alguno de los cinco americanos heridos o alguna de sus bestias en que se batieron?
>
> EL FISCAL: No, sólo los dos mejicanos muertos y uno de sus caballos.
>
> ORTIZ: ¿Cuándo los cinco americanos vinieron a avisar a Vdes. que habían dado muerte a los dos mejicanos, alguno de los cinco o todos manifestaron a Vdes. algún documento u orden de las autoridades del Estado de California o de algunas autoridades competentes del Territorio de Nevada, por donde constara que podían perseguir o parar o arrestar a los dos mejicanos en el camino?

EL FISCAL: No mostraron ninguna orden ni cosa parecida, pero después han venido de otras partes a reclamar parte de las bestias, y como han jurado que era suyas, se les han entregado.

ORTIZ: ¿Cuántas bestias encontraron Vds, en poder de los muertos?

LOS EMPLEADOS: Tenían ocho. Cuatro mulas, tres caballos y un muerto.

ORTIZ: ¿Después de muertos los dos mejicanos, mostraron Vds. a los vencedores la propiedad que tenían o poseían los difuntos?

LOS EMPLEADOS: Si, todo lo reconocieron y dijeron que nada era de ellos.

ORTIZ: ¿Y pueden Vds. darme por escrito un tanto de la última pregunta?

LOS EMPLEADOS: Sí, la dio el juez gratis.

ORTIZ: ¿Podrán Vds. darme una copia de la causa que se ha versado en el jurado por escrito?

LOS EMPLEADOS: Sí la daremos. Cortaron un pedazo de periódico de Virginia City, creo era del papel nombrado Paqut y como decía lo mismo que el original lo tomó Ortiz.

ORTIZ (DESPIDIÉNDOSE): Señores empleados, tanto el señor anciano como yo, damos a Vdes. las gracias por el trabajo que han tenido para despacharnos, advirtiéndoles que yo no supongo en este asunto más que de intérprete y sin interés particular, viniendo en obsequio de la humanidad a acompañar a este señor anciano, que aunque no es mi paisano, siempre es de la misma raza, y les diré a Vdes. que yo no conocía la conducta de los dos muertos; pero señores empleados como quiera que tomen Vdes. u otras personas civilizadas, lo que sobre este asunto se versa y cualquiera que haya sido la conducta de los difuntos yo creo por todo lo que se ve que ha sido una arbitrariedad que se ha cometido contra los dos mejicanos, contra las leyes de los Estados Unidos de Norte América, contra el derecho de gentes, y contra los tratados que los Estados Unidos tiene con las demás naciones.

Lo que ha pasado en este negocio, dice el editorialista, es de tal manera irregular y contrario a los principios más triviales del derecho común, que nunca hubiéramos creído que en un país civilizado, en donde la administración de justicia debe ser una verdad, pudieran cometerse hechos de tal naturaleza, quedando impunes los autores, de tan escandalosos atentados, bajo el pretexto de que *no hubo quien pidiera en favor de los muertos.* Así es que la vindicta pública, la sociedad que se encuentra interesada en la represión del crimen, base única sobre la que pueden reposar las garantías individuales, quedan completamente burladas, desde que el que ha sucumbido a las tiros alevosos de un asesino, no tiene allí de luego a luego, algún deudo o persona de corazón recto que pida justicia y nada más que justicia. Preciso es convenir que esta situación es peor que la del salvaje.[7]

EL CLAMOR PÚBLICO (1855-1859)

Es éste el periódico abanderado de las críticas más agudas y constantes contra los linchamientos. De sus 200 editoriales, una buena parte tienen que ver con las injusticias que se cometían sistemáticamente contra la población española (es decir, mexicana y chilena mayormente) por todo el Estado de California con los asesinatos o linchamientos. La compilación de estos editoriales (unos cincuenta) es imprescindible para conocer la gran implicación de la población hispanounidense y de sus intelectuales en la erradicación de estas prácticas salvajes de hacer justicia porque son documentos incuestionables del amor a la libertad y a la justicia del pueblo mexicano de los EEUU, y también la prueba irrefutable de que la lucha por los derechos civiles (y humanos) de la población mexicana de los EEUU empezó inmediatamente después del Tratado de Guadalupe Hidalgo en 1848. El joven californio Francisco P. Ramírez (contaba sólo con dieciocho años en 1855) se reveló contra la falta de garantías civiles existentes para muchos segmentos de la sociedad decimonónica estadounidense pero sobre todo para las minorías y puso toda su ideología liberal al servicio de su gente. Militaba en el partido republicano (el partido antimonárquico, anti esclavista, anti filibustero, anti *squatters* de aquel entonces) y le costó el exilio (vivió más de la mitad de su vida en México: en Ensenada, Baja California) por oponerse al aparato del poder, a los demócratas esclavistas que pululaban, y controlaban de norte a sur todo el Estado de California. De igual manera, condenaba los linchamientos sin paliativos, desde todos los puntos de vista: el cristiano, el legal, el humanitario, el político. Puso toda su capacidad de convencimiento en sus escritos para poder explicar a sus lectores la barbaridad de los mismos, la crueldad que era matar a un semejante sin las garantías legales en un estado de derecho y basándose sólo en la presunción de culpabilidad por ser quienes eran miembros de una raza definida por el sistema opresor como instintivamente criminal. El linchamiento de Miguel Soto nos lo describe en el periódico así:

> El jueves pasado, Mr. Cyrus Sanford, de la Misión, fue atacado por Miguel Soto y dos otros. Mr. Stockton fue a su socorro, y la pelea continuó por algún tiempo bastante encarnizada. Sanford le dio un balazo a Soto en el muslo; y

---

7. *El Nuevo Mundo*, San Francisco, California, 26-VII-1864.

Soto le dio cuatro balazos al caballo de su antagonista. Soto estando herido, dejó su caballo y corrió a pie, a refugiarse en una especie de ciénaga que estaba cerca. Se cubrió allí todo el cuerpo con lodo y ramas. A este tiempo varios ciudadanos de El Monte (Houstin, King y Ward) llegaron y le pegaron fuego a la yerba hasta que se consumió toda. Esto expuso la posición del astuto ladrón, cuando uno de la partida le tiró un balazo y le dio en el corazón. Inmediatamente le cortaron la cabeza al ladrón y fue llevada a El Monte donde fue reconocida por Mr. Wm. H. Petterson como la cabeza de Miguel Soto, que había sido examinado por el juez Sackett por el robo de la tienda de Mr. Twist hace algún tiempo.

(. . .) Hace unos días, un mexicano llamado Miguel Blanco, fue arrestado y alojado en la cárcel. Ha confesado que Soto, que fue muerto por el pueblo de la Misión, tuvo algo que hacer con el robo de Twist. También ha confesado su propia participación en aquel asalto, y los nombres de toda la cuadrilla. (. . .) Soto, que fue muerto en la Misión por Stockton y Sanford, llevaba una mula cargada de provisiones, y una escopeta reconocida por ser de Don Francisco Mellus, que le prestó a Barton antes de salir en su expedición. Si todo esto es cierto no hay duda que era un criminal; pero su muerte no deja de ser terrible.

Nos dicen de que cuando le pegaron fuego a las ramas y yerbas donde se había ocultado, en la agonía del dolor y de la desesperación hizo un hoyo con las manos para enterrarse. Allí fue muerto: cortada la cabeza y su cuerpo fue abandonado para alimento de los animales y las aves. Por malo que sea un hombre, y halla cometido crímenes que lo hagan detestable a los ojos de la sociedad, siempre el corazón noble se compadece de él; siente lo que es la humanidad, y no persigue a sus semejantes como si fueran otros tantos animales del campo[8].

El 14 de febrero *El Clamor Público* vuelve a dar información de lo que pasó en esta cacería, y lo hace en un especie de "diálogo" con *Los Angeles Star*. Se comparte lo siguiente:

Habiendo visto en *El Clamor Público* del sábado, enero 31, una noticia falsa de los acontecimientos que tuvieron lugar en San Gabriel el jueves anterior consideramos necesario dar una relación correcta de los hechos como fueron.

En la mañana de jueves los Sres. Cyrus Sanford, Gifford y Totten, procedían para la misión. Cerca de la Ranchería vieron venir hacia ellos en

---

8. *El Clamor Público*, Los Angeles, California, 7-II-1857.

el mismo camino, a Wm. M. Stockton a caballo junto con un mexicano; al mismo tiempo había otro mexicano acercándose de un lado, en ángulos rectos con el camino como si para cortarlo y juntarse con Stockton y su compañero. Este hombre había salido de la Misión en compañía con el otro que iba con Stockton, pero se había separado, tomando un camino diferente, que corría casi paralelo. Al ver que Stockton alcanzó al mexicano en el camino de abajo, su compañero cruzó aparentemente como para juntarse con él. Al acercarse, la partida de Sanford que llegaba al mismo tiempo, viendo Stockton que el mexicano que venía estaba armado y de una apariencia sospechosa, le dijo: "Tenga v. cuidado con ese hombre, es un ladrón." Entretanto, Stockton, después de haberse acercado con el mexicano que venía en su camino, le habló, y la siguiente conversación tuvo lugar.

Stockton le preguntó a dónde iba. Él le respondió: "A la casa de Don Julián." Mr. Stockton replicó, "Aquí no vive ningún Don Julián." El extranjero (esto es el mexicano) le respondió: "Sí, es un mexicano." A la que le respondió Stockton: "Está v. equivocado, porque yo conozco todas las casas mexicanas en estos alrededores y no hay tal individuo." El mexicano entonces le dijo, "Pues bien, si v. sabe tanto ¿por qué pregunta?" y volvió su caballo hacia Stockton quien lo evitó. Al mismo tiempo, Sanford, que había oído la advertencia que se le había hecho que tuviera cuidado con el otro hombre que venía, volteó su caballo contra él, viendo esto, los dos extranjeros se echaron a correr y sacaron sus pistolas, Sanford y sus compañeros, con Stockton, los siguieron, otros se juntaron con ellos, pero todos, con excepción de Stockton y Sanford, estando mal montados, no pudieron acercárseles bastante para hacerles un servicio.

Al tiempo de la pelea y corrida, se vio a Diego Navarro montado en un buen caballo, haciendo esfuerzos para unirse con los mexicanos. Se le habló que volviera, oyó pero rehusó obedecer, pero fue alcanzado a lo menos a dos millas y quizás tres millas de su casa, en donde según las representaciones de *El Clamor Público,* estaba echando "brea." Habiéndosele preguntado por qué no se paró cuando se le habló, dijo que uno de los hombres que corría y tiraba a Sanford, le debía un poco de dinero y que había ido para que le pagase. Se le preguntó también cuál era el nombre del hombre, y no lo pudo dar. En la pelea, el caballo de Mr. Sanford recibió tres balazos, dos en el pecho y uno en el pescuezo. Unos de los mexicanos, que había descargado todos sus tiros, dejó su caballo y se metió en una especie de ciénega detrás del molino de Mr. Courtney. Mr. Van Deusen y otros, le prendieron fuego inmediatamente y descubrieron al mexicano enterrado hasta el cuello en el cieno. A este tiempo, llegó Mr. King del Monte. Y viendo al ladrón le dijo que se saliera y se rindiera, lo cual rehusó, y lo despachó con su rifle.

Ahora, tuvo lugar un registro general y un gran número de personas sospechosas fueron tomadas prisioneras, entre ellos a Pedro López y Juan Valenzuela. Fue nombrado un jurado de doce personas por los ciudadanos reunidos, entre los cuales había algunos hijos del país, se les formó un juicio imparcial; en prueba de lo cual un gran número de ellos fueron puestos en libertad. Se probó que Navarro era hombre de mal carácter y peligroso para permitirle vivir en una comunidad pacífica, y que tenía comunicación con partidas de ladrones. Juan Valenzuela es un ofensor viejo. Se le aprobó su participación en varios robos y atentados, y finalmente de haber robado unos carneros, hacía unas noches. A Pedro López se le juzgó como criminal de haber robado una mula y vendida la misma a un tal Hamilton, que perdió 120 dólares por la operación. Además de esto, jamás se le ha visto trabajar, manteniéndose peleando gallos y robando ganado. Cada uno de estos hombres fue sentenciado a morir, y fueron ejecutados. La fábula de que uno de ellos cayó muerto en los brazos de su esposa, jamás tuvo ninguna verdad en ella, pero es una clase de artículos que demasiadas veces, durante el año pasado, han aparecido en aquella publicación incendiaria titulada *El Clamor Público*.

Esta es una traducción tan literal como puédamos [sic] hacerla, del artículo que apareció en el último número de *La Estrella*, con el objeto aparente de atacar y desmentir la noticia que dimos nosotros de aquellos lamentables sucesos, pero para cubrir y paliar la atrocidad de esos ultrajes.

Según esta relación, desde el primer encuentro con los dos mexicanos en el camino, empezó aquella provocante malignidad tan común entre gentes de tan poco valor, y por consiguiente, al ver que Mr. Sanford volteó su caballo contra ellos, sacaron sus pistolas para defenderse, y se echaron a correr. Uno de ellos se vió muy apurado y se metió en la ciénega mencionada en donde quemaron la yerba que estaba alrededor y fue muerto de dos balazos. Su cuerpo fue llevado a la Misión en una mula, en donde recibió los más execrables insultos.

El "gran número de personas sospechosas" que dice, fueron todos los mexicanos o individuos de raza española que había en San Gabriel. A todos los tomaron prisioneros y los reunieron en frente de la iglesia. Allí estaban cuando trajeron el cuerpo del mexicano que había sido muerto en la ciénega. Uno de los mexicanos que fueron arrestados, en cuya veracidad ponemos la mayor confianza por hacer mucho tiempo que lo conocemos, nos ha dado la información siguiente: "Cuando trajeron el cuerpo, un Juez de Paz de la Misión sacó su cuchillo y le cortó la cabeza, (aunque varios americanos se oponían a ello) y la rodó con el pie como si fuera una piedra; después le clavó el puñal varias veces en el pecho con una brutalidad raras veces vista entre los mismo bárbaros. Soy de opinión que no hubo jurado ni juicio ninguno, porque apenas hacía quince minutos que habían sido tomados prisioneros Juan Valenzuela, Diego Navarro y Pedro López, cuando vimos salir de un cuarto al mismo Juez de Paz con las cuerdas en las manos. Aunque todo esto sucedía a nuestra vista, no creíamos que iban a ejecutar a estos pobres hombres, tan precipitadamente, sin un juicio formal y sin pruebas de su crimen."

Fueron conducidos a un árbol y allí los suspendieron, pero como se les cortó la cuerda, cayeron al suelo y fueron muertos a balazos. Estamos listos para probar que "la fábula de que uno caía muerto en brazos de su esposa" es demasiada verdadera. La esposa de Diego Navarro se abrazó con él después de había recibido el golpe fatal y expiró (Navarro) entre sus brazos.

Al tiempo que Diego Navarro estaba echando "brea," su padre lo llamaba para esta ciudad, y se preparaba a salir con una carreta de trigo, e iba a traer los bueyes. Con este objeto montó a caballo, y si fue perseguido con siniestras intenciones, su propia seguridad le obligaba a huir de sus asesinos, lo cual es muy susceptible que todos lo hubieran hecho bajo las mismas circunstancias. Navarro era el más inocente de todos, era natural de este pueblo, y los que lo conocen aseguran que jamás se ha sabido nada contra su conducta. El testimonio de todos los hijos del país es suficiente para refutar la desvergonzada aserción que se hace contra él como que era "hombre de mal carácter y peligroso para dejarlo vivir en una comunidad pacífica." ¡Hasta dónde llega el cúmulo de la desfachatez y la mentira!

Con respecto a la "fábula" de los carneros que "robó" Juan Valenzuela, diremos en dos palabras cómo tuvo su origen. Se habían perdido unos carneros al Sr. Muñoz, y preguntando por ellos, un amigo le dijo que en la noche anterior le parecía haber oído el balido de un carnero en la casa de Juan Valenzuela, pero como estaba tan atemorizado por los temblores, no le aseguraba si era cierto o no. El Sr. Muñoz puso muy poca atención a ese aviso, porque no creía que una persona como Juan Valenzuela fuese capaz de robarle. Pedro López era un pobre y como es bien sabido que los infelices no tienen "voz ni voto" como se dice generalmente, fue ejecutado alevosamente por una cuadrilla de "hombres," que olvidándose de las leyes y del honor de su país, usurparon la autoridad y el nombre sagrado del "pueblo," con el objeto de conseguir un vil venganza.

Es falso que hubo jurado nombrado por el "pueblo," y que entre éste había algunos hijos del país, porque todos fueron tomados prisioneros; o se quiere decir que los prisioneros se juzgaron unos a los otros, es una nueva invención de "justicia." Y si hubo jurado ¿quién le dio autoridad para asesinar a sus conciudadanos? ¿las leyes de los Estados Unidos autorizan semejantes procedimientos? ¿En qué tiempo vivimos? ¿Es barbarie o civilización lo que nos enseña? ¿En qué país se ha visto a los jueces de paz condenar a la pena capital? Estas son cuestiones, que si no se reflexiona su solución por un momento, traerán a la imaginación la horrorosa atrocidad de los acontecimientos de San Gabriel, que para siempre serán una marca indeleble de infamia para los que tomaron parte en ellos.

Se ha dicho en honor del pueblo americano, que muchos de ellos se desesperaron por salvar a los infelices; hicieron todo lo posible para conseguirlo; pero con solo esto jamás se nos olvidará su noble conducta. Los buenos ciudadanos de este pueblo también han condenado con indignación aquellos asesinatos con excepción del redactor de *La Estrella,* que no solo aprueba tan horribles procedimientos, sino que desgarra el corazón de sus padres, madres, esposas y hermanas, publicando al mundo entero que eran "unos criminales de la más baja clase." ¡Pobres padres, desventuradas esposas, hermanos desgraciados! ¡Hasta qué grado de infamia os ha puesto la acrimonia de este escritor! Pero ya murieron: compadezcámonos de su suerte: olvidemos sus faltas: respetemos su memoria: porque eran nuestros hermanos. El que muere por malo que sea, debe ser respetado: ya está tranquilo en el sepulcro, y no se gana nada con recordar sentimientos desagradables.

Ahora nos falta decir una palabra al editor de *La Estrella.* Siempre que ha tratado de nosotros, ha preguntado al pueblo por qué nos protege y nos sostiene. Hace tiempo que solo se ocupa en divulgar calumnias contra *El Clamor Público,* hemos hecho poca atención a sus ataques, despreciando la bajeza servil de su autor. Pero si su objeto es derribar a este periódico, esperábamos que lo hiciera más caballerosamente, que titulándonos de "incendiarios" porque muchos que no pueden entender la verdad, llegan de creerse de sus falsas representaciones. Que para darnos semejante título se funda en la defensa que hacemos de los infelices que fueron sacrificados en San Gabriel, tenemos el honor de informarle, si no ignora, que este periódico ha sido establecido con el único objeto de defender a nuestros hermanos y compatriotas, que por todas partes son vejados y atropellados, y que si hubiera más garantías individuales, podríamos publicar ciertas verdades que serían demasiado amargas para este tiempo, sin embargo creemos que todo sea inútil porque es lo mismo que predicar en desierto.[9]

Podemos ver los discursos contradictorios de ambas realidades. Lo que encoraginaba a personas como Francisco P. Ramírez era que ante el beneficio

---

9. *El Clamor Público,* Los Angeles, California, 7-II-1857.

de la duda estas huestes del poder popular decidían por su cuenta y riesgo contra la vida de las personas y el estado protector, que supuestamente estaba ausente, se hacía el desaparecido. Y estaba ausente para perseguir al delincuente y estaba ausente para perseguir a los que tomaban la justicia por su mano. El estado era cómplice del genocidio que se estaba perpetuando, nos dicen los textos de la prensa mexicana.

En otra ocasión Francisco P. Ramírez reflexiona sobre la muerte de Cipriano Sandoval, que, más tarde, se demostró que era inocente del cargo que se le imputaba, la muerte del Mayor General Bean, y dice en un escrito:

> Como para demostrar cuánta precaución es necesaria en los movimientos populares contra el crimen, aun cuando los motores tengan el mayor conocimiento y el mejor corazón, mencionaremos un hecho casi olvidado en nuestra historia. Entre siete personas que han sido ahorcadas en la loma de esta ciudad, o en otra parte, durante los últimos siete años, por el pueblo de Los Ángeles, sin autoridad legal, uno era enteramente inocente del crimen que se le imputaba
>
> ¡Uno era pues inocente¡ -¡Oh verdad terrible!
>
> El nombre de aquel desgraciado era Cipriano Sandoval. Su mismo nombre indica su nacimiento. Era un trabajador simple y obscuro, que tuvo la desgracia de hallarse en San Gabriel, en donde vivía sobrio y tranquilo y trabajaba industriosamente en su oficio, en la época cuando un distinguido ciudadano, el Mayor General J. H. Bean, a deshoras de la noche fue herido mortalmente en la calle. El resto de su historia es muy breve. Las mujeres indias de aquel vecindario señalaron al autor de este hecho; y muchos de los más juiciosos creían que estas mujeres no tenían motivo para mentir. Es terrible reflexionar que el infeliz zapatero, Cipriano, fue sacrificado al lado de dos supuestos asesinos, y en medio de la graciosas felicitaciones prodigadas sobre uno cuya mejor fortuna era de tener amigos ricos e influyentes. Las lamentaciones moribundas de este último, revelaron poco después toda la verdad, si no era bastante conocida anteriormente.
>
> Este acontecimiento sucedió en el año de 1852. Aquellos que por si acaso se acuerden de algunos pormenores de esto, preguntarán por los lugares una vez ocupados por los autores principales en aquella tragedia; y ojalá sean perdonados. ¡Oh Dios eternamente justo, si creen, "cuán inescrutables son tus designios" y que la retribución no pertenece al hombre, pero queda en tu mano poderosa! El castigo del inocente; el triunfo del crimen orgulloso y potente. Esta es la justicia de este mundo. ¡Grande y solemne misterio!
>
> Creemos que hubo una propiedad singular, aunque sin pensarlo, en cambiar el lugar de ejecución, cuando el séptimo fue lanzado a la eterni-

dad el sábado pasado; porque consagrada estaba ya la tierra en donde había caído ya la sangre de la inocencia. Todo aquel cuyo corazón sea susceptible de las más tiernas sensibilidades, al ver las áridas crestas de aquella loma fatal, que derrame una lágrima—no sin una oración—por el alma del pobre Sandoval ¡Descanse en paz!"[10]

EL RANCHERO Y EL BEJAREÑO (SIGLO XIX)

Los periódicos de San Antonio, Texas, *El Ranchero* y *El Bejareño*, publicados en el siglo XIX, también confrontaron la discriminación y la carencia de derechos y el aniquilamiento civil a los que se enfrentaba la población mexicana por los seguidores de los *Know-Nothings* y de otros partidos. En *El Ranchero* de San Antonio, José Agustín Quintero (1829–1885), expone la ideología racista y sectaria de los *Know-Nothings* del siguiente modo:

> Con indignación hemos leído un artículo publicando en el *Bastrop Advertiser*, periódico que hace algún tiempo ha declarado guerra a muerte a todo lo que no es americano, y que por la hiel como desahoga su ira contra los mexicanos, lo mismo que por la degradación y cobardía de su redactores, ha alcanzado algún renombre en la arena periodística. Al publicar algunos extractos del mencionado artículo nos anima la esperanza de que el mayor número de nuestros lectores comprenderá cuán grave es la situación actual y cuán imperiosa la necesidad de que se unan todos como un solo hombre bajo la bandera democrática, para repeler los ataques de un enemigo implacable que no duerme y ha tiempo busca la ocasión de dividir a los demócratas para obtener la victoria. Recuerden nuestros lectores que en algunas ciudades el partido *Know Nothings* ha alcanzado el triunfo empleando la fuerza, el engaño, el crimen y el asesinato.
>
> El pueblo mejicano no puede, ni quiere, ni debe cooperar de ningún modo al éxito de aquellos que no les tratan como conciudadanos sino como viles ilotas a quienes se niegan los derechos más puros al hombre libre. Véase, pues, la necesidad de no abandonar las filas de nuestro partido, de marchar todos juntos como hermanos bajo el pendón de la igualdad y de la fraternidad y prescindir de la amistad que sintamos hacia algunos malcontentos o alucinados que han desertado de la falange democrática sin pensar que su imprudente conducta puede tener tal vez por resultado la división y derrota de nuestro partido. He aquí lo que dice el *Bastrop Advertiser*: "El

---

10. "Cipriano Sandoval (Una reminiscencia)." *El Clamor Público*, Los Angeles, California, 21-II-1857.

pueblo de Texas tiene más de la mitad de la población alemana, suficiente en número para dar una influencia preponderante a cualquier partido, hay sin embargo otro elemento todavía más peligro y destructivo. Aludimos a los mejicanos que votan. No tenemos documentos a mano para presentar a nuestros lectores el número exacto de *greasers* a quienes se permite el derecho al sufragio; pero suponemos por observación personal que en la parte occidental del río de San Antonio no hay menos de cuatro mil de esos cobrizos bribones. Dicen que se lo mandan sus amos. Sería un insulto al buen sentido del pueblo de Texas procurar describir el carácter de esta clase de votantes. Todos los hombres francos de cualquier partido que sean, admiten que son incapaces de apreciar los derechos y privilegios que se les han concedido y ninguno negará que son ignorantes, venales, prostituidos, viles y estúpidos. Apenas hay un rasgo bueno en el carácter mejicano y vanamente se el buscaría en la raza entera que hay en Texas. Educadlos y será traidores. Dadles riquezas y poder y abusarán de ellas. Y sin embargo estos hombres en conexión con los alemanes abolicionistas de Tejas, contrariaron cinco o seis mil votos de hombres blancos y vencieron la boleta americana. A los lectores que piensen (no importa a qué partido pertenezcan) hacemos esta pregunta. ¿Queréis reconocer a los mexicanos como vuestros iguales social, moral o políticamente? ¿queréis que el compañero de vuestros criados y el marido de vuestra esclava esté al lado de vosotros durante la elección o anule vuestro voto que ha sido dado con todo el conocimiento de los hombres y de las medidas que se discuten? ¿Queréis que esa raza donde ninguno es superior a vuestros negros en moral, educación o delicadeza y con frecuencia aún mucho más serviles compitan con vosotros el inestimable privilegio de votar? Nosotros os decimos conciudadanos de Tejas (y no nos importa si estáis opuestos o en favor del movimiento Americano) si animáis a los mejicanos a que voten, alimentaréis una serpiente que os está envenenando ahora y continuará emponzoñando el punto más vulnerable que tengáis. Vosotros dais vida política y poder a aquellos cuyas afinidades y simpatías no son por vosotros sino por vuestros esclavos. Vosotros armáis una banda de hombres que os despojará de vuestras propiedades como ya lo han hecho con otros. Vosotros incorporáis bajo la bandera de la Democracia un ejército de abolicionistas, bajos, ignorantes y estúpidos. Vosotros saludáis como vuestros hermanos políticos a aquellos a quienes aborrecéis y despreciáis en las relaciones sociales. Vosotros desencadenáis el viento. Fuerza será que tengáis por fruto la tempestad. No nos oponemos a darles poder político porque estén congregados contra el partido americano. Nosotros queremos privarles de los derechos y privilegios de un ciudadano libre porque son *instrumentos de un sacerdocio corrompido, forzados a obedecer al mandato de todo fraile y villano* de capucha que pasa alegremente la vida yendo del fandango de media noche al confesionario, y del burdel al altar. Nosotros queremos privarles del derecho de votar en la elecciones porque un hinchado Jesuitismo gobierna sus conciencias, guía sus juicios y les dicta como han de dar su voto. Queremos impedir su intervención en todo asunto público porque la misma religión que profesan es Anti-americana y contraria a los republicanos. Finalmente les queremos privar de todo derecho porque son un estorbo social y porque queremos que sean Americanos los que gobiernen la República."[11]

REGENERACIÓN (PRIMERAS DÉCADAS DEL SIGLO XX)

Por último, Práxedes G. Guerrero (1882–1910), ya en el siglo XX, a menos de dos meses de su propia muerte en los albores de la Revolución Mexicana, escribe un artículo demoledor a raíz del linchamiento de Antonio Rodríguez en Rocksprings, Texas el 4 de noviembre de 1910:

Quemaron vivo a un hombre.

¿Dónde?
En la nación modelo, en la tierra de la libertad, en el lugar de los bravos, en el pedazo de suelo que todavía no sale de la sombra proyectada por la horca de John Brown; en los Estados Unidos, en un pueblo de Texas, llamado Rock Springs.
¿Cuándo?
Hoy, en el año décimo del siglo. En la época de los aeroplanos y los dirigibles, de la telegrafía inalámbrica, de las maravillosas rotativas, de los congresos de paz, de las sociedades humanitarias y animalitarias.
¿Quiénes?
Una multitud de "hombres" blancos, para usar del nombre que ellos gustan: "hombres blancos, blancos, blancos."
Quienes quemaron vivos a ese hombre no fueron hordas de caníbales, ni fueron negros del África Ecuatorial, no fueron salvajes de la Malasia, no fueron inquisidores españoles, no fueron apaches ni pieles rojas, ni abisinios, no fueron bárbaros escitas, ni trogloditas, ni analfabetas desnudos habitantes de las selvas; fueron descendientes de Washington, de Lincoln, de Franklin; fue una muchedumbre bien vestida, educada, orgullosa de sus virtudes, civilizada; fueron ciudadanos y *hombres* blancos de los Estados Unidos.

---

11. "Los mexicanos y los *Know-Nothings*." *El Ranchero*, San Antonio, Texas, 4-VII-1856.

Progreso, Civilización, Cultura, Humanitarismo. Mentiras hechas pavesas sobre los huesos calcinados de Antonio Rodríguez. Fantasías muertas de asfixia en el humo pestilente de la hoguera de Rock Springs. Hay escuelas en cada pueblo y en cada ranchería de Texas, por esas escuelas pasaron cuando niños los *hombres* de la multitud linchadora, en ellas se moldeó su intelecto, de ahí salieron para acercar tizones a la carne de un hombre vivo y decir días después del atentado, que han hecho bien que han obrado justicieramente. Escuelas que educan a los hombres para lanzarlos más allá de donde están la fieras.[12]

CONCLUSIÓN

Vemos por estos textos que el pueblo mexicano del norte de México vencido en la Guerra Mexicano-americana de 1847, sufrió lo indecible como tal y que se revolvió contra la conquista de su tierra por medio de la palabra y de los pocos recursos legales que tenía a su disposición. Esta imposición fue percibida por los méxicanoamericanos que quedaron en los territorios ocupados no como un avance con respecto a la etapa histórica anterior bajo el México independiente, como quiere hacernos ver la historiografía norteamericana sino al contrario, los mexicanos (tejanos, californianos, arizonenses, nuevomexicanos, colorenses) se vieron a sí mismos retrocediendo en todos los aspectos de su vida personal, social, política y cultural. Los linchamientos contra ellos y contra las demás minorías raciales, como negros, indios, y chinos (e incluso contra los anglos pobres), son una prueba de ello. Irrefututable también es el hecho de que no predominaba en estos territorios el imperio de la ley ni se hacía uso de los mecanismos para imponerla. La prosa de estos textos, hermosos en su forma literaria y rotundos en sus planteamientos lógicos, consideraron, desde un principio, a los linchamientos como actos cometidos por un pueblo bruto e incivilizado que nada tenía que ver con la Constitución norteamericana de 1787. Aquello era un territorio sin ley o dominado por la ley del más fuerte, del vencedor, sin instituciones democráticas o alteradas, viciadas y vaciadas de valor a punta de pistola. Las tradiciones e instituciones políticas mexicanas de corte liberal heredadas de la Revolución Francesa, de las Cortes de Cádiz, y de los pensadores que impulsaron los movimientos insurgentes de los países hispanoamericanos que predominaban en los territorios conquistados, fueron abolidas o aniquiladas por completo. Sus habitantes se convirtieron de la noche a la mañana en extranjeros en su propia tierra y

---

12. Práxedes G. Guerrero, "¡Blancos, blancos!" *Regeneración*, Los Angeles, California, 19-XI-1910, pág. 2, cols. 2–3.

subyugados por un sistema déspota y racista que les impidió conservar sus tradiciones, lengua y cultura en general.

Ante las mayores aberraciones e ignominias cometidas contra ellos por el nuevo poder impuesto desde Washington sólo podían defenderse desesperadamente y poner su propio punto de vista en los desgarradores relatos de las mismas. Hoy, estos textos son una prueba de la madurez cultural y superioridad moral de este pueblo frente al agresor. Son un ejemplo de coraje, entereza e inteligencia ante la adversidad y el crimen de estado, un ejemplo para afrontar los retos culturales, políticos y sociales de hoy en día por parte de la comunidad hispanounidense de los EEUU.

OBRAS CITADAS

Bassets, Marc. "La memoria rescatada de los mexicanos linchados." *El País*. 1 Mar. 2015. http://internacional.elpais.com/internacional/2015/02/28/actualidad/1425159560_545362.html. Web.

Carrigan, William D. and Clive Webb. *Forgotten Dead. Mob Violence against Mexicans in the United States, 1848–1928*. New York: Oxford Press, 2013. Print.

———. "When Americans Lynched Mexicans. *New York Times*. 20 Feb. 2015. http://www.nytimes.com/2015/02/20/opinion/when-americans-lynched-mexicans.html. Web.

"Cipriano Sandoval (Una reminiscencia)." *El Clamor Público*, Los Angeles, California, 21-II-1857. Print.

Gonzales-Day, Ken. *Lynching in the West*. Durham, NC: Duke UP, 2006. Print.

Guerreo, Práxedes. "¡Blancos, blancos!" *Regeneración*, Los Angeles, California, 19-XI-1910. Print.

"Los mexicanos y los Know-Nothings." *El Ranchero*, San Antonio, Texas, 4-VII-1856. Print.

McWilliams, Carey. *North from Mexico: The Spanish-Speaking People of the United States*. New York: Praeger, 1949. Print.

"Muerte a los Españoles." *El Clamor Público*, Los Angeles, California, 28-VIII-1855. Print.

"Muerte de Miguel Soto en San Gabriel." *El Clamor Público*, Los Angeles, California, 7-II-1857. Print.

Retes, Manuel. "Expresión simultánea del pueblo de California," *El Clamor Público*, Los Angeles, California, 24-VII-1858. Print.

CONTRIBUTORS

ABOUT THE EDITORS

JESÚS ROSALES was born in Durango, Mexico, and raised in Santa Barbara, California. He received his BA from the University of California, Los Angeles, and his MA and PhD from Stanford University. Rosales's main research interests deal with Chicana/o literary history and Chicana/o literature written in Spanish. He has written *Thinking en español: Interviews with Critics of Chicana/o Literature* (University of Arizona Press, 2014) and *Alejandro Morales: Encuentro, historia y compromiso social* (Peter Lang, 1999). Rosales is the founder and editor of *Puentes: Revista méxico-chicana de literatura, cultura y arte*. He is currently an Associate Professor of Chicano literature at Arizona State University.

VANESSA FONSECA was born and raised in New Mexico. She received her BA in Spanish and her MA in Southwest Hispanic Studies from the University of New Mexico. Her PhD is in Spanish Cultural Studies, with an emphasis in Chicano literature from Arizona State University. She has published in *Puentes: Revista méxico-chicana de literatura, cultura y arte*, *Chicana/Latina Studies: The Journal of Mujeres Activas en Letras y Cambio Social,* and *Chiricú: Latina/o Literatures, Arts, and Cultures,* among others. She is the Co-Director for the *Following the Manito Trail* project, which looks at the Hispanic New Mexican, or Manito, diaspora from the mid-1800s to the present. She is currently an Assistant Professor of English at Arizona State University.

ABOUT THE CONTRIBUTORS

JULIO CAÑERO is an Associate Professor in the Department of Modern Philology and Director (2013–present) of the Benjamin Franklin Institute of North American Studies at the University of Alcalá-Henares (Spain). He also coordinates the Master's program in North American Studies. Cañero received his MA and PhD in English Philology from the University of Alcalá. His research focuses on the study of U.S. literature, society, and culture and has published the following books: a co-edited collection titled *The Chicano Imagination: A Collection of Essays by Francisco Lomelí* (2012) and *Nuevas Reflexiones en torno a la literatura y cultura chicana* (2010), which includes his chapter "Dos décadas de estudios de España sobre la población hispana en los Estados Unidos: El Instituto Franklin y la presente edición como ejemplos." Cañero is the Assistant Editor of *Camino Real*, a peer-reviewed and multidisciplinary journal associated with the Franklin Institute, whose focus is Hispanic North American studies.

CARMEN LYDIA FLYS JUNQUERA is an Associate Professor of American Literature in the Department of Modern Philology at the University of Alcalá, Henares (Spain). She is also a member of the board for the Benjamin Franklin Research Institute of American Studies. Her areas of interest include contemporary ethnic American literature—including Latinos, African Americans, and Native Americans—sense of place, ecocriticism, environmental justice, border issues, and cultural and literary mestizaje. In 2010 Flys Junquera was elected President of the European Association for the Study of Literature, Culture, and Environment (EASLCE) and currently serves on the advisory board for the organization. She has co-edited the following books: *El Nuevo Horizonte España/Estados Unidos* (2001); *Family Reflections: Representing the Contemporary American Family in the Arts* (2007); *Paisajes culturales: Herencia y Conservación / Cultural Landscapes: Heritage and Conservation* (2010); and *Ecocríticas. Literatura y Medio Ambiente* (2010). She has served as co-guest editor of special volumes on ecocriticism for the following Spanish journals: *Nerter* in 2010 and *Revista Canaria de Estudios Ingleses* in 2012. She is the general editor of *Ecozon@. European Journal of Literature, Culture, and Environment*. She also is the coordinator of the research grant *Cultura, Literatura y Medio Ambiente* (CLYMA), which aims to create an ecocritical book series at the Benjamin Franklin Institute.

VÍCTOR FUENTES received his PhD in Romance Languages and Literatures from New York University in 1964. He taught at the University of California, Santa Barbara, from 1965 to 2003, where he served as Professor of Spanish Literature and for several years as Chair of the Department of Spanish and Portuguese. In 2003 he was named Professor Emeritus at UCSB. Fuentes's most important works include *La marcha al pueblo en las letras españolas: 1917–1936* (2006); *El cántico material y espiritual de César Vallejo* (1981); *Galdós, demócrata y republicano: escritor y discursos 1907–1913* (1982); *Benjamín Jarnés: biografía y metaficción* (1989); *Buñuel en México: iluminaciones sobre una pantalla pobre* (1993); *Buñuel, del surrealismo al terrorismo* (2013); *California hispano-mexicana: una nueva narración histórico-cultural* (2014); *César Chávez y la Unión: una historia victoriosa de los de abajo*

(2015). Fuentes's creative works include *Morir en Isla Vista* (1999) and *Bio-Grafía americana* (2008).

JUAN PABLO GIL-OSLE completed his doctorate at the University of Chicago and is currently an Associate Professor of Spanish Golden Age literature at Arizona State University after having held positions at the University of Michigan and Arkansas State University. His recent publications focus on the representations of friendship in early modern culture, on the relationship between word and image, and on gender studies. In the book *Amistades imperfectas: del Humanismo a la Ilustración*, Gil-Osle explores similarities and divergences between premodern and modern social models of friendship. His emphasis on the connection between early modern transformations of the institution of friendship and the opposition between current, contrasting social models grounded in solidarity, on one hand, and individualism, on the other, makes the book relevant to a deeper understanding of the history of intellectual debates on neoliberal and welfare policies in the United States and Europe. In addition, Gil-Osle's interest in visual and digital portrayals of the Golden Age has resulted in his presidency of the Early Modern Image and Text Society (Emit Society), and his co-editorship of the journal *Laberinto*. Upcoming projects include a book about gender and visual culture in the representation of early modern friendship, a monograph on patronage in Tirso de Molina's Los Cigarrales de Toledo, and a number of publications on the matrix between new media commemorations of Spanish and Basque early modern culture, history, and nationhood.

MANUEL M. MARTÍN-RODRÍGUEZ is Professor of Literature and founding faculty at the University of California, Merced. He has published the books *The Textual Outlaw: Reading John Rechy in the 21st Century* (co-edited with Beth Hernandez-Jason, Universidad de Alcalá de Henares, 2015), *Cantas a Marte y das batalla a Apolo: Cinco estudios sobre Gaspar de Villagrá* (Academia Norteamericana de la Lengua Española, 2014), *With a Book in Their Hands: Chicano/a Readers and Readerships Across the Centuries* (University of New Mexico Press, 2014, edited; recipient of a 2015 International Latino Book Award), a scholarly edition of Gaspar de Villagrá's *Historia de la nveva Mexico* (Universidad de Alcalá de Henares, 2010), *Gaspar de Villagrá: Legista, soldado y poeta* (Universidad de León, 2009), *Life in Search of Readers: Reading (in) Chicano/a Literature* (University of New Mexico Press, 2003), *La voz urgente: Antología de literatura chicana en español* (Editorial Fundamentos, 1995, 1999, and 2006), and *Rolando Hinojosa y su "cronicón" chicano: Una novela del lector* (Universidad de Sevilla, 1993). His scholarly articles have appeared in edited volumes and journals, including *PMLA, Modern Language Quarterly, The Bilingual Review, The Americas Review, La Palabra y el Hombre, Hispania, Revista Iberoamericana, Latin American Literary Review, REDEN*, and *Aztlán*, among others. Martín-Rodríguez is also the publisher of alternaCtive-publicaCtions, a virtual press that has featured numerous Latino/a authors. He serves on the National Committee of the Tomás Rivera Mexican American Children's Book Award, and is an elected Académico de Número (permanent member) of the Academia Norteamericana de la Lengua Española.

ARMANDO MIGUÉLEZ is the Director of the Academic Language Institute (A.L.I.) in Alicante, Spain, and Director of the Centro de Estudios Hispanounidenses of Miguel Hernández University. His undergraduate studies were completed at the Universidad de Salamanca and the Universidad Complutense de Madrid, and his graduate studies in Madrid and the United States. He has done extensive research to recover Spanish-language literature in the United States, with emphasis on the literary production of Mexican Americans prior to the Chicano movement. His publications include *Literatura de la Revolución Mexicana en el exilio: Fuentes para su estudio* (México D. F.: UNAM, 1997) and *Antología histórica del cuento literario chicano 1887–1959* (PhD dissertation, Arizona State University, 1981). He also has published material on language development for heritage speakers of Spanish, including *Jauja: Método integral de español para bilingues* (Englewood Cliffs, NJ: Prentice Hall, 1986), and has taught in both Spain and the United States (MIT, University of Arizona). He is currently a corresponding member of the U.S. Royal Academy of the Spanish Language.

CAROLINA NÚÑEZ-PUENTE is an Associate Professor in the English Department at the University of A Coruña (Spain). She has an MA in English from the University of Santiago de Compostela, (Spain), an MA in Women's Studies from Rutgers University, and a PhD in American Literature from the University of A Coruña (Spain). She has been a teacher and research fellow in various universities on both sides of the Atlantic; she also has been a member of different group projects, working on topics such as (post)colonialism, gender, ecocriticism, and immigration. Núñez-Puente is the author of *Feminism and Dialogics: Charlotte Perkins Gilman, Meridel Le Sueur, Mikhail M. Bakhtin* (2006); "Queeremos a Gloria Anzaldúa: Queering Poetry, Difference, and Dialog" (*Queerness in Anzaldúa: Post/Borderlands*, 2016); "Reading (from) the Afro-Caribbean in Hurston's 'Sweat:' an Eco-womanist Voyage" (*Transatlantic Visions: Women's Studies Collection, Vol. 9*, 2016); "From Genealogies to Gynealogies: Comparing *Borderlands* to Its First All-Poetry Manuscript" (*El Mundo Zurdo 3*, 2013); "Cantos de sanación. Una entrevista con Renato Rosaldo, antropoeta" (*Aztlán*, 2012); and "The Yellow Hybrids: Gender and Genre in Gilman's Wallpaper" (*Short Story Theories: A XXIst Century Perspective*, 2012). Her current work revolves around women's writing, film studies, and affect theory.

ANA SÁNCHEZ-MUÑOZ received a PhD in Linguistics from the University of Santiago de Compostela (Spain) and a PhD in Hispanic Linguistics from the University of Southern California with the dissertation topic "Register and Style Variation in Speakers of Spanish as a Heritage and as a Second Language." Sánchez-Muñoz currently serves as Full Professor in the Chicana/o Studies Department and the Linguistics/TESL Department at California State University, Northridge, where she has taught since 2007. Since 2015 Sánchez-Muñoz has served as Associate Chair of the Department of Linguistics/TESL. Muñoz's book publications include *Navigating the Great Recession: Immigrant Families' Stories of Resilience* (Dubuque, IA: Kendall/Hunt, 2011); *Spanish as a Heritage Language in the United States: A Study of Speakers' Register Variation* (Saarbrücken, Germany: Verlag Dr. Müller, 2009); and *Learning English/Learning America: Latino and Asian Ameri-*

can Voices (Dubuque, IA: Kendall/Hunt, 2008). Chapter contributions in peer-reviewed books include "Shifting Identities: The Spanish of U.S. Latino/a Speakers" (In A. Nikčević-Batrićević and M. Krivokapić, eds., *Mapping the World of Anglo-American Studies at the Turn of the Century*. Newcastle upon Tyne, UK: Cambridge Scholars Publishing, 2015); "Identidad y confianza lingüística en jóvenes latinos en el Sur de California" (In D. Dumitrescu and G. Piña-Rosales, eds., *El Español En Los Estados Unidos: E Pluribus Unum? Enfoques Multidisciplinarios*. New York: ANLE, 2013); and "Different Words for Different Contexts: Intra-speaker Variation in Spanish as a Heritage Language" (In S. Rivera-Mills and D. Villa, eds., *Spanish of the Southwest: A Language in Transition*. Madrid/Frankfurt: Editorial Iberoamericana/Vervuert, 2010).

CARMEN SANJUÁN-PASTOR is an Associate Professor of Spanish, Latin American & Caribbean Literatures and Cultures at Scripps College in Claremont, California. She holds a PhD in Spanish and Portuguese from Stanford University. Her recent works include "Imágenes del margen en la ciudad global española: la 'mujer de la calle' como metáfora espacial en *Todo sobre mi madre* (1999) de Pedro Almodóvar y en *Princesas* (2005) de Fernando León de Aranoa," in *Letras Femeninas* 39.1 (2013); "*Fígaro*: crónica/s de un suicidio anunciado. Una aproximación comparada a la lectura de 'El día de difuntos de 1836' y 'La Nochebuena de 1836,'" in *Cuadernos De ALDEEU* 27 (2014); and "'Am I Catalan, Mom?' Figuring a 'Shared Public Culture' in Najat El Hachmi's *Jo També Sóc Catalana* (2004)," in *Pacific Coast Philology* 50 (2015). She is completing a book that explores the impact of global migrations on the racial and cultural landscape of Spain as represented in texts produced by Iberian, African, and Afro-Iberian authors. Of particular interest are themes of identity, citizenship, conflict, mestizaje, and intercultural debates around notions of value, reason, and modernity.

RICARDO F. VIVANCOS-PÉREZ is an Associate Professor of Spanish and Latino and Latina Studies at George Mason University, where he also serves as Director of Graduate Studies in Foreign Languages. He received his PhD from the University of California, Santa Barbara, and specializes in transnational Chicana/o, Latina/o studies, Latin American studies, Exile studies, and Feminist and Queer theories. Vivancos-Pérez has written numerous articles on social movements in Spain and Latin America, on exile and immigration in Hispanic literatures, on transatlantic Hispanic studies, and on the relationship between human rights, feminisms, and literary forms. His most recent work includes *Radical Chicana Poetics* (Palgrave Macmillan, 2013).

INDEX

accommodation theory, 8, 77
Acuña, Rodolfo, 113
Adair, Doug, 96, 98, 98n16
AFL-CIO, 102, 103n20, 104
African American, 12, 129, 136; communities, 127–28; cultures, 126; exodus, 128; garden arrangements, 129; gardens, 129 (see also garden); interest in ecofeminism, 127; literary traditions, 14; rights, 128; short story, 11; traditions, 12; women, 129, 135; writing, 12, 127
agriculture, 128
Alarcón, Justo S., xii, 4, 4n4, 119; Chicano studies at Arizona State University, 4; *La Palabra: Revista Chicana*, 4
Alarcón, Norma, 62
Almaguer, Tomás, 113
Alurista, x
Alvar, Manuel, 110
Alvarez, Esther, 114, 119–20
Alvarez, Román, 122
Amazigh, 10, 35n2, 42
American literature, 86n8, 111, 122
Anaya, Rudolfo, 13, 29, 29n18, 31, 82, 86n8, 112, 114, 139–40, 145, 147; *Bless Me, Ultima*, 29, 82–84, 86–88; *Heart of Aztlán*, 145; *Jemez Springs*, 148; *Río Grande Fall*, 148; *Shaman Winter*, 148; Sonny Baca detective series, 13, 147; *la tierra*, 13, 140; *Zia Summer*, 148
Anaya, Rudolfo A. *See* Anaya, Rudolfo
Anzaldúa, Gloria, 1, 6–7, 11, 12, 35, 35n1, 38, 38n6, 39, 45, 47n24, 49, 54, 59, 60n2, 60–64, 61n3, 73; *sus plumas al viento*, 12, 132, 134; *This Bridge Called My Back: Writings by Radical Women of Color* (Moraga and Anzaldúa), 59, 126–29, 132–36, 133nn4–5
Arias, Ron, 5, 29; *The Road to Tamazunchale*, 5, 29–30
Arizona, xii, 99–100, 109, 137; Arizona State University, 4, 5n4, 82n1; University of Arizona, 112
arraigo, 13, 140, 147, 150; *sentido de arraigo*, 140
arrebato, 10, 60. *See also arrebatos*
arrebatos, 7, 63–65, 66
Atherton, Gertrude, 23; *Rezánov*, 23
Atlantic, 10, 109–11, 117, 119, 122; *Perspectivas transatlánticas en la Literatura Chicana: Ensayos y creatividad*; transatlantic, 85, 111, 114
Atxaga, Bernardo, 82. *See also Obabakoak*
Las aventuras de Don Chipote o cuando lo pericos mamen (Venegas), xii, 5, 25–26, 90
Aztec, 128; aesthetics, x; goddess Coyolxauhqui, 62. *See also* Coyolxauhqui
Aztlán, ix, 13, 112–14, 121, 133, 135, 141; *Aztlán: Essays on the Chicano Homeland* (Anaya et al.), 140; Becas para Aztlán, 2; cultural capital of Aztlán, 113; *Floricanto en Aztlán* (Alurista), x; *Heart of Aztlán* (Anaya), 145

Baca, Jimmy Santiago, 13, 139, 141, 147; *The Importance of a Piece of Paper*, 13, 141,

146; *Matilda's Garden*, 13, 146. See also garden
Baez, Joan, 95, 99
Barrera, Mario, 113
Basque: "Basqueness," 86; Country, 11, 84, 86–87, 113; culture, 177; intellectuals, 86; island, 87; language, 9, 10, 82, 84, 86–88; literary canon, 84
Becas para Aztlán, 2. See also Aztlán
El Bejareño, 14, 157, 169
bildungsroman, 31n24, 149
Bilingual Review Press, 121
Black (race), 129, 136: Black Urban Growers, 129; community, 128; ecofeminist, 132; farmers and urban gardeners, 129; man, 132; men, 67; spiritual song, 131; washerwoman, 132; woman, 67; women, 130–31
Blanco Aguinaga, Carlos, xiin7
Bléser, Nathalie, 114
Bless Me, Ultima (Anaya), 8, 82–83, 86, 86n8, 87–88
Borderlands/La Frontera: The New Mestiza (Anzaldúa), 1, 7, 38–39, 60, 60n2, 61–62, 64, 73, 126, 133, 133n5, 134, 136. See also border
Brito, Aristeo, 112
Buxo Rey, María Jesú, xii

Cabello, Margarito, 100
Cabeza de Baca, Fabiola, xii; *We Fed Them Cactus*, xii
Cabeza de Vaca, Alvar Núñez, 109–10
Calderón, Carlos R., 102
Californios, x, 22, 24, 162
Calvo Buenaz, Tomás, xii
Camarillo, Albert, xi; barrioization, xi; *Chicanos in a Changing Society: From Mexican Pueblos to American Barrios in Santa Barbara, 1848–1930*, xi
Camino Real, 2, 122; Colección Camino Real, 2
Cañero, Julio, xii, 10, 14, 109–25, 112
Caracol, 1
Caras viejas y vino nuevo (Morales), 2n1, 5, 29
Carpentier, Alejo, 85; *The Kingdom of This World*, 85
Carrillo, Adolfo, 119

Cartes al meu fill (El Kadaoui Moussaoui), 50, 50n26, 51–53
Castillo, Ana, 5, 13, 30, 117, 139, 143; *So Far from God*, 13, 117, 143; *The Mixquiahuala Letters*, 30
Catalan-Amazigh, 6, 35, 46n22
La Causa, 101
Cervantes, Miguel de, 21, 24–25, 110, 117n2; *Don Quijote*, 6, 21–22, 22n4, 24; Instituto Cervantes, 117
Chacón, Eusebio, xii, 5, 24, 24n8, 25; *Tras la tormenta la calma*, xii, 5, 24–25. See also *Tras la tormenta la calma*
Chávez, César, 9, 90–94, 95n11, 97–100, 102, 102n19, 103; *César Chávez y la Unión: una historia victoriosa de los de abajo* (Fuentes), 104n23; fasting, 96–97
Chávez, Denise, 115
Chávez, Fran Angélico, 22n4
Chican@: cultural critic, 66; culture, 60, 61, 63; and Latin@ scholarship, 59; and Latin@ studies, 7; scholars, 61; scholarship, 7, 61; studies, 59, 63–64, 66–69
Chicana, 7, 31, 47n24, 58, 60–62, 116–17, 135; activista, 98n15; and African American women, 135; and African American writing, 12; *Antología de la literatura chicana* (ed. Gaona), 2n1; Asociación de la Prensa Chicana, 97 (see also Chicano Press Association); author, 31, 111, 114–15; *comunidad*, 113; *cultura*, 114, 117; cultural production, 58, 60, 63; ecofeminist activists, 127; *excepcionalidad*, 114; experience, 5, 31; farmworker, 132; feminism, 38, 58, 65 (see also feminism); feminisms and rap music, 11; feminist, 58, 61, 61n3, 64, 66 (see also feminist); feminist principles, 7 (see also feminist); feminist theory, 36 (see also feminist); feminist thought, 59, 60, 64 (see also Anzaldúa, Gloria; feminist); group awareness, 31; group consciousness, 6; intellectuals, 135; lesbian, 64; lesbians and eroticism, 65; lesbian writing, 64; literary critics, 6, 120; *literatura*, 114; literature, 30, 115; Mexican/Chicana and African American traditions, 12; narrative, 30; National Association for Chicana and Chicano Studies (NACCS), 1 (see also Chicano; National Association for Chicana and Chicano Studies [NACCS]); *Nuevas reflexiones en torno a la literatura y cultura chicana*, 117; *La*

Palabra: Revista Chicana (Alarcón), 4; *Perspectivas transatlánticas en la Literatura Chicana: Ensayos y creatividad* (ed. Herrera-Sobek et al.), 2; poet, 31n22; poetics, 63, 66; Postmodern Chicana Generation (1985-95), xii; and Puerto Rican literature, 116; radical, 60, 62-63; as radical artists, 59; *Radical Chicana Poetics* (Vivancos-Pérez), 58, 62; radical poetics, 60; and Riqueñas, 117; scholarship, 7; story, 58, 62; *telenovela*, 117-18; writer, 5, 62, 117

Chicana/o, 73, 120; author, 127; biculturalism, 121; bilinguals, 80; critics, 127; English, 75; identity formation, 71; literary identity, 121; literature, 117; scholar, 67-68; self-identification, 74; Spanish, 74; speakers, 75; studies, xiii, 68; workers, 133

Chicano, ix–xi, xiii, 1–3, 5, 7, 11–13, 45, 58–60, 62–63, 65–66, 73–74, 78–80, 102, 110–11, 113–16, 120, 126–28, 133, 136, 143, 146, 149, 153; ancestors, 12; artistic creation, 115; artistic expression, 117; artists, 112; authors, 2, 3, 13, 111, 114, 118–19, 121, 139; *El bandolero, el pocho y la raza: imágenes cinematográficas del chicano* (Maciel), 2n1; bilingual literature, 118; in borderlands, 12; borders, 9; campesino newspaper, 10; *Chicano Narrative: The Dialectics of Difference* (Saldívar), 1, 45; Chicano Press Association, 97; *Chicanos: Antología histórica y literaria* (Villanueva), 2, 2n1; *Chicanos in a Changing Society: From Mexican Pueblos to American Barrios in Santa Barbara and Southern California, 1848-1930* (Camarillo), xi (*see also* Chicano Press Association); Chicano Studies Center at UCLA, xn3; communal literary consciousness, 6; community, 11–13, 146; conferences, 112; creations, 114; critical consciousness, 10; criticism, 15; critics, xii, xiin7, 2, 10, 121–22; cultural identity, 115; cultural makeup, 10; cultural nationalism, 10; cultural nationalists, 10; culture, 2, 5, 10, 112, 114; discourse, 7; English, 75; ethnic issues, 3; experience, 9; films and murals, 115; folklore, xi, xin6; folklorists, xin6; heritage, 150; identity, 3, 8, 79, 139, 141; identity and traditions, 153; koiné, 80; language, 132; letters, 3, 4, 10; literary and cultural studies, xii; literary criticism, 1, 4, 116–17; literary critics, 111–13, 120; literary history, 3; literary journals, 1; literary productions, 127; literary scholars, 15; literary traditions, 14; literary works, 6; literature, ix, xiin7, xiii, xiiin8, 1–5, 5n4, 10, 11, 13–15, 20, 27, 31, 86n8, 110, 112–14, 117–20, 122, 139; literature and culture, xii, 4, 119; "los periódicos chicanos," 97; male depictions of family, 31; masculinity(ies), 116; Moratorio, 102; movement (movimiento), ix, xi, 1, 22, 26–27, 68, 86, 102; movement literature, 5, 26; National Association for Chicana and Chicano Studies (NACCS), 1; non-Chicano, 3, 7, 58–59, 62–63, 66–76; poetry, 11, 114, 133; popular culture, 115; professor, 64; readership, 87; reality, 5; *Revista Chicano-Riqueña*, ixn1; *Rolando Hinojosa y su "cronición" chicano* (Martín-Rodríguez), 29n17 (*see also* Hinojosa, Rolando); scholar, 7, 10, 11, 65–67, 122; social issues, 7; soldado, 98; Spanish, 7, 72–76, 76 table 2, 77–78; studies, 1, 3–4, 7, 11, 67–68, 110–11; texts, 1–2; tragedy, 145; work, 3, 110, 119; worldview, 140; writer, 10–11, 29, 112, 119–22

Chicano/a, xiii, 7, 133, 133n5, 134, 136; audience, 27, 31; authors, 27; critical scholarship, xiii; critics, xii, xiin7, xiii, 127; experience, 27; Folklore, xin6; letters, 26; literary curriculum, 22; literature, xiii, 5, 12, 19–20, 27, 133; narrative, 29; presses, 27; reality, 27; studies, xiii; workers, 26, 133, 133n5; writers, 29, 115

Chicano Movement, ix. *See also* Chicano

Chicano Narrative: The Dialectics of Difference (Saldívar), 1. *See also* Chicano

Chicano Press Association, 97. *See also* Chicano

Chicanos: Antología histórica y literaria (Villanueva), 2, 2n1

Cisneros, Sandra, 5, 6, 30–32, 39, 48, 119; *Caramelo*, 119; "A House of My Own," 6, 31–32; *The House on Mango Street*, 6, 30–32, 39, 45, 48–49. See also *The House on Mango Street*

City of Night (Rechy), 27

El Clamor Público, 14, 156, 156n2, 157, 157n3, 157n5, 159n6, 162–63, 163n8, 164–65, 167, 167n9, 169n10

Coachella, 101, 102

code switching, 8, 74–75, 79–80, 118

colonial: ban, 22; censorship, 23; Center of Study and Investigation for Decolonial Dialogues, 2; and class-based system,

130; Decolonizing Knowledge and Power: Postcolonial Studies, Decolonial Horizons, 2; and dictatorial ashes, 85; era, ix; languages, 72; Latin America, 22; mind-set, 134; neocolonialist, xi; past, 6, 73; period, 20; *Postcolonial* (Spivak), 63; postcolonial Feminist studies, 68; postcolonial identities, 45n20; (post) colonialism, 134; postcolonialism, 2; postcolonial subjects, 45, 49; postcolonial theories, 85; powers, 14; practices, 12; project, 14, 52n30; "The Search for Decolonial Love" (Moya), 41n14; ways of being, 136

colonization, 129; effects of colonization, x; as framework, 83; internal, 11; Spanish, x; Spanish and Anglo, 133; and rape, 134

conquest, 114; 500th Anniversary of the Conquest of the Americas, xi; American, 151; effects of, x; of the land, 151; past of, 114; political, 151; Spanish, 151; Spanish reconquest, 10

conquista, 172; *conquistado*, 155; *conquistador*, 155; *del Norte de México*, 155; "Spanish conquistador," 64; *territorios conquistados*, 172

Convención de la Unión en Fresno, 101

Corcoran, California, 96

Cortés, Hernán, 109

Coyolxauhqui, 62, 63, 115

Cruz, Sor Juana Inés de la, 65; *Carta Atenagórica*, 65; *Sor Juana's Second Dream*, 65

curanderos, 8

De Colores, 1

Delano, 91, 97–98, 100, 102n19, 105

De Soto, Hernando, 109

Díaz, Porfirio, 100

diglossia, 8, 77

Domínguez, Antonia, 115

Don Quijote (Cervantes), 6, 21–22, 22n4, 24. See also Cervantes, Miguel de

Don Quixote (Ruiz de Burton), 22n5, 23

Dreams of Trespass: Tales of a Harem Girlfriend (Mernissi), 50–51

Durán, Isabel, 117, 120

ecocriticism, 11–12, 14, 127

El Eco del Pacífico, 14, 157–58, 159n6

ecofeminism, 11–12, 35, 126–27, 127n1, 129, 132, 134. See also feminism

ecofeminist, 134–35; Chicana ecofeminist activists, 127 (*see also* Chicana); criticism, 134; ethic, 130; literary criticism, 118; pastoral literature, 128; perspective, 127n1; project, 148; statement, 135; viewpoint, 126; working class fashion, 132

ecology, 126, 148, 151, 153; of dispossession, 127

Eguíluz, Federico, xii, 112–14

Elizondo Griest, Stephanie, 119; *Mexican Enough*, 119

English department, 68, 111, 113

environmental, 11; awareness, 139, 141; cruelties, 12; environmentalist, 148, 152; issues, 152; justice, 127; landscape, 11 (*see also* landscape); literature, 127; meaning, 140; nonenvironmental problems, 127; rhetoric, 139; spaces, 12; understanding, 139; writing, 12

environmentalism, 12

epistemic privilege, 40, 40n11

Español Vernáculo de Los Angeles, 74

Espinosa, Aurelio M., xi, 23; Chicano folklore, xi. See also Chicano

La Estrella, 165, 167

farmworker: Chicana, 132 (*see also* Chicana); El Farmworker Movement Documentation Project, 104n22; voice, 9. See also *Voz del campesino*

Faulker, William, 111

feather, 132–33, 133n4, 134

feminism, 14, 35, 114, 126–27; Chicana, 11, 38, 58, 65 (*see also* Chicana); ecofeminism, 11–12, 35, 126–27, 127n1, 129, 132, 134 (*see also* ecofeminism); *Feminism and Dialogics* (Núñez-Puente), 130n2, 135. See also Núñez-Puente, 135; third world, 6, 35n1, 38n6, 39, 49, 58, 65; white, 38

feminist, 6, 38, 38n6, 40, 61, 66, 115, 118, 131; African feminist ancestor, 131; anthologies, 61; Bakhtinian, 130n2; border subject, 64; Chicana, 7, 38, 58–61, 61n3, 64, 66 (*see also* Chicana); Chicana feminist theory, 36 (*see also* Chicana); critics of Islam, 42; definition of *epistemic privilege*, 40 (see also *epistemic privilege*); discourse, 38, 66; feminist-oriented border subject, 64; Hispanic-feminist-oriented-male-writer, 66; ideology and practice, 38; interventions, 38; liberal feminist theory, 38n6; *mestizaje,* 50; *mestizaje* theories, 6, 35; 35n1, 50; *mestizo* thinking, 43; philosophy, 60, 63; postcolonial Feminist studies, 68; queer feminist quill, 134; radical, 7; radical feminist poetics, 59; radical feminist thought, 68; research, 64; scholars, 7, 64–65; studies, 64, 67–69; thinkers, 66; thinking, 38; thought, 60, 64; "U.S Third World Feminists" (Moraga and Anzaldúa; Sandoval), 38

Fernández de Pinedo, Eva, 116

Flesler, Daniela, 52, 52n29

Floricanto en Aztlán (Alurista), x

Flys Junquera, Carmen Lydia, 13–14, 139–54

Folkart, Jessica, 38n6, 41n13

Fondo de Cultura Económica, 2

Fonseca, Vanessa, xiii, 1–15

Franklin Institute, xii, 139n2. *See also* Instituto Franklin de Investigación en Estudios Norteamericanos

Fuentes, Víctor, 9, 90–105

"Funes the Memorious" (Borges), 85

Gallo Wines, 103

García, Linda, 105

garden, 11–12, 126, 128–30, 132–33, 135–36, 146–47: African American, 129 (*see also* African American); arrangements, 129 (*see also* African American); biblical, 132; community, 128; Floating Garden of Xochimilco, 128; gardener, 128–29; gardening, 12–13, 128–29; literary, 126; "Matilda's Garden" (Baca), 13, 146 (*see also* Baca, Jimmy Santiago); of Eden, 12, 132; outdoor, 126; outdoor and literary, 135; spaces, 11–12; vegetable, 129; "Wild Cosmopolitan Gardens" (Flys Junquera), 139n1

Gasca, Luis, 100

Gaspar de Alba, Alicia, 59, 64–65, 112, 116

gender, 22, 38, 49, 54, 64: abuse, 130; and class, 22–23; and ethnic groups, 68; expectations, 22; gendered experience, 44; gendered position, 45; gendered subject, 40; gender-undifferentiated, 31; identity, 37, 42, 65, 68; oppositions, 131; politics, 41n14; relations, 38n6; violence, 31, 130, 141

Germersheim, Germany, xii; first international conference on Chicano literature and culture, xii

Gil-Osle, Juan Pablo, 8, 82–89

Girard, René, 83, 84

gobierno, 103, 159; *federal,* 157

Gonzales, Rodolfo "Corky," x

Gonzales-Berry, Erlinda, 112

González, Carmen, 115

González, Deena, 63

Gramsci, Antonio, 94n10

Granada, 16, 110, 112–13; Universidad de Granada, 10, 112

Grande, Reyna, 121

Gruzinski, Serge, 85, 85n5

guerra, 92n6, 155, 169; *de Vietnam,* 98; *expansionista,* 155; *Guerra de Secesión,* 159; *Guerra Méxicano-americana,* 172; *justa,* 155

Guijarro, Juan Ignacio (Nacho), 115

Gurpegui, Juan Antonio, xii, 10, 110–13, 118, 121; conference on Chicano literature in Torredembarra, Spain, xii; the Franklin Institute at the Universidad de Alcalá de Henares, xii

El Hachmi, Najat, 35–36, 36n4, 37, 39, 40–41, 41n13, 43, 43n17, 44–46, 46n23, 47–48

Henríquez, María, 112

Herrera-Sobek, María, xin6, 112

hierarchy: between intellectual and manual work, 135; economic, 129

Hinojosa, Rolando, 3, 29, 112, 114; Premio Casa de las Américas, 3; *Rolando Hinojosa y su "cronición" chicano* (Martín-Rodríguez), 29n17

Hinojosa-Smith, Rolando. *See* Hinojosa, Rolando

Hispanic, x–xi, 66, 73, 75, 82, 109–11, 118, 143; background, xi; border cultures, 83; communities, 110; Decade of the Hispanic, xi; *Handbook of Hispanic Cultures in the United States* (eds. Kanellos and Esteva-Fabregat), xi; *herencia Hispana,* 121; *Hispana,* 111; Hispanic/Latino, 72; Hispanic Period (1519–1521), x; Latino/Hispanic, 72, 74; Latino/Hispanic population, 72 table 1; Latino/Hispanic studies, 4; minority, 110 (*see also* minority); "El Poder Hispano," 111; population,

8, 111; spaces, 8; studies, xii, 4; United States, 109; U.S. Hispanic Literature, 118; world, 82–83, 85
HispaUSA, 11, 120, 120n3, 121n4
The House on Mango Street (Cisneros), 31–32, 39–40, 45, 48–49
Huerta, Dolores, 94, 96, 99
humor, 25, 66, 116
Hurston, Zora Neale, 126–32, 134–35; *Sweat*, 12, 126, 128–29, 131–32, 134

I am Joaquín (Gonzales), x
Ibarrarán Vigalondo, Amaia, xii, 113
immigration, x, 2, 46, 53n31, 64, 72, 121
imperialism: cultural, 38; ecological, 151
indigenous, 88: background, xi; connection, 79; cultural makeup, 10; cultural past, x, xi; girl, 83n2; peoples, 20, 151; and pre-Columbian traditions, 127; subjugation, x; traditions and lifestyles, 152
Instituto Franklin de Investigación en Estudios Norteamericanos, 2, 11, 116, 120, 122 (*see also* Franklin Institute); Colección Camino Real, 2, 2n2
The International Conference on Chicano Literature, 109; First International Conference on Chicano Language and Literature, 112; Second International Conference on Chicano Literature, 113; Third International Conference on Chicano Literature, 114; Fourth International Conference on Chicano Literature, 115; Fifth International Conference on Chicano Literature, 116; Sixth International Conference on Chicano Literature, 117; Seventh International Conference on Chicano Literature, 118; Eighth International Conference on Chicano Literature, 119; Ninth International Conference on Chicano Literature and Latino Studies, 120; 10th International Conference on Chicano Literature and Latino Studies, 120; 11th International Conference on Chicano Literature and Latino Studies, 122
Islas, Arturo, 116

Jackson, Jesse, 98
Joaquín Mortiz, 2; Chicano novels published, 2n2

El Kadaoui Moussaoui, Saïd, 35–36, 36n5, 48–53
Kanellos, Nicolás, 26n11
Keller, Gary Francisco, 121
Kennedy, Edward, 100
Kennedy, Robert F., 97
King, Coretta, 99
King, Martin Luther, 97
Know-Nothings, 169, 171n11
koinéization, 77

land, 13, 109, 129, 139–42, 145–47, 150–51, 153; appropriation, x; attachment, 13, 147, 149; barren, 87; betrayal, 146; borderland, 6, 12, 35, 35n1, 43n17, 50–51, 84; borderland consciousness, 38; borderland identity, 36; borderland location, 48; borderland subject, 49, 54; *Borderlands/La Frontera: The New Mestiza* (Anzaldúa), 1, 7, 38–39, 60, 60n2, 61–62, 64, 73, 126, 133, 133n5, 134, 136 (*see also* Anzaldúa, Gloria); conquest of, 151; grant, 141–42, 145, 149 (*see also* land grant); history, 152; homeland, 13, 50–51, 117; importance and appreciation, 13, 145, 148; inheritance, 13, 141; Land Allotment Acts, 142; land-based practices, 13; land-holding Californios, x; Land of Enchantment, 144; Land of Entrapment, 144; language of, 148; lifestyle, 147; linguistic borderlands, 84, 86; loss, 13, 142–45, 147; and nature, 13; overuse, 143; Promised Land, 2; reconnection, 149, 153; relationship, 141, 147–49; rights, 141; sacredness of, 151–52; transborderland, xiiin8; violation of, 134; wasteland, 83
land grant, 141–42, 145, 149
landscape, 44, 62, 118, 139–40, 148–49, 153; changing, 118; environmental, 11, 72; epiphany, 140; and language, 11; linguistic, 11, 72, 76, 80; literary, 119; multicultural, 2; narrative, 48; pastoral, 12, 128; of the southwest, 140; spiritual, 118; urban, 72, 80
The Last Patriarch (El Hachmi), 36n3
Latin America, 22, 109, 112; *Latin American Literary Review*, 154; Latin American countries, 72, Latin American literatures, xiii; Latin American studies, 59
Latino, 109–11, 116–17, 120, 122, 128–29, 136, 176–77; community, 120; courtyards, 128;

culture, 109; Latinoist movement, 136; population, 109; studies, 120

Leal, Luis, ix, 66; "Mexican American Literature: A Historical Approach," xin6

Límites y fronteras (El Kadaoui), 6, 35–36, 48–53, 53n31

Limón, José, xin6

linchamiento, 13, 155–56, 162, 172; *de Antonio Rodríguez*, 171; *como crímen de estado*, 155; *espontáneos o repentinos*, 155; *de los méxicoamericanos*, 155–56; *de Miguel Soto*, 162; *perpetrados*, 155

linguistic, 7, 72, 80; aspect, 88; attitudes, 72; behavior, 71; borderlands, 84n3, 86; borders, 84; code, 8, 83; campaigns, 86; and cultural politics, 82; cornucopia, 85; differences, 10; diversity, 72; expression, 73–74, 82; fabric, 71; factor, 83; features, 78; heritage, 79; hybridization, 80; identity, 71, 78; influence of Spanish in English, 118; landscapes, 11, 72, 76, 80 (*see also* landscapes); manifestations, 10; mark, 75; metalinguistic, 87; minorities, 85; of nationalism, 83; *Nepantla*, 75; notions, 76; outcomes, 76; phenomena, 73, 75–76; policies, 83, 85–86; politics, 8; prestige, 74; repertoire, 73; resources, 8, 75, 80; situation of Los Angeles, 77; sociolinguistic interviews, 78; sociolinguistic lab, 72; sociolinguistic space, 79; space, 79, 80; strategy, 75; third space, 8, 80

Lomelí, Francisco A., ix–xiv, 24n8, 121–22

Long Road to Delano, 105

Lorca, Federico, García, 59

Lorenzo, Eusebio de, 120

Maalouf, Amin, 36, 50n26, 51–52, 52n27, 53, 53n31

Madrid, 2, 110, 119–20

magic, 8, 82–84; cultural, 9; of language of border identity, 84; magical, 84; magical realism, 83; magical realism mode, 151; magical real play of time, 151; (non)curative, 83–84; nonhealing, 9; pseudo-magical, 37, 42; and religion, 86; of shaman, 83, 83n2; of tradition, 83; veil, 82

magic realism, 9

El Malcriadito, 9, 104–5

El Malcriado, 9, 90, 90n3, 91, 91n4, 92–93, 93n7, 94, 96–99, 99n17, 100–103, 103n20, 104, 104n22; *Don Coyote*, 92; *Don Sotaco*, 92; *Ranchero*, 92

La Malinche, 114, 134

Márquez, Antonio, 112

Márquez, Teresa, 112

Martín, Alejandro, 115

Martín Junquera, Imelda, 11, 112, 118

Martín Rodríguez, Manuel M., xii, 4, 4n3, 5, 10, 19–34

Méndez, Carmen M., 120

Méndez, Miguel, 112

Mernissi, Fatima, 42, 42n15

mestiza consciousness, 35n1, 38–39, 47n24. *See also* Anzaldúa, Gloria

mestizaje, 35, 35n1

Mexican American, 14, 22, 73, 110; literature, 22, 25; "Mexican American Literature: A Historical Approach" (Leal), ix (*see also* Leal, Luis); Mexican-American War, 14–15; Tomás Rivera Mexican American Children's Book Award, 4n3; writers, 22

Mexican Revolution, 127

Miguélez, Armando, xii, 14–15, 119, 155–73

mimesis, 5, 6, 19–21, 21n3, 22, 24–27, 30–31

minority, 40, 75, 84, 117; Hispanic, 110 (*see also* Hispanic); identities, 48n25, 54; internally colonized, 113; languages, 83, 86–87; literatures and cultures, 15; positions, 54; subjugated, 114

modernity, 13, 53, 148–49; destabilizing elements of, 139; rationalism of, 85

Mohanty, Chandra Talpade, 38–39

Montes-Alcalá, Cecilia, 118

Montoya, Rubén, 102

Mora, Pat, 31, 31n22

Moraga, Cherríe, 6, 35, 38, 45, 49, 59, 61, 61n3, 64, 114–15; theory in the flesh, 6, 38

Morales, Alejandro, 2, 2n1, 5, 29, 112; *Caras viejas y vino nuevo* and *La verdad sin voz*, 2n1; *El olvidado pueblo de Simons*, 2

Moratorio Chicano, 102

Moroccan-Amazigh, 36–37, 42

Movimiento Chicano, 102

Moya, Paula, 35n1, 41n14, 47n24, 48n25, 54

muerte, 163, 171; *amenazas de*, 97; *de Cipriano Sandoval*, 168; *a los dos mejicanos*, 160; *extrajudiciales*, 157; *del Mayor General Bean*, 168; "Muerte a los Españoles" (*El Clamor Público*), 157; *de Rubén Salazar*, 102; *sentencia de*, 56; *a todo lo que no es americano*, 169

National Association for Chicana and Chicano Studies (NACCS), 1. *See also* Chicana; Chicano

nature, 12–14, 88, 118, 127n1, 129–32, 134–35, 140, 142–43, 146–51; and environmental understanding, 139; motif, 150; writing as genre, 127

New Mexico, x, xn4, xii, 1, 24, 29, 29n19, 149, 153; attraction of, 152; of *Bless Me, Ultima*, 82; conquest of, 151; Las Vegas, 145; mountains of, 82, 84; Oñate incursion, 151; and sense of place, 153; seventeenth-century, 20–21; University of New Mexico 4n3; and Yucatán, 8

Nixon, Richard, 97, 101

Nogales, 109

nos/otros scholarship, 67

El Nuevo Mundo, 14, 157, 159, 162n7

Núñez-Puente, Carolina, 11, 12, 14–15, 126–38, 132n3; *Feminism and Dialogics*, 130n2. *See also* feminism

Obaba (Armendariz), 8, 82, 86

Obabakoak (Atxaga), 8, 82, 86, 86nn7–9, 87–88

Olivares, Julián, 28

Oliver, María Antonia, xii, 112, 119

El olvidado pueblo de Simons (Morales), 2

Orlando furioso (Ariosto), 20–21

La Palabra: Revista Chicana, 4. *See also* Alarcón, Justo

Papa Pío VI, 104

Paredes, Américo, xin6

partido, 169–70; *demócrata*, 100; *Know Knothings*, 169; *republicano*, 162

pastoral: antipastoralism, 127; canon, 12; landscape, 12, 128 (*see also* landscape); literature, 128

Perles Rochel, Juan Antonio, 112, 114

Perspectivas transatlánticas en la literatura chicana: Ensayos y creatividad, 2

Pita, Beatriz, 22

Plan de Santa Barbara, 3

Portillo Trambley, Estela, 30

Posada, Guadalupe, 98

property, 128, 145–46; communal, 141; community, 144; private, 141

pueblo (community/town), 28, 91, 98–99, 158–59, 166–67, 172–73: *americano*, 159, 167; *bruto e incivilizado*, 172; *Chicanos in a Changing Society: From Mexican Pueblos to American Barrios in Santa Barbara and Southern California, 1848-1930* (Camarillo), xi (*see also* Chicano; Camarillo, Albert); "Expresión simultánea del pueblo de California" (Retes), 157n5; *de Los Angeles*, 168; *mejicano*, 169; *mexicano*, 162, 172; *de la Misión*, 163; *El olvidado pueblo de Simons* (Morales), 2 (*see also* Morales); *de Texas*, 170–71; *victimizado*, 155

Pueblo: Indians, 140; Indian cosmology, 150; ways, 151

queer, 65; feminist quill, 134 (*see also* feminist); and lesbian cultural production, 60; sexuality, 133n4; studies, 2, 7, 61, 69

Quintana, Miguel de, xi

Quinto Sol, 27, 29

Quinto Sol Generation, xii

racial: and cultural difference, 48; and cultural landscape, 179; and economic ideologies, 45; ethnoracialized and sexualized female body, 62; gendered, racialized, and classed position, 45; identities, 38; interracial themes, 130; *minorías raciales*, 172; mixing, 35n1; mixtures, xn2; multiracial, 98; overtones, 132; racialization of class, 129; racialization of work, 135; racially contentious issues, xn4; racial minority, 40; segregation of work, 130

Radical Chicana Poetics (Vivancos-Pérez), 58, 62

El Ranchero, 14, 157, 169, 171n11

Raza Unida Party, 2

Reagan, Ronald, 98

Rechy, John, 27

Recovering U.S. Hispanic Literary Heritage Project, xi

Regeneración, 14, 157, 171, 172n12

Revista Camino Real, 2, 122

Revista Chicano-Riqueña, ixn1; Nicolás Kanellos and David Dávalos, ixn1. *See also* Chicano

Revolución Mexicana, 92, 171

rights: of African Americans, 128; civil, ix, 73; Civil Rights Groups, 97; community, 142; individual, 142; to land, 141; and planetary peace, 53; and shared human traits and values, 53; water, 152; of women, 22

Rio Grande, 109, 133, 152; *Rio Grande Fall* (Anaya), 148, 150 (*see also* Anaya, Rudolfo); Rio Grande valley, 152

Ríos, Isabella, 30

Rivera, Tomás, 5, 27–28, 31; *. . . y no se lo tragó la tierra*, 5, 27–29

The Road to Tamazunchale (Arias), 5, 29

Rodríguez, Néstor E., 86n9

root, 117, 149, 151; deep, ix; Iberian, xi; Moroccan or Imaziguen, 53; of soul, 145; of trees, 150

rooted, 7; in the body, 60; in land, 139; in Latinidades and Hispanidades, 59; rootedness, 139–40, 152–53; uprooted, x, 146–47

Rosaldo, Renato, 63

Rosales, Jesús, xiii, 1–15, 110

Ruiz de Burton, María Amparo, xii, 5, 22–25

sacred: land, 152; sacredness of land, 151; sacrifice, 83

Salazar, Rubén, 102

Saldívar, Ramón, 1, 40, 48

Saldívar-Hull, Sonia, 6, 38

Sánchez, Rosaura, 22

Sánchez-Muñoz, Ana, 7–8, 10, 71–81

San Diego, 109, 138

Sandoval, Chela, 6

Sanjuán-Pastor, Carmen, 6, 10, 35–57

sense of place, 13, 139, 140–41, 147–49, 151–53. See also *arraigo*

serpent, 134; Serpent Skirt or Coatlicue, 134

serpiente, 170

slave, 134; narratives, 127; slavery, 39, 127, 129; slavery system, 12

Sor Juana's Second Dream (Gaspar de Alba), 65

Southwest (American or North American), x, 3, 14, 86, 110, 143; landscape, 140 (*see also* landscape); university, 68

Spain, xi–xiii, 1–4, 6, 8–11, 20, 35, 37, 43–44, 46, 46n22, 50, 52, 63–64, 67, 82–83, 86, 109, 110–17, 119–22, 145; cultural boundaries, 9; multicultural realities, 10; southern, 7; Spanish government, 111

Spaniard, 109–11, 119, 121, 133; *Spaniard*, 114

Spanish department, xiin7, 111, 121

Spanish scholars, 110, 112, 114, 117–19; *de acá*, 4, 17, 119; *de allá*, 4, 10, 14–15, 112–13, 120

Spivak, Gayatri Chakravorty, 63, 68; *An Aesthetic Education in the Era of Globalization*, 68, 69; *Postcolonial*, 63

The Squatter and the Don (Ruiz de Burton), xii, 5, 22–23

subjectivity, 36, 38, 45, 48; alternate, 66; multicultural, 52; of narrator, 41n13; rupture, 45, 47, 49; of sense of place, 140; speaking, 130

Taller de Gráfica, 92

Taller Gráfico, 99

Teamsters, 101, 105

telenovela, 117–18

theory in the flesh, 6, 38. See also Moraga, Cherríe

This Bridge Called My Back: Writings by Radical Women of Color (Anzaldúa and Moraga), 59–60

tierra, 13, 139, 140, 153, 157, 169, 171–72; *Mi lucha por la tierra* (López Tijerina), 2n1; *. . . y no se lo tragó la tierra* (Rivera), 5, 27, 29 (see also *. . . y no se lo tragó la tierra*; Rivera, Tomás); *sagrada*, 140; de los yaquis, 100

tongue, 47, 133–34; *deslenguada* (without tongue), 135; domesticated, 135; wild, 135

Torredembarra Conference, xii

Torrijos, Mar Ramón, 119

Tras la tormenta la calma (Chacón), xii, 5, 24–25

Tratado de Guadalupe Hidalgo, 162

Ulibarrí, Sabine R., xii

L'últim patriarca (El Hachmi), 6, 35–38, 38n6, 39–40, 41n13, 42, 44, 44nn18–19, 45, 45n20, 46, 48–49, 54

UFW, 9, 102, 103nn20–21, 104, 105. See also United Farm Workers

Un embrujo (Carrera), 8, 82, 83n2, 84, 86

La Unión, 90, 93, 95, 95n11, 96, 98, 98n15, 99, 99n16, 100–102, 102n19, 103, 103n20, 104, 104n23, 105

Unión de Campesinos, 90. See also La Unión

United Farm Workers, 102, 103. *See also* UFW

United States, xii, xiii, 1, 3–4, 6–8, 10, 14–15, 22, 25, 30, 64, 67, 69, 73–74, 80, 83, 87, 109–11, 114–22, 128, 134; *Handbook of Hispanic Cultures in the United States* (Kanellos Esteva-Fabregat), xi; Hispanic past, 109; *North from Mexico: The Spanish-Speaking People of the United States* (McWilliams), 157n4

Universidad de Alcalá de Henares, xii, 2, 110, 111, 116

Universidad de Alicante, 117

Universidad Nacional Autónoma de México (UNAM), 1, 2

Universidad de Oviedo, 11, 119–20

Universidad del País Vasco, 11, 113

Universidad de Salamanca, 122

Universidad de Sevilla, 115

University of California, Santa Barbara, 3, 110, 121

Valdez, Luis, 95

Valenzuela, Liliana, 119

Varela, Félix, xi; *Jicoténcal*, xi

Varsava, 19, 30

Vásquez, Alfredo, 100

Vázquez de Coronado, Francisco, 109

Venegas, Daniel, xii, 5, 25, 90

Villagrá, Gaspar, Pérez de, xi, 110; *Historia de la Nueva México,* xi

Villar Raso, Manuel, xii, 112

Villarreal, José Antonio, xii, 27, 112; *Pocho,* xii, 27

Villa y Corte, 110

Viramontes, Helena María, 116

Virgen de Guadalupe, 116–17

Viriato, 109

Vivancos-Pérez, Ricardo F., 5, 7, 10, 15, 58–70

Voz del campesino, 9

Walker, Alice, 45, 126, 131, 133; *The Color Purple,* 45

water, 11–12, 128–29, 131–32, 152; derivatives, 126, 129, 132, 134; imagery of, 12, 126, 129–30; life-giving, 152; notion of, 126; rights, 152; of Río Grande, 133; running, 51; themes of, 12; watering, 129

Wehbe-Herrera, Aishih, 116

Whitman, Walt, 111

Who Would Have Thought It (Ruiz de Burton), xii, 22

Yarbro-Bejarano, Yvonne, 35n1

. . . y no se lo tragó la tierra (Rivera), 5, 27–28

Zamora, Bernice, 30

Zermeño, Andy, 92, 95

Zilles, Klaus, 114

GLOBAL LATIN/O AMERICAS
FREDERICK LUIS ALDAMA AND LOURDES TORRES, SERIES EDITORS

This new series focuses on the Latino experience in its totality as set within a global dimension. The series will showcase the variety and vitality of the presence and significant influence of Latinos in the shaping of the culture, history, politics and policies, and language of the Americas—and beyond. We welcome scholarship regarding the arts, literature, philosophy, popular culture, history, politics, law, history, and language studies, among others. Books in the series will draw from scholars from around the world.

Spanish Perspectives on Chicano Literature: Literary and Cultural Essays
    EDITED BY JESÚS ROSALES AND VANESSA FONSECA

Sponsored Migration: The State and Puerto Rican Postwar Migration to the United States
    EDGARDO MELÉNDEZ

La Verdad: An International Dialogue on Hip Hop Latinidades
    EDITED BY MELISSA CASTILLO-GARSOW AND JASON NICHOLS